90-DAY GUIDE FOR SUCCESS

PATHWAYS TO THRIVE IN THE VIRTUAL, REMOTE, AND HYBRID WORLD

JENNIFER J. BRITTON

90-DAY GUIDE FOR SUCCESS

Pathways to Thrive in the Virtual, Remote, and Hybrid World

Jennifer J. Britton

Published by
Potentials Realized
Ontario, Canada

Copyeditor: Lynette Smith, www.AllMyBest.com
Cover and Interior design: Yvonne Parks, www.PearCreative.ca
Proofreader: Clarisa Marcee, www.AvenueCMedia.com

ISBN: 978-0-9937915-7-4 (paperback)
        978-0-9937915-8-1 (eBook)

Quantity discounts are available on bulk purchases of this book for educational, gift purposes, or as premiums for increasing magazine subscriptions or renewals. Special books or book excerpts can also be created to fit specific needs. For information, please contact Potentials Realized, PO Box 93305 Newmarket, Ontario, Canada L3X 1A3.

Dedicated to everyone who has a Day One in starting a new role, new quarter.

CONTENTS

ACKNOWLEDGMENTS

As I bring this book across the finish line, I am conscious of the ongoing changes that are continuing in our world, yet, how relevant these topics continue to be. As I recently shared with a group of Chief Talent Development Officers (CTDOs), the more things change, the more important it is to go back to the basics. While our processes and technology will change, the foundations of great work in the virtual, remote, and hybrid space is often more about simplification rather than adding on more layers of complexity. People are at the heart of great work at any time, and this guide is to support you as an individual. I hope that the Guide will be like having a coach in your corner every day for the 90 days, inviting you to pause, reflect and envision what's possible.

The Guide is geared to be consumed one-day-at-a-time, which is how it was written. This book was first birthed during the 2019 National Novel Writing Month, pre-pandemic. Day by day during the month of November 2019 this book took shape, initially as a brainstorm on cue cards (which took up several tables).

As someone who has lived and operated in the virtual, remote, and hybrid space for the bulk of my career over the last three decades, I felt that it was important to create a resource to support others in the onboarding process, especially when they were new to role in the remote space. I know that in most of my roles I was not able to benefit from a resource like this, and that missing piece has shaped what I put attention on now when I coach leaders and teams, entrepreneurs, and organizations.

As the pandemic has continued to evolve, it has become very apparent that it's EVERYONE who could benefit from a resource like this, not just new-to-role employees. So whether you are a seasoned hand like myself, or simply looking to inject some new energy into your next 90 day cycle, I look forward to hearing how you use the resource and where you take it. Be sure to share your photos and ideas over on Instagram, with the hashtag #ReconnectingWorkspaces90DayGuide.

A big thank you to my team:

The Reconnecting Workspaces Certified Coaches (RWCC) – I have been thrilled by our hours of dialogue and am excited to see how you are taking this body of work out into the world with your clients, influencing remote, hybrid and virtual conversations in a wide variety of industries and geographic locations.

My vision for my work and writing is to impact the work of 5 million virtual, remote, and hybrid professionals this decade, and the RWCCs are instrumental in making that happen. If you are a coach, I hope you will consider joining us! You'll find out more about this ICF-CCE approved program over at ReconnectingWorkspaces.com.

To Janica Smith, a huge thank you as always. It's been wonderful to bring this book forward with your continued expertise and thank you for continuing to pave the way to get my body of work out into the world.

A big thanks to Lynette Smith and Clarisa Marcee for your editorial and proofreading support, and to Yvonne Parks of Pear Creative for her wonderful design work.

I also want to give a shout out to the amazing colleagues I have met this summer at the inspirational Muskoka Collective in Bracebridge. It's more than I could ask for as a co-working space! It also hosted me for my TEDx talk this summer, which we think may have been the most northernly TED talk recorded in Ontario (at least for now!).

Huge appreciation to my family who have respected how important my walking time has been these last few years. The track here in Bracebridge has seen many an edit happen on it during the summers of 2020 and 2021, in my daily walks.

This book has been shaped by a lifetime of work and conversations. As this book has been coming to completion from my amazing "remote-remote" location of Muskoka in the summer of 2021, I am so appreciative of the decades of ongoing learning my career has afforded me. It hasn't always been easy, but I have made sure that it's been fun and has had an impact.

Thank you to those around the world who have shared a pathway with me⊠whether you've been a teammate, a client, or an organization who has adopted me, thank you for sharing the remote road, or hybrid highway, with me for a while. I look forward to the next time our paths connect!

And to readers, stay tuned for more adventures of the Digital Dozen™! There are several more manuscripts in process, and books to come in what I envision to be a series of twelve! For now, continue to listen in at the Remote Pathways podcast.

WELCOME TO THE
90-DAY GUIDE FOR SUCCESS

Remote, virtual, and hybrid work continues to grow in scope and volume. It's been estimated that remote work grew by 159% since 2005 up to 2020.[1] During March 2020, it was estimated that more than 3 billion people needed to work remotely in response to COVID-19. A Gartner study on March 17th found that 88% of organizations "encouraged or required employees to work from home."[2]

From office professionals working remote several days a week, to entire organizations which are virtual, to the creative solopreneur who moves from side-gig to full-time hustle, remote work is here to stay, with hybrid work becoming a new reality for many teams and organizations.

Many who have experienced the freedom from the world of the cubicle are not keen to return anytime soon. The pathways to remote work are all varied and will be explored in a separate book in the Reconnecting Workspaces series, which will feature a Choose Your Own Pathway.

While many books are geared for leading remote teams, there has been a missing focus around how to get started and keep running when you move remote or into a hybrid working context where you blend both in-person and remote work.

For many years it's been stressed that the first 90 days of a person's new role can make or break the experience. Many of us don't get an "Operations Manual" when we are in the remote and hybrid workspace. This guide addresses many of the practical areas we may not necessarily consider as we move to remote or virtual work, whether a few days a month or full time. The *Guide* is written so each day you'll have the opportunity to dig into a core area geared to get you up to speed with your role and work within the remote and hybrid space.

This work has been inspired by my own remote career, which has spanned continents, pathways, and technologies over the last three decades. From my early work as a leader supporting teams in South American jungles to managing subregional teams from another continent, since 2004 I've been growing and leading a virtual business supporting professionals around the world, remote work is not only my passion, it's my practice.

Throughout the *Guide* you will explore the many pathways to remote work. This conversation is expanded in the *Remote Pathways* podcast launched in late 2019, which you can find on your favorite podcast player. It's also explored in my 2021 book, *Reconnecting Workspaces: Pathways to Thrive in the Remote, Hybrid and Virtual World*.

FOUR PRINCIPLES

The *Guide* is written with four principles in mind:

1. **Daily Steps + Consistent Action creates the traction and momentum we need in business.** Just as the tagline in the planner/workbook I created for virtual and remote workers in 2019—*PlanDoTrack*—"Daily Steps + Consistent Action = Momentum." It's the cumulative events that add up. Key to remote work is getting into action and keeping in action. Consistency is one of the 7 Remote Enablers to success. We've seen how powerfully daily steps add up in the *21 for 21 series of Virtual Co-working Sprints.*

2. **Keep it simple—These are bite-sized pieces that don't need to take a lot of time.** Each day you are encouraged to build in 15 minutes to take a look at that daily tip, and consider the conversations and questions associated. With the idea that small steps add up, 15 minutes a day of reading and journaling can create a valuable treasure trove of learning and insights you can return back to. Miss a day? Not a problem, return back.

3. **These ideas are generic to role and function.** Throughout my writing and the story line of the *Remote Pathways* podcast is the backstory of 12 different remote workers. Explore these backstories in the Meet the Digital Dozen section.

4. **Everyone in the remote space needs skills and leadership capabilities.** Building capacity and empowering the entire team is important in the remote space.

The tips fall across a range of areas including:

Ways of Working	You as a Remote Worker	Skills
Context of Remote Work	Team Topics	Time Management
Tools	The Iceberg of Remote Work	Your Relationships

FREQUENTLY ASKED QUESTIONS

In addition to daily steps, this resource provides you with "In Focus" spotlights. The Guide explores key questions and areas remote workers have, including:

- What are the benefits of working remote?
- What are the biggest challenges people find with this work?
- What apps do people use when they are working remote?
- What are the things people miss about face-to-face work?
- What questions can I ask in building new relationships?
- What project management fundamentals should I be aware of?
- What are key words I should note in communicating effectively?

- What are tips for managing up?

- I'm having conflict with a colleague. What might be at the core?

- As a team, what can we do to get better at results?

- What are some core planning tools we can use?

- What types of courses are going to help me keep learning?

- What are the skills remote workers need?

- What are the skills remote entrepreneurs need?

- What is intrapreneurism?

- What informal learning opportunities can I tap into?

- I have multiple matrix relationships. What can I do to say no? I have too much work already.

- Where do I begin with my workflow? How do I manage my time?

- What activities can I undertake to demonstrate follow-through?

- I have a colleague who doesn't follow through. What can I do?

- What actions create consistency?

- What different ways can I work on creating my vision? Is this something we want to do as a team?

- How do I adjust my style?

DESCRIPTION OF THE GUIDE

The *Reconnecting Workspaces 90-Day Guide* is geared for remote and hybrid workers of all kinds who want a step-by-step/incremental bite-sized approach of practical and tactical things you can do to ease into, or continue to flow through, your remote and hybrid role.

This is broken down into three monthly sets: Days 1–30, Days 31–60, and Days 61–90. We know that the first 90 days of any job are critical for a leader's success. So is the first 90 days of a remote or hybrid worker's world. This guide will be of interest to those stepping into the remote space.

At the same time, the focus on 90-day cycles is gaining popularity in many industries. A 90-day focus is often seen as just enough time to be designing and implementing projects. With this in mind, seasoned remote and hybrid workers will also find this guide of benefit.

With a tip every day, the *90-Day Guide for Success* focuses on:

- Ways of Working

- You as a Remote Worker

- Skills for Today's Remote and Hybrid Workspace

- Exploring the Context

- Key Relationships for Success

- The things you think you might want to do

While remote work is often "bucketed" under one term, it's anything but similar or homogenous. Therefore, the *Guide* incorporates the adventures of twelve different types of remote workers.

In the sections titled "Meet the Digital Dozen," I hope you will find yourself in one or more of the different pathways in which remote workers find themselves. As my Remote Pathways podcast co-host Michelle Mullins indicated to me recently, "Jenn, you've been almost all of these." And I have. "Softening the silos" is key to remote work, as is finding common ground across what might seem like huge differences in terms of role, space, and geography.

Throughout the *90-Day Guide*, we're going to be meeting a variety of remote teammates—

1. Mel, a professional business coach,
2. Malcolm, a mentor,
3. Sam, who has scaled and is selling her business,
4. Sujit, a project manager,
5. Jo, a virtual team leader,
6. Victor, who is working in the voluntary sector,
7. Jane, a virtual facilitator,
8. Serge, a seasoned serial entrepreneur,
9. Mo, a creative solopreneur,
10. Alex, who works from anywhere,
11. Sally, a sales professional, and
12. Ned, someone new to the role.

These are all characters we explore in the *Remote Pathways* podcast. You can check it out at RemotePathways.com.

HOW TO USE THIS GUIDE

The *90-Day Guide* is geared for new and seasoned hybrid and remote workers of all kinds. As individual contributors, as project managers, as team leaders, and as entrepreneurs, we all have a Day One.

It's been a long-held adage in the HR world that the first 90 days of any professional's career sets the foundation for success. What is going to help you do your best work?

This guide is structured into 90 days of prompts you can follow consistently. Each day includes a quote and also takes a deeper dive into the *What and Why* of each topic via the subheads of *What? So What?* and *Field Work—Now What?*

- The *What?* includes a description of what the topic is, some key details, or a case study.

- The *So What?* includes more detail about what's important about this topic, including implementation ideas.

- The *Now What?* includes a prompt or potential activity for you to take the action forward.

- There is also a *Did You Know?* section for most days, providing interesting factoids or resources to explore.

You are encouraged to share these on a daily basis with those around you, given that remote work does not happen in isolation. As I like to say, "No person is an island." See Day 4 for more on building relationships in the remote space!

You will notice that each week is broken down into a meta-theme as well. A key practice of helping navigate complexity is finding patterns or common ground. The meta-themes of each week will serve as an umbrella of connectivity, and a larger theme to think about throughout the week. Each one of these is a fundamental element of success with remote work.

Here are the weekly themes for our 90 days:

Week 1—Trust

Week 2—Connection

Week 3—Clarity

Week 4—Learning by Doing

Week 5—Resilience and Change

Week 6—Loneliness

Week 7—Leadership

Week 8—Focusing and Getting Things Done

Week 9—Additional Conversations to Have

Week 10—Technology

Week 11—Tricky Issues

Week 12—Experimentation

Week 13—Moving It Forward/Track

90-Day Guide for Virtual, Remote, and Hybrid Work Success

SUNDAY	MONDAY	TUESDAY	WEDNESDAY	THURSDAY	FRIDAY	SATURDAY

WEEK 1–FOUNDATIONAL FOCUS: TRUST

☐ 1	☐ 2	☐ 3	☐ 4	☐ 5	☐ 6	☐ 7
Welcome. Getting Started.	You–Areas of Focus, Getting Clear on Your Role.	Remote Work: Similarities, Differences, Advantages	Vision	Setting Up Your Office	Building Trust and Relationships	Team Effectiveness

WEEK 2–FOUNDATIONAL FOCUS: CONNECTION

☐ 8	☐ 9	☐ 10	☐ 11	☐ 12	☐ 13	☐ 14
Goals	Core Skills for Success	Relationship Building: Your Boss	Relationship in Focus: Your Peers	Context and Navigating VUCA	Strengths	Communication

WEEK 3–FOUNDATIONAL FOCUS: CLARITY

☐ 15	☐ 16	☐ 17	☐ 18	☐ 19	☐ 20	☐ 21
Systems for Working remote	Planning	Personal Brand	Time Management and Staying at Peak	Motivation	Prioritization	Teams in Focus: Types of Teams

WEEK 4–FOUNDATIONAL FOCUS: LEARNING BY DOING

☐ 22	☐ 23	☐ 24	☐ 25	☐ 26	☐ 27	☐ 28
Styles	Metrics Matter	Project Management	Networking	Personal Productivity	Focus (and Attention) Getting It Done	Teams in Focus: Matrix Teams

WEEK 5–FOUNDATIONAL FOCUS: RESILIENCE AND CHANGE

☐ 29	☐ 30	☐ 31	☐ 32	☐ 33	☐ 34	☐ 35
The Iceberg: Introduction and Values	Mentoring and Month One Check-In	Obstacles and Challenges	Trouble-shooting and Decision Making	Getting Unstuck	Coaching	Teams in Focus: Team Identity and Culture

WEEK 6–FOUNDATIONAL FOCUS: LONELINESS

☐ 36	☐ 37	☐ 38	☐ 39	☐ 40	☐ 41	☐ 42
Iceberg: Beliefs, Habits	Boundaries	Getting Organized	Change and the Dip	Routines	Problem Solving	Teams In Focus: Performance Measures and Roles

WEEK 7–FOUNDATIONAL FOCUS: LEADERSHIP

☐ 43	☐ 44	☐ 45	☐ 46	☐ 47	☐ 48	☐ 49
Assumptions	Perception Does Not Equal Reality	The Messy Middle and Mid-Point Check-in	Influence	Empathy	Presentations 101	Teams in Focus: Team Practices and Commitment

WEEK 8–FOUNDATIONAL FOCUS: FOCUSING AND GETTING THINGS DONE

☐ 50	☐ 51	☐ 52	☐ 53	☐ 54	☐ 55	☐ 56
Mindset	Ongoing Learning	High-Leverage Activities	Meetings 101	Get It Done: Consistent Action	Collaboration	Teams in Focus: Tools in Your Toolbox

WEEK 9-FOUNDATIONAL FOCUS: ADDITIONAL CONVERSATIONS TO HAVE

☐ 57	☐ 58	☐ 59	☐ 60	☐ 61	☐ 62	☐ 63
Virtual Conversation Skills	Feedback	Difficult Conversations	Trouble-shooting and Month Two Check-In	Pitfalls	Negotiation	When Are You at Your Best? Circadian Rhythm

WEEK 10-FOUNDATIONAL FOCUS: TECHNOLOGY

☐ 64	☐ 65	☐ 66	☐ 67	☐ 68	☐ 69	☐ 70
Reliability	Alchemy, Blends, and Follow-Up	Visibility	Productive or Busy?	Conflict	To Do/Not to Do	Chunk It Down

WEEK 11-FOUNDATIONAL FOCUS: TRICKY ISSUES

☐ 71	☐ 72	☐ 73	☐ 74	☐ 75	☐ 76	☐ 77
Memora-bility	Micro-Monitor: Challenges and Opportunities	Intercultural Mindset	Delegation	Working across Time Zones	Simplify and Keep It Simple	Co-Working

WEEK 12-FOUNDATIONAL FOCUS: EXPERIMENTATION

☐ 78	☐ 79	☐ 80	☐ 81	☐ 82	☐ 83	☐ 84
Leveraging Your Support Network	Lightbulb Moments and Innovation	Flexibility	Renewal/Release Valve/Well-Being	Experimentation	What's Beyond the Screen	What Doesn't Get Scheduled, Doesn't Get Done

WEEK 13-FOUNDATIONAL FOCUS: MOVING IT FORWARD/TRACK

☐ 85	☐ 86	☐ 87	☐ 88	☐ 89	☐ 90	☐ 91
Integration	Remote ≠ Disconnected: DNA of Remote	Track	Questions	Creativity	What's Next?	Bonus: Wrap It Up

For more ideas to support you in your work, check out the *Remote Pathways*™ podcast, where we explore the people, pathways, and processes of remote work. For the podcast, visit RemotePathways.com and also check out the ReconnectingWorkspaces.com website for more resources related to this book.

The 90-Day Guide for Success provides you with a different daily focus for 90 days, as a three-month roadmap. Each day is broken down into a *What? So What?* and *Field Work—Now What?* Here's what you can expect in each of these three daily sections:

WHAT?

The *90-Day Guide* was written for those of you starting a new role, starting remote or hybrid work for the first time, or scaling into more work.

Are you a new remote worker who is looking for daily structure to support you in exploring *what* you need to know as you move into your first 3 months of your work? Are you a seasoned remote worker looking to amplify your results?

The *What?* section of each daily focus sets the foundation, and includes tips for remote working success at any stage.

Unfortunately, we don't all have our manager down the hall, or a colleague to ask at the water cooler. We usually need to find our way in a new remote post, *alone*.

There are differences with remote and hybrid work, and onboarding is one of them. While the *90-Day Guide* is not meant as a replacement to your own organizational onboarding process (if there is one), this resource will provide you with a daily theme and focus.

SO WHAT?

Typically, at the start of a lifecycle of a new employee you have a program where you get to meet with people, and you have support all around you. Getting up to speed in the remote space is not as easy as focusing in on your list. Or running down the hall.

In the remote space, we are usually left to figure it out ourselves.

The *So What?* section explores what's important about the daily topic at any stage of your remote or hybrid career. The *So What?* sections help you think about the *Why* of an issue—the implications the topic may have on your role, or your work, as well as application opportunities.

With decades of experience of supporting new team members, and designing many onboarding processes, this *90-Day Guide* is meant as a daily touchpoint, to get you thinking about *what* you need to do, *where* you can go, and *what* follow-up activities you can undertake.

FIELD WORK—NOW WHAT?

The *Field Work—Now What?* is about getting into action. What are you going to do now?

As we quickly find when working in the remote space, action is even more important than words. The *Field Work—Now What?* offers you an invitation to take action around that area. It might include an action step, or something to journal on.

Here are some next steps for you as you get started:

- If you don't have a journal already, be sure to grab one.
- Download the 90-Day Calendar at ReconnectingWorkspaces.com and make it visible.
- Schedule in 15 minutes every day for the next 90 days to read, reflect, take notes, and take action on the daily prompts.
- Bring your insights to your discussions with your peers, your boss, and others who support you in your professional journey.
- Follow the *Remote Pathways* podcast at RemotePathways.com/podcast to acquire more tips and ideas around remote work.

Enjoy!

WHERE TO GO IN THE FIRST 90 DAYS

Michael D. Watkins is well known for his focused writing on ramping up in a new role. His book, *The First 90 Days—Proven Strategies for Getting up to Speed Faster and Smarter*, is now into a new edition.

Watkins identifies the following critical focus areas as you start a new role, particularly if you are a leader. Consider how these may be an important area of focus as you get started:

- Delegation
- Transition traps
- Sticking with what you know
- Falling prey to the "action imperative"
- Setting unrealistic expectations
- Attempting to do too much
- Coming in with "the answer"
- Engaging in the wrong type of learning
- Neglecting horizontal relationships[3]

-The First 90 Days, pp 5 and 6

The following strategies help you "dramatically accelerate your transition into your new role." Watkins' whole book focuses on the following main areas. (Listed in pages 9–12)

- Prepare yourself.

- Accelerate your learning; "you must be systematic and focused about deciding what you need to learn and how you will learn it most effectively."

- Match your strategy to the situation.

- Secure early wins. "Early wins build your credibility and create momentum . . . ." In the first 90 days, you need to identify ways to create value and improve business results that will help you get to the break-even point more rapidly.

- Negotiate success, "carefully planning for a series of critical conversations about the situation, expectations, working style, resources, and your personal development."

- Achieve alignment.

- Build your team.

- Create coalitions.

- Keep your balance.

- Accelerate everyone[4].

What is important to you as you get moving?

At Potentials Realized, it is important for us to Plan. Do. And Track. With that in mind, be sure to check off the days on the 90-Day Calendar as you complete them.

90-Day Guide for Virtual, Remote and Hybrid Work Success

WELCOME TO WEEK 1

Welcome to Week 1. Are you ready to get started? I hope so. As indicated already, the goal of this guide is to provide you with a quick daily touchpoint around key issues of importance for remote and hybrid professionals over a 90 day period. This may be your first 90 days at work, or you may be moving through a new quarter.

Whether you are a corporate employee, a freelancer, a digital nomad who is traveling the world, or someone building their own digital empire, we all have a Day One.

This week gets you working on your foundation for remote work success. Taking time to focus on these items can mean the difference between a house built on quicksand and one anchored firmly in the ground which won't shift, regardless of the freeze and thaw cycles of business.

This week's focus is going to be on our foundations, with our Week 1 roadmap including:

- Day 1—Welcome to Your Role
- Day 2—You: Areas of Focus, Getting Clear on Your Role
- Day 3—Remote Work—Similarities, Differences, Advantages
- Day 4—Vision
- Day 5—Setting Up Your Office
- Day 6—Building Trust and Relationships
- Day 7—Team Effectiveness

Each week is also going to have a foundational theme. These meta-weekly themes are cross-cutting across our work.

This week we start off with the Theme around Trust. Trust is one of the currencies of business, an enabler to great remote work.

As we get started, here's an invitation for you to grab a new notebook, file, or journal and dedicate it to the learning throughout this guide.

As you get started each week, be sure to write down your top 3 goals for the week, keep them visible, and be sure to use the daily tracker to capture additional notes.

Ready to go? Let's get started!

WHAT ARE YOUR TOP 3 GOALS THIS WEEK?:

1. _____

2. _____

3. _____

By the end of the week I want to be sure that . . .

_____

WEEK 1 · TRUST

"Consciously managing boundaries in a group setting is an essential way to
sustain and deepen the safety that people feel."
—William Isaacs

Trust takes on new meaning in the remote and hybrid space. It's an essential element ensuring that I not only show up but that I show up ready to do my best work.

When people are working on their own every day, we need to ensure that trust is occurring across multiple levels—self-trust that I will get my work done, trust with my team that they have my back, and trust that we can get it done.

As Stephen Covey writes, "Trust begets Trust." Trust is a two-way street. I need to give it in order to get it.

What are the things we can do to create more connection, trust, and safety in our remote and hybrid spaces?

Consider: how do you demonstrate trust in the remote and hybrid space?

We'll be coming back to *trust* as a core area over the next 90 days. At the start, trust comes down to specific, observable behaviors that others can see or read. This is even more important when the windows of time we are together are limited and usually infrequent in the remote space. Our connection may be framed by the screen, and others may never see the full picture of our context and work. This has implications for what I share, and how I choose to connect with others. What we do share, and what others see, becomes pronounced.

In building trust, it's important to remember that these actions individually are simple and straightforward and add up to create a vibrant working environment. It includes things like being sure we:

- Show up and be present (not multi-tasking).
- Are clear with expectations—what can others expect from me? What can I expect of them?
- Are explicit with deadlines, end product required, and what success will look like
- Micro-monitor, not micro-manage.

- Follow through—do what I say I will.

- Are clear in communicating—what's expected, who is responsible, and how tasks fit together.

Trust is often measured by our activities, which aren't seen consistently in the remote and hybrid space. Consider what you need to do to maintain and build trust with those you work with. Some of the more common ways are listed here.

9 Ways to Build Trust as a Remote Worker

On an individual level, building trust may include these behaviors:

- Walk the talk—do what you say you are doing. Follow through.

- Be fair—How are your actions being perceived? Are you treating everyone equally?

- Build on strengths.

- Take ownership—for what works and what doesn't.

- Be transparent—with process.

- Create connection. Find the common ground. Connect in ways that are meaningful to others.

- Create clear expectations you can live by—with your boss, your peers, and other stakeholders.

- Communicate, communicate, communicate—be sure that key messages are being reinforced. Don't assume they are being read or are even getting through! Match the importance of the message with the right channel. Don't over-rely on technology. Remember, there is a human being on the other side of the conversation!

- Regular one-on-ones—personal touch is key in the remote space, and relationships are important. Regular one-on-ones or conversations with your boss, your peers, and stakeholders are key. Remote does not mean invisible!

How are you doing on each of these? What are you doing in each of these areas? Which could benefit from some attention?

_____

_____

_____

_____

And what if your rating is low?

Simon Sinek writes, "When we are not on a trusting team . . . we often feel forced to lie, hide, and fake to compensate. We hide mistakes, we act as if we know what we're doing (even when we don't) and we would never admit we need help for the fear of humiliation, reprisal or finding ourselves on a short list at the next round of layoffs."[5]

The cost of low trust is very high.

TRIAD OF TRUST, SAFETY, AND CONNECTION[6]

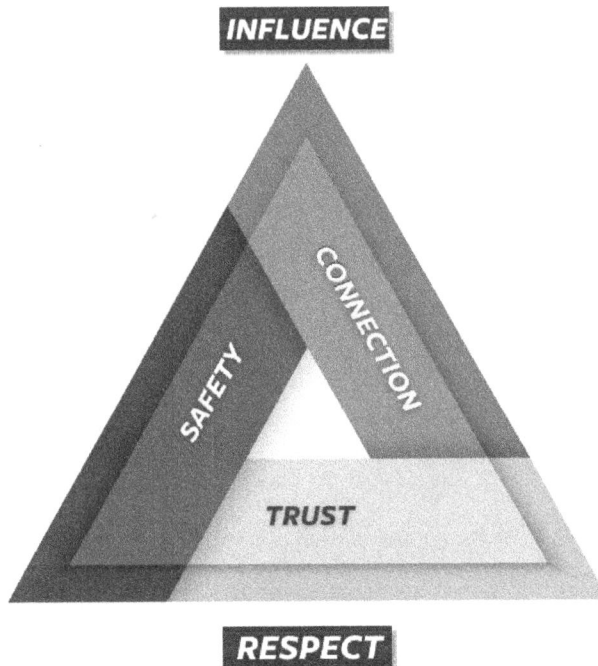

Trust has an important connection to other enablers to great work in the remote space—Connection and Safety. I term these the Triad of Trust, Safety, and Connection. Lack of any of these can impact results and relationships. Like the project management triple constraint, impact on one will also impact on others.

A phrase you will hear regularly throughout this guide is that "No person is an island." We don't operate in isolation. In fact, in the remote space, trust may play an even bigger role around longer-term engagement and movement. Connection is key; and even if we can't see our colleagues, they are there.

"Part of safety," said Professor Robin Ely, "is being able to admit mistakes and being open to learning—to say, 'I need help, I can't lift this thing by myself.'"[7]

Trust impacts many business results—from flow of information to the ability to take risks. Simon Sinek notes in his most recent writing, "When we work on a Trusting Team, we do so with the confidence that our boss or our colleagues will be there to support us."[8]

Sinek quotes Brene Brown in her book, *Dare to Lead*, "Trust is the stacking and layering of small moments and reciprocal vulnerability over time. Trust and vulnerability grow together, and to betray one is to destroy both."[9]

Trust occurs on multiple levels, including organizational trust, team trust, and self-trust.

Trust is usually demonstrated via our behaviors. A challenge in the remote space is that these behaviors may not be:

- **Visible.** Given that our touchpoints are infrequent, and we usually can only be seen via the frame of our screen, the windows into our world of work are magnified, as are the behaviors (good and bad) which are seen.

- **Understood as we intended.** Remember that our actions in the remote space are usually through a small window on the screen for a micro-part of our week. What can we do to expand the screen to provide more context? What can we do to check that what we share and how we interact is what's needed?

- **Seen in context.** Given that we are a distributed team, we do not see each other's context. What is important to share about "What's beyond your screen?"

With these factors in mind, it means that we need to be more explicit with setting the context and being proactive in indicating what is important.

Things that we can do to build trust include:

- Follow-through.

- Addressing issues immediately before they are too big and have festered.

- Adopting a win-win mindset—Reinforce with the other party or your partner how important it is to have a shared focus and shared outcome for both people.

Some trust models, such as Reina and Reina's, include competence (how well we do things) and character (how we are perceived).

Consistency may also be linked to trust. How consistent are our actions? If we are not being seen regularly enough, it may serve to erode trust.

Communicate regularly. Whether it's communicating things that are working, or things that aren't, ongoing communication in multiple channels is essential. Without this it is hard to focus.

Highlight what may be different for a remote worker vs. leader vs. entrepreneur.

COMPLETE THE SELF-ASSESSMENT AROUND TRUST

Take a few minutes to work through the following self-assessment on these trust behaviors:

WHAT IT IS:	WHAT IT LOOKS LIKE:	MY RATING ON A SCALE OF 1–10 (1 = LOW, 10 = HIGH)	WHAT I CAN DO TO IMPROVE IT?
Walk the talk			
Be fair			
Build on strengths			
Take ownership			
Be transparent			
Create connection			
Set clear expectations			
Communicate, Communicate, Communicate			
Hold regular one-on-ones			

Questions to consider:

- What is the state of trust in your team right now?
- What is the state of trust in your organization?

- What is your level of self-trust?

- What actions do you need to take?

- Now what do you want to do less of? *or* What do you want to build capacity around?

Remote workers have many different opportunities open up, and our work may evolve very quickly. Those who are good at this work will find that their reputation will spread—even from country to country. Being of service and constantly adding value is key. So is developing relationships which are grounded in trust and connection. Going the extra mile to anchor in solid relationships with your colleagues will help you stand out. Given that we can't congregate around the "water cooler," what role can you play in bringing people together?

There are lots of different opportunities and options to bring people together to build trust and connection.

Safety is also important. If people do not feel safe, they will not raise the real issues which need to be addressed. Having an "open door" policy will not work in the remote space if people do not trust you or if they feel like they will have their job impacted. This can also have interesting connotations. We'll be looking at safety as our theme of Week 2.

Trust-Building Conversation Sparkers

Creating the space for conversation around trust can be important. Consider incorporating questions like these trust builders, which are geared to help others learn a little more about each other:

- Tell me about your greatest success.

- What's the resource you go to all the time?

- What are the things you think I should learn to do in these first 90 days?

- Who should I meet with?

- What resource should I refer to?

- What should I always second-check?

- What else is the important thing to focus on?

For more on this topic, refer to the Reconnecting Workspaces Tip: Chapter 5—The Triad: Trust, Safety, and Connection.

DAY 1
WELCOME TO YOUR ROLE

"A new job is not a new beginning. It is a path to create a new ending."
—Unknown

FOCUS QUESTION:
What's possible for you in the next 90 Days?

WHAT?

Welcome to remote and hybrid work. Whether you are new to your role or have been doing this for a while and are using this guide to get some traction for the next 90 days, welcome!

What are you excited about? What do you want your rhythm of work to look like?

As we'll see in coming weeks, there are many different pathways to remote work, from those who WFA (Work from Anywhere) to those who WFH (Work from Home) to those who are project managers or creative solopreneurs. Despite the different roles, most of us share these ideals as remote workers:

- Flexibility
- Global focus
- Independence
- Autonomy
- Freedom
- Creativity
- Environmental focus—reducing our carbon footprint

9 Core Skills for Remote Workers[10]

What's important to you?

Keep these factors in mind, as these are likely to be motivators for you. Motivation is a key topic to understanding what we love and what keeps us going in the remote space. We'll return to this topic later in the *Guide*.

As with any first day on the job, it can be useful to spend time today getting yourself set up, connecting with others, and clarifying what your work will entail.

What is your role? What are the main components? What is going to help you do your best work?

A wide variety of skills can help us excel in the remote space. I introduced these in Chapter 10 of *Effective Virtual Conversations* and share them again in Section 1 of *PlanDoTrack*. Also refer to the Teamwork and Leadership chapters in *Reconnecting Workspaces*.

As you consider your work right now, which areas could benefit from more attention? Stay tuned as we dive a little deeper into these topics throughout the *Guide*.

So, what's going to help you?

Settling In—Ten Essentials

Ten things remote workers need as they get settled:

1. Technology that works

2. Power/juice—something to keep charged

3. A work space—quiet or stimulating; it often doesn't matter

4. A way to communicate with colleagues—Skype, Zoom, WebEx

5. A routine and ways to renew

6. Peers and mentors and ways to get advice

7. Connection with your boss and team

8. Feedback cycles

9. Easy ways to connect in on work instructions

10. Ways to keep things visible

SO WHAT?

Getting Settled into Remote Work Practically

As you get started with remote work, here are several things you will want to consider:

- **Creating space in your office**—If you work in a small space what are the areas you want to earmark for work?

- **Creating boundaries**—boundaries will help you excel. What are your boundaries around WHEN you work (when you are on and when you are off) and WHERE you work (what space do you have to get your work done)?

- **Creating shared agreements**—what do you need to do? What's your role? What's expected of you?

- **Creating habits**—what are the habits that will keep you grounded? Focused? Healthy? Productive? Connected?

- **Creating relationships**—reaching out to others in your organization. Reaching out to others outside your organization. Creating space for co-working.

We'll be looking at these as we go.

Space > Boundaries > Shared Agreements > Habits > Relationships

Part of the transition to remote work can be tiring. Without the normal signals and routines of in-person office work, you may find yourself questioning if this was the right move. Perhaps there was not a choice when shifting to working in the remote or hybrid space.

AREAS TO CONSIDER

What are the routines you want to get into? Just like working in the face-to-face realm, what are the activities you want to do on a regular basis? If you swim, look into the swimming schedule—block it in. If you want to learn how to cook, schedule that in. Put it in the calendar. As Michael Hyatt wrote, "What doesn't get scheduled, doesn't get done."[11]

Clarify the basics. What are the required work hours? Many organizations operate on a common working hours frame. Whether it's 11–1 or 10–2, what are the hours that you are going to have to be "On"? These may be times when you want to, or need to, schedule routines, as well as times when one-on-one meetings can be scheduled. Beyond that, consider your circadian rhythms and think about whether you want to get started early in the day or later.

Track your time. Notice where your time is going. Research undertaken by Stanford's Nicholas Bloom found that remote workers studied over a two-year period working from home were 13.5% more productive and had a 50% lower attrition rate. HR professionals have for years earmarked turnover as costing 1.5 times an employee's salary.

Establish "office hours" and communicate this to friends, neighbors, and family.

Watch for "errand creep." It can be easy to offer to walk the neighbor's dog or pick up the mail. Interruptions at work can take upwards of 22 minutes to get back on track, according to Dr. Gloria Mark.[12]

What are the core activities you need to get completed each day? Are you considering starting the day with a list of your top 3–5 goals? Pick up a digital copy of my *PlanDoTrack* planner, which includes weekly, monthly, quarterly, and annual tools.

What work schedule is going to work best for you? Consider your circadian rhythms, or what is commonly referred to as your internal clock. According to Daniel Pink, some of us are larks and love to start work in the early hours of the day, and some of us are night owls and work into the wee hours of the night. Chronobiology has found that we each have optimum times during which we like to work, and rest.

So, what's going to help you?

FIELD WORK—NOW WHAT?

Take some time today to:

- Set yourself up for success. Review Settling In—10 Essential Elements.
- Consider what space you need and what's going to make it work.
- Consider your boundaries and start communicating them.
- Clarify and design your shared agreements around work, hours of work, roles, and responsibilities.
- Consider the habits and routines you want to cultivate.

Also, consider the key relationships you want to be cultivating in these first few weeks. Today it may simply be starting to create a list of everyone you want to or need to meet. If you don't know who you need to meet, start asking around.

HOW FAR WE'VE COME! THE CONTEXT OF REMOTE WORK

The context of remote work continues to shift in amazing ways. Think of some of these times:

- 1990s—fax and long distance. Do you remember when we moved from the internet only available in university environments to the bigger world?
- 2000s—cell phones and flip phones ushered in the advent of Blackberry and a small keyboard to be able to type in. Online courses made their entry.

- 2010s—iPhone/Android wars . . . . Apps. Devices.

- 2019—digital minimalism—Cal Newport, and his focus on the areas of digital detox.

- 2020s—wearable devices—take phone on your wrist, heart tracker, sleep tracker. Virtual reality. Augmented reality became a reality. Automatic tools.

- 2020–2021: COVID-19—Physical distancing and remote work becomes the new normal.

- What's ahead—AI and impact to work. Empathy and the *way* we work will become more important.

The world of the remote space has changed dramatically—from the days of fax to the days of "talking heads" and conference calls, today we are able to stream without too much effort. It's become a common way of working.

Where were you as we were stepping into Y2K; what was it like in 1999? I remember the excitement and anxiety that technology might just stop as we moved into the new decade. I think for many it was a time of learning to contingency-plan, which was quickly forgotten once things kept going.

What do you recall from the 2000s? Think about your work as you stepped into the 2010s. What were you doing? The iPad had been around for 3 years. It was already revolutionizing how things were doing. While you might not remember it, it was as if we could "cut the cord" from our desks.

Flashback to 2009. The average size of the phone. It was more common to have cordless phones, but laptops were still outside of the norm. My laptop at the time was a whopping 11 pounds. It made up the entire luggage allowance I had!

It can be interesting to consider the markers in life. Consider how much things cost in 2009[13]:

- Average cost of new house $232,880.00

- Average income per year $39,423.00

- Average monthly rent $675.00

- Cost of a gallon of gas $2.73

- US Postage Stamp 42 cents

- 1 lb. of bacon $3.19

- Movie ticket $7.50

- Loaf of bread $1.77

- In-state college tuition $6,585.00

- Price of gold per ounce (September 1st, 2009) $958.00

- Price of oil $53.56 per barrel

The underbelly of technology change and remote work is that everything is moving *very* quickly. While for many years *always being on* was the norm, there is pushback in terms of creating boundaries in our work. There is also a pushback about how you want to connect. Not everyone wants to be connected in a 365-day, 360-degree way. Consider what boundaries might be useful for you.

What's changed in the time that you have been working remotely?

NOTES AND REFLECTIONS:

DAY 2
YOU: AREAS OF FOCUS, GETTING CLEAR ON YOUR ROLE

"Concentrate all your thoughts upon the work at hand. The sun's rays do not burn until brought to a focus."
—Alexander Bell

FOCUS QUESTION:
What's important to focus on? What's important to get clear?

WHAT?

As you step into day 2, it can be key to get clear on your role and understand what your main areas of work are in the remote and hybrid space. Today, consider exploring these questions:

- What are your main responsibilities? Review your job description and/or meet with your boss.

- What are your main areas of focus?

- What does success look like around those areas?

- Who do you report to? Are you part of any matrix relationships? (Note: in the remote space you may have several leaders and be part of several teams.)

- Who do you need to know? Where does your role connect in with others? Whom do you connect with?

As you consider your work—this year/this quarter/this month—ask yourself:

- What's a must do? In other words, needs to get done, no matter what?

Versus

- What's a nice to do? In other words, what would be nice to do or learn?

Versus

- What can be outsourced or delegated to others?

In addition to your specific job function, check out how important it is to include a focus on:

- Reporting
- Budgets
- Business Planning—Annual Planning
- Business Development
- What else?

Top 10 How Tos

10 things remote professionals need to know:

1. How to build relationships across distance.

2. How to ask questions to elicit the information you need.

3. How to make decisions when you may not see all the information.

4. How to prioritize across the remote space.

5. What to learn about different cultures and their own cultural bias.

6. How to read energy and tone in a call where you might not see the other party.

7. How to keep energy moving.

8. How to help people connect into what's important for them.

9. How to follow up.

10. How to prepare yet be ready to move

SO WHAT?

Focus and *motivation* are going to be critical for us as remote workers. We are our own engine.

On a personal level, ask yourself: *Where do I want to be one year from now?*

_____

_____

_____

_____

_____

With that in mind, what do you need to *focus* on? In other words, what do you need to say *Yes* to right now in order to get to it? What do you need to say *No* to?

_____

_____

_____

KEY SUCCESS FACTORS FOR REMOTE WORK

Several activities and behaviors help remote workers thrive in both the short and medium term:

- **Be visible**—it can be very important to be visible in the remote space. This means going out of your way and being proactive in scheduling meetings, attending industry events, undertaking outreach for one-on-ones, and participating in training. What can you do to be more visible in your organization? With your peers? In your network?

- **Offer value**—it's important to offer something of value. Trust begets trust. What is the value you are bringing to your team members? To your organization? To the stakeholders and/or customers you support?

- **Be consistent**—consistency is key in today's VUCA context. VUCA stands for *volatile, uncertain, complex,* and *ambiguous.* With so much uncertainty, being consistent can create more trust and connection.

  - o Consistency takes several forms—from being consistent in your outreach strategies (e.g., you are going to blog once a week) to writing or focusing on the same topic regularly. What does consistency mean for you?

Be Visible | Offer Value | Be Consistent

Collaborate | Be Present and Be Visible | Follow Through

Find Common Ground | Leverage Strengths | What's Beyond the Screen?

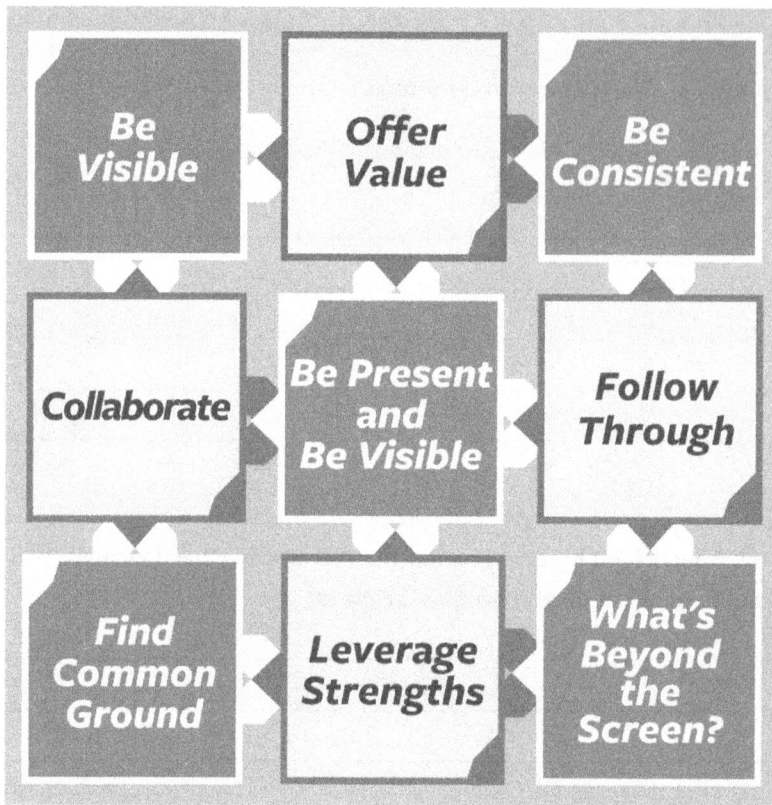

- **Collaborate**—no person is an island. Your results may be inherently linked with others with whom you are connected but cannot see. Consider how collaboration is key for success.

- **Show up, be present, and be visible**—some days your focus may get fractured with multiple meetings. It's important to be present and visible. Make a practice of proactive outreach with key stakeholders such as your boss, peers, and mentor. Schedule it in.

- **Follow-through**—follow-through is a strong signal for reliability. Where do you need to follow through more? What could that look like for you?

- **Find the common ground**—in building solid, trusting relationships, finding common ground is key. What is similar? What are common opportunities and challenges you face?

- **Leverage your strengths**—given the independent nature of remote work, you will likely need to lean more into your own abilities than if you were part of an in-person team. At the same time, be sure to be reaching out to your colleagues and peers, as teamwork may be expected in your role.

- **What's beyond the screen?**—sharing more about you, your context, and your priorities as a remote worker can go a long way. Depending on the people you are working with, rapport and relationship building can be the essential precursor to business success. Taking a few minutes to inquire after current events or sharing something that is wider than the screen you can see can be of immense value. What is it that you would like to share from behind your screen?

IN THE SPOTLIGHT—DIGITAL DOZEN: WHAT DO OTHERS SAY?

Top 10 recommendations from the Digital Dozen on being successful in the remote and hybrid space:

1. **Be proactive in flagging issues which need attention.** This might require a meeting with multiple stakeholders, or multiple solutions (not just one or two) to be generated.

2. **Always get clear on what the outcome and output is.** If it's not shared, ask!

3. **Focus first on the work that needs to get done.** It's easy to become very reactive in any role, and we want to make sure that the "big rocks" are taken care of. Just like Stephen Covey illustrated in his work back in the 1980s, if we start first with the big rocks, it's easier to fit in the smaller tasks around that.

4. **Consider what is needed in terms of time, people, and resources for project completion.** Make requests from those who can help you get these.

5. **Get to know others.** We do not work in isolation in the remote space. No person is an island. Work still occurs through others.

6. **Prioritize.** And know what the priorities of your key partners (boss and peers) really are.

7. **Focus in on the things which are going to get high leverage.** What's going to give you the most impact?

8. **Chunk or batch tasks.** It's easy to get stalled in remote work, especially around projects that feel large. First, break these down by creating a mind map of all the tasks that go into it. This may help you chunk them down, or make them smaller. Then consider batching them into "like tasks," thereby reducing what is known as "cognitive load." More mental energy gets expended when we shift tasks.

9. **Get good at negotiating.** It's easy to have work piled on. What are the things you need to create boundaries around or take a stand for?

10. **Discern.** What is a *need to have* (absolutely essential), and what is a *nice to have* (nice, but not essential)?

FIELD WORK—NOW WHAT?

Use today to get clear on what you are required to do. Reach out to your boss and have a dialogue about their expectations.

_____

_____

_____

Identify your assumptions of what you think you are going to need to do and check this.

_____

_____

_____

Make a list of what's required with your work. Think about how you are going to get your work done.

_____

_____

_____

_____

_____

_____

Identify _who_ you are going to need to connect with.

_____

_____

_____

Foster the space for different activities:

- Innovation
- Creativity
- Relationship development

> ## Remote Work Principle
> Know what is required; everything is on steroids

Most things are magnified in the remote space, framed by the small screen we see. The following are core areas you will want to pay attention to:

- Establishing trust
- Clear communication
- Consistent messaging
- Systems to ensure fluidity and flow
- Systems and tools so that people can work from the same materials
- Managing and navigating roles
- And ensuring that communication flows

NOTES AND REFLECTIONS:

REMOTE WORK: SIMILARITIES, DIFFERENCES, ADVANTAGES

"One thing is for sure; you cannot choose not to change when the world around changes. Response to change is mandatory. The only choice is how to respond."
—Simon Harris

FOCUS QUESTION:

As you think about virtual, remote, and hybrid work, what do you see as similar and different? What do you see as the advantages and disadvantages?

Today's focus explores the similarities and differences in remote and hybrid work you might see, as well as some of the advantages and disadvantages. If you are new to remote work but not new to the role, it may feel like there are a lot of similarities.

WHAT?

Many factors have lead to today's resurgence of virtual teams and remote work. In *Effective Virtual Conversations* I highlighted these factors influencing the space for virtual conversations, teamwork, and learning:

- The move to just-in-time and real-time processes
- Time efficiency
- Reduction of the carbon footprint—with commute times flourishing, there can be better ways to work. Britain's Open University found that eLearning consumes 90% less energy than traditional courses. They found that the amount of CO_2 emits (per student) is also reduced by up to 85%[14]

- Bringing expertise together

- Bringing peers together from a wider cross section

From ecological considerations to a focus on flexible work, many compelling stats exist for remote work today.[15]

STATE OF REMOTE WORK–2015

As I shared in Teams365 post #994, learning how to be an effective virtual professional is one part of the equation of moving to a more mobile, and engaged, workforce. Another key part is creating an enabling environment for virtual and remote work, which may include ensuring there are adequate resources, policies, and expectations around virtual work.

Here's some research around the drivers for developing a more remote workforce. Softchoice's study, the "Death of the Desk Job," found through its survey that:

- 62% of employees believe they are more productive working outside the office.

- 61% of employees prefer working the equivalent of an eight-hour workday broken up over a longer day, rather than in a single 9-5 block.

- 57% of employees work on personal and or sick days, and 44% of employees worked on their last vacation.

- 24% of organizations have set clear policies and expectations around appropriate work activities after business hours.

- 74% of North American employees would quit their job for one that allows them to work remotely more often.

- 70% would quit in favor of a position that offers increased flexibility. [16]

Did You Know?[17]

According to Flexjobs.com, here's the total environmental impact for the current remote worker population of 3.9 million workers who work from home at least half time:

- Vehicle miles not traveled: 7.8 billion

- Vehicle trips avoided: 530 million

- Tons of greenhouse gases (GHG) avoided (EPA method): 3 million

- Reduced traffic accident costs: $498 million

SO WHAT?

What's the end of the cubicle world?

From health outbreaks, to environmental pressures, to political constraints, the world of the remote worker is morphing the way we work around boundaries that exist.

Whether it's VUCA, the Great Resignation, politics, COVID-19, changes to borders, or economic instability, many forces influenced the changes taking place in this decade of the 2020s.

VUCA is a term originally coined by the US Army. It stands for *volatility*, *uncertainty*, *complexity*, and *ambiguity*. VUCA has characterized most of this decade and is rapidly shaping the way we work.

ADVANTAGES TO REMOTE WORK

The wide variety of advantages to remote work range from cost savings to time netted. It's no wonder that remote work grew by 159% since 2005, before the pandemic even started. Let's explore some of the more common reasons cited.

More productive

A survey spearheaded by Cloud Solutions found that employees reported being 77% more productive.[18]

Another study found reduced turnover by 50% when the work from home option is available.[19]

2015—Stanford University study found remote workers to be more productive than their in-office counterparts.[20]

Happier employees

Happiness—Those who work from home one day a month are 24% happier according to an OWLLabs 2019 study.[21]

Shorter commute time

Cost-saving on commute time—Toronto has some of the highest commute times in North America. According to the 2016 census, more than 21% of Canadians had a commute of more than 60 minutes. The average cost estimate for travel time, using minimum wage, was $273 per week. Over 52 weeks, that would equal $14,913 CDN.[22]

Lower travel costs

Cost—remote work saves $10,000 per employee on commercial real-estate.[23]

Fostering cross-sectoral and cross-functional learning

Working from anywhere creates an opportunity for employees to collaborate with many different types of colleagues, both internal and external. As the pandemic illustrated, virtual learning events created opportunities for people to come together from across the world, leading to learning occurring across industries and silos.

Fewer interruptions

Enhanced ability to focus on work—what are some of the distractions? A recent study on office acoustics found that 70% of global workers are facing office noise, including these areas:

- Conversations and chitchat among employees
- Phone conversations
- Phones ringing
- People walking around[24]

Reducing ecological footprint

Tracking by World Wildlife Federation found that the pandemic lockdowns meant a contraction of the ecological footprint of three weeks, with the annual Earth Overshoot date shifting in 2020 from July 29 to August 22.[25]

Harnessing the best of global talent

Finally, remote work provides an opportunity for talent to be sourced from anywhere, not just from a geographically convenient location to the office. The geographic-independence of remote and hybrid work allows for talent to come from multiple locations.

This is on top of such additional distractions as email coming in, ongoing meetings, and lack of focus.

Who is supporting remote work?

Prior to the pandemic, the age of the manager might have had an influence. A 2018 Upwork Future Work Report found that millennials led the pack in terms of enabling remote work: "69% of these younger managers say they allow their team members to work remotely, compared to 59% of generation X managers and 58% of baby boomers." [26]

> "Two out of five full-time employees will work remote in the next three years."
> —Greg Katz

Talent LMS found that in their survey group, 31% worked out of a home office and 27% worked out of their living rooms.

THE DOWNSIDE TO REMOTE WORK

While a lot has changed, many things still stay the same. Early studies found that successful telecommuters "stay connected with coworkers and boss, are well organized, get out of the house, separate work from home, make tech a friend, know when to take a break." [27]

The same study notes that remote work is not for:

- Employees who have a high need for social interaction
- Employees who are easily distracted by outside demands and interruption
- Employees who need the office setting to provide an environment conducive to work.

What are some of the biggest challenges people find with this work?

- Loneliness
- Isolation
- Boundaries
- The blending of our different roles and hats that we wear (parent, employee, caretaker, spouse . . .)

What are the things people miss about face-to-face work? Several things, including:

- **The social interaction.** While having people drop by to chat might not have been your favorite activity, remote professionals can feel isolated. Without opportunities to see people face to face—in the hallways, at the watercooler—it's important to be proactive in reaching out to others to keep the social conversations going. In *Effective Virtual Conversations*, I also share the idea of doing virtual lunches, potlucks, and co-working sessions on a regular basis. These may be more informal in nature and provide opportunities for people to "get to know each other" and share information.

- **Commute time.** While commuting can be extended for many in larger cities like Toronto and LA, the commute time can also be an impetus to do reading or learning. If you like a change of pace, is it possible to work offsite from your regular location a few hours or days a week? It might be a library or coffee house.

Here are two practical things you can do to counter the isolation with remote work:

Get active in local communities. Being active in your local community events can also provide the social interaction you need on a daily basis, making your outreach with others in your organization more targeted and specific. What are the events you'd like to be active in? If you are a parent, do you want to be part of the PTA? Can you link into the local chamber of commerce? Participate in Meetups locally for those in your network? What does being active in local communities look like for you?

Connect in social channels. While social media can be a "time sucker," it may be useful to dedicate time in the social channels. If you are a solopreneur or business owner, might there be a social community builder in the process? Whether you host or are active in one, social channels can be a great place to build a brand and be active.

Establish Routines. As many found during stay-at-home or quarantine experiences during COVID-19, establishing routines is key to success for remote and hybrid work. What are the things you'll be doing throughout the day? What do you want to make sure you leave time for?

COUNTER VOICES TO REMOTE WORK

What are the arguments against remote work?

Yahoo's CEO was a great example of "bringing people in" to the office. Their research found that their workers were not as productive.

ARGUMENT AGAINST REMOTE WORK	THE MYTH OR THINKING BEHIND THE ARGUMENT	WHAT YOU NEED TO DO TO AVOID THIS
You are not going to work on your own.	An older mindset of leadership would assert that professionals cannot work on their own.	Clarity around end results, touchpoints, regular communication, and reporting.
You are going to sit in your pajamas.	Laziness	Establish a routine—get up and go to work.
No one is going to know what you are going to do.	A mindset of "out of sight equals out of mind"	Continue team meetings on a regular basis.
No one is going to know what to do.	Individuals need to be "directed" and monitored at all times.	Need to clarify tasks and roles
You are not going to work as hard, or focus as much, when working outside the office.	Employees need to be supervised in an official office. Offices provide a distraction-free place to be creative and innovative.	Focus on output rather than time spent on activities. Explore what does generate the conditions for productivity, creativity, innovation, and focus.

You need face-to-face communication.	We can't communicate well virtually.	As many have found, streaming by video may be as clear as being face to face.

FIELD WORK—NOW WHAT?

What do you see as:

Similar with remote, hybrid, and face-to-face work?

_____

_____

_____

_____

Different with remote work?

_____

_____

_____

_____

Advantages of remote or hybrid work?

_____

_____

_____

_____

Disadvantages of remote or hybrid work?

_____

_____

_____

_____

Unique Things That Hybrid and Remote Workers Can Do

- Employ MacGyver technology—find innovative fixes for making it work

- Know how to work both Zoom and audio

- Always start with the question

- Know introductions or hellos/greetings in multiple languages

- Host a function, making people feel at ease

- Get as comfortable at working in the virtual space as we do in the in-person space

- Be comfortable in thinking about how work needs to flow so that it impacts others (maybe not unique to remote workers)

- Be adept at getting time-zone conversions right (so we show up at the right time!)

- Be able to focus

- Have exposure to a lot of different ways teams work—because they are typically part of several different teams themselves!

- Consider time-management apps their second-best friend

- Know exactly how much time it takes to do something

NOTES AND REFLECTIONS:

D A Y 4
VISION

"Vision helps us through the ebbs and flows of business."
—Jennifer Britton

FOCUS QUESTION:
What's your vision for your work?

WHAT?

As a remote worker we are left to our devices a significant amount of the time. While we have goals related to our work, it's likely that we will also be setting goals related to our own focus as well.

Our vision is larger than our goals. It's imagining where we want to go and what we want our work, or world, to look like down the road. Visions may be 3 years from now, 5 years from now or even 10 years from now.

Why is it important to take time to create your own vision?

- Developing a vision helps to create clarity on what we want to create in our business.
- A vision helps us decide where we want to focus and where we don't want to—this can help us say *yes* and *no*.
- A powerful vision can help us through the ebbs and flows of business.
- From our vision comes our goals—large and strategic, as well as granular and immediate.
- From our goals, we can create a roadmap and break down our goals into concrete, regular action steps.[28]

ACTIVITY

Today's activity gets you to create a list of your goals for the next decade. Over the last few years, the notion of a *bullet journal* has taken root in popular culture. Bullet journals are characterized by lots of open space.

Start a part of your journal or notebook around what your goals are for this decade. While a goal list may seem daunting, think of yourself 10 years from now:

- What do you want your work to look like?
- How do you want to spend your time?
- What do you want to have accomplished?
- What milestones will you have reached?
- What life experiences do you want to have completed?
- What are you known for?

Make a bullet list—or bucket list—for all the things you hope to achieve. What are your goals for this role?

Dream big, don't limit yourself!

12 Things Remote and Hybrid Workers Are Grateful For

1. The freedom and flexibility remote work entails
2. Being able to get a global perspective without having to leave their house
3. Not having to jump in the car and commute two-plus hours a day
4. The ability to work around other important parts of their life
5. Not having to spend a ton of time in meetings every day—unless we opt into this
6. The autonomy to do work in a way that works for us
7. The ability to schedule our workflow to outputs rather than schedule
8. The ability to collaborate with other intriguing minds
9. Exposure to a lot of ideas/topics that we might not have if we sat at a desk in a regular office
10. Mindset shift
11. Perspectives that are wider than our own
12. Opportunity to be part of matrix teams from across an organization or industry

SO WHAT?

CREATING A POWERFUL VISION—10 DIFFERENT WAYS

Here are 10 ways to work with vision:

1. Use a series of reflective questions which you can journal to.

2. Ask people to create their own story line or drawing of what it could look like.

3. Create a roadmap to indicate milestones along the way. Look at the following Roadmap image I use to support clients in chunking down parts of their vision. What are your four road markers along the way?

4. Create a vision board of the vision.

5. Get people to reflect on their sweet spot: What they are good at? What are they passionate about? What does their target audience want, need, and prefer?

6. Use the *5 Ws and an H* to get clearer on different parts of the vision. What is the Who, What, Why, When, Where, and How of your vision?

7. Chunk down parts of an annual vision into monthly components.

8. Infuse vision with some fun tools like Visual Cards like the Conversation Sparker Deck (ConversationSparker.com), Points of You, or Visual Explorer.

9. Roll the dice and get inspiration from the Reconnecting Workspaces Dice or Rory's Story Cubes.

10. Participate in a "Draw Your Future" process.

We don't always want to hold long-term visions too tightly. Many times, they are aspirational; and with that, we need to trust in *how* they will come to be. If we spend too much time thinking about the *how*, we may, in fact, limit ourselves.

Questions to consider:

- What is your vision for your work—Next quarter? A year from now? Five years from now?
- What are the things that you aspire to?
- If you had no limits, what would you focus on? What would you do?
- What can you do to cultivate or incorporate more of that into your work?
- Who will you be 10 years from now, and how will you reflect on this moment now?

Envision your future—your brain can't discern between what you see and what your brain thinks you see. Visualization can be a powerful tool to manifest things into reality. It thinks your thoughts are today's focus.

Today is a new day of a new chapter of your work. It's likely that this is one of the many different chapters you are likely to be engaging with in your work.

FIELD WORK—NOW WHAT?

Your vision is critical in terms of helping you move forward. Without a vision, you are unlikely to be able to manage the rough and rocky seas which are at play. Consider these questions and take note:

- What type of journey do you want?
- What role do you want to play?
- What connections do you want to make in your environment?
- What is going to be the pathway which will lead you there?
- Who else do you need to bring on the journey?
- Who do you need to be in order to not only survive but thrive?
- Who do you need to surround yourself with? (We are a product of the average of the five people around us.)
- What are the elements that you want to bring in—*fire, water, air, earth*—what can they combine to make or create?
- What is the chapter you want to be working on?
- What are the frustrations you have in your work?
- What are the stressors that hold you back?
- What detracts from your journey?
- What else do you need to pay attention to?

- What conflict might you need to resolve?

If you want to take a deeper dive around this topic:

- Check out Episode 4 of the *Remote Pathways* podcast—released January 1, 2020, at RemotePathways.com/Podcast
- Check out the Vision questions found on page 95 of *Coaching Business Builder* or page 99 of *PlanDo Track*
- Use the Annual Plan template found in Section 5 of *PlanDo Track* or *Coaching Business Builder*

CONNECTING IN WITH THE DIGITAL DOZEN:
WHO WILL YOU BE 10 YEARS FROM NOW?

Having a medium and long-term vision of where you want to go is very powerful. Let's check in with some of the members of the Digital Dozen to hear about their words of wisdom about where they want to go in 10 years.

- With the pace of change, 10 years may feel a little too long, so make it 3 or 5.
- Some of you may hope to be in a team leader role like Jo—confident and secure in supporting your team.
- Others may hope that they have refined more project management skills and plan on reaching out to Sujit in order to do that.
- Others may want to learn from Serge, the serial entrepreneur, who has a focus on innovation and experimentation.
- Others may want to start their own company one day and, with that in mind, realize that they need to develop skills in all the different areas they are being exposed to.
- From the tutelage of Sam, who is selling her enterprise, we can learn about how she has empowered different staff members. This has been key in quickly scaling the business.
- From the insights of Malcolm, the mentor, we are encouraged to pass on our skills.
- Mo, the creative solopreneur, is encouraging us to think about the blend and how this may lead into other elements.

GOING BEHIND THE SCENES AS A REMOTE WORKER

I'm always intrigued to explore the behind-the-scenes view of work. What is the behind-the-scenes day for you as a remote worker?

What I find interesting is that as much as our work may be varied, it's quite possible that the work process you are undertaking as a remote professional attached to an organization may be very similar to mine as a remote solopreneur. Likewise, the bucket of work and ways of working for a remote project manager may be very similar to that of a serial entrepreneur.

Regardless of what time you get up, think about these typical components of work:

- Prioritizing the key 3–5 activities
- Checking email and what items have received feedback
- Team Meetings
- Project kick-offs and project wrap-ups
- Engaging in a learning activity—how to do . . . (because there are always different activities and tasks we need to take on as a remote worker)
- Meeting with other teams
- Meeting with core stakeholders
- Sending emails again to someone on the project team
- Follow-up from meetings
- Fitting in exercise time (at home or elsewhere)
- Fixing something
- Moving to an in-person meeting
- Getting dinner on or a task done
- Fitting in writing and being able to focus on items
- Scheduling time for self
- Finding out what's important about our work

What is your typical workflow? What makes your role unique?

Beyond Your Vision—The Why

In addition to vision, you will have your *Why*. If you have not read Simon Sinek's work, *It Starts with Why*, you must. As he writes in his book, *The Infinite Game*:

> Think of the WHY like the foundation of a house, it is the starting point. It gives whatever we build upon it strength and performance. Our Just Cause is the ideal vision of the house we hope to build. We can work a lifetime to build it and still we will not be finished.

However, the results of our work help give the house form. As it moves from our imagination to reality it inspires more people to join the cause and continue the work . . . forever.

. . . A Just Cause inspires us to stay focused beyond the finite rewards and individual wins. The Just Cause provides the context for all the finite games we must play along the way. A Just Cause is what inspires us to want to keep playing.[29]

His model is circular and includes five essential practices—Just Cause, Trusting Teams, Worthy Rival, Existential Flexibility, and Courage to Lead. [30]

ACTIVITY

What is your vision? Write it down here.

_____

_____

_____

_____

_____

What is your *Why?* Write it down here.

_____

_____

_____

_____

_____

_____

NOTES AND REFLECTIONS:

DAY 5
SETTING UP YOUR OFFICE

"Three Rules of Work: Out of clutter find simplicity; from discord find harmony; in the middle of difficulty lies opportunity."
—Albert Einstein

FOCUS QUESTION:
What office environment will help you thrive?

WHAT?

Whether you are an entrepreneur or attached to a large company, in setting up your remote office, the landscape is inherently similar. There may be some distinctions around the types of support you have and what you need to link into. Today's topic connects into the business of working remote, and is another key success factor for getting your best work done while working remote or hybrid.

In setting up your office, we are going to look at the following:

- Office Essentials
- Getting Organized: Creating Focus and Creating a Space that Works for You
- Security

Today's focus wraps up with a checklist for you to use in setting up your office.

Did You Know?

Ergonomics refers to "the study of people's efficiency in their working environment"

—Oxford Dictionary

The physicality of your work can have long-term implications, from the impact of too much time on keyboards, leading to carpal tunnel syndrome, to some long-term impacts we don't know, like the long-term effects of blue light on the retina.

Consider and explore these typical ergonomic areas:

Keyboard — Desk Height — Screen Height

While some of these factors may not have an immediate impact, over time they will have a significant impact on your health, which could have even wider implications for your productivity and well-being.

SO WHAT?

In terms of getting your best work done, this section explores three key areas—Office Essentials, Getting Organized, and Security.

Area 1—Office Essentials

In order to do your best work, consider the essentials you need in your office. Introducing the Ideal Remote Worker Workspace!

Office supplies you may need are a printer (with ink), scanner, basic supplies, white board, great webcam, mouse, ergonomic chair, standing desk, bookcase, and locking file cabinet.

Other essentials can involve getting your tech working, managing apps, and being clear on administrative tasks such as invoicing, reporting, and tracking (capturing what you are doing). For more on these, check out Episode #32 of the Remote Pathways podcast—Top 10 Tools to Get Things Done. You will find it on your favorite podcast player or at https://www.remotepathways.com/podcast/ep32-top-10-tools-to-get-things-done-in-the-virtual-remote-hybrid-world.[31]

To keep yourself moving as a remote worker, you may tap into a variety of different apps and software. Check out what's currently available in the following areas:

- **Instant messaging and data sharing**—across teams Slack has been a way to communicate and share information. Some teams will use Microsoft Teams, while others may use Slack, or event Google Drive.

- **Document storage**—Drop Box or Google Drive may be another storage facility you turn to. What are the platforms which will help you with information flow and storage?

- **Project management**—having a shared project dashboard can support teams in keeping projects moving with the requirements in place. From Monday.com to Trello to Asana, project management software will be of benefit when everyone is using it in the same way.

- **Creativity tools such as mind-mapping software**—given that new projects may require brainstorming, consider such individual or shared brainstorming platforms as MindJet, MindMeister, or Coggle. What projects are you needing to expand upon, or elaborate?

Area 2—Getting Organized

What things do you want to put in place in order to get moving in the way you want to?

As a remote worker, you may find a need to get organized and use systems in several areas. Consider:

- Communication
- Files and information
- Financials
- Client files
- Marketing Systems

List the different systems you want to make.

Getting organized can involve more than having good systems. It might also entail:

- Having a way to file information.
- Having a place for everything—consider the things you are going to need to use on a regular basis. What things will you want to reach regularly?
- A way to keep different projects and pieces of work separate.
- A way to access things offline and online.

What's going to help you get organized?

Many organizers indicate that organizing approaches can be contingent on your style. So, if you have a preference for visual learning, it may be useful to have open cupboards (or be able to open a door and take a look at what you have). For those who are minimalists, a place to put things away and close off on business may be a preference.

What do you know about your own preferences for how you like to work and see things?

To go deeper into this topic, check out *PlanDoTrack (Section 3)*.

Back up or peril!

Practices for remote and hybrid work:

- *Always* have a backup. If you are leading meetings or training, have a backup!

- Consider what is going to help you focus and do your best work.

- Be sure to back up. When and how do you back up your work?

Create a space that works for you.

Area 3—Security

Security issues abound in the remote workspace, and you are encouraged to reach out to your HR and/ or IT department to find out about the specific data security issues and policies for your organization. A big upsurge around cyber-security issues was found in March and April 2020 as so many people started working remotely. Check out this article from March 2020, which includes 6 security tips for remote work: www.welivesecurity.com/2020/03/26/6-tips-safe-secure-remote-working/

Security requirements will range across the virtual space, depending on where you work from and who you work for. This area can become quite complex, so check with your HR department and/or IT department about the requirements for the following:

- Data
- Information
- Legal agreements
- Insurance on your location
- What to do if something is compromised
- What to do if something is lost
- What to do if something is stolen
- What things you need to secure in your work

Industrial espionage. While not every worker will think about espionage, it is important to note that as a remote worker you may be an easy way into a business system.

An increasing concern for organizations with remote workers is security. Each staff member could be the weakest link.

Security involves multiple levels, including data security, device security, and paper security.

Reach out to your IT department about what you need to do in this area.

Here are two other blog posts which address this issue:

- "10 Security Tips for Remote and Mobile Working," By Carl Henriksen: https://minutehack.com/guides/10-security-tips-for-remote-and-mobile-working
- Cybersecurity issues with remote work: https://heimdalsecurity.com/blog/cybersecurity-issues-with-remote-work/

FIELD WORK—NOW WHAT?

Work through the following checklist to figure out what office space works best for you.

I work best when:

☐ People are around me	☐ I am on my own
☐ There is nothing to distract	☐ There is lots to look at
☐ It is quiet	☐ There is noise
☐ I can focus on one task at a time	☐ I can bounce back and forth between items
☐ No one knows where I am	☐ I am available to everyone
☐ I am able to work in short blocks	☐ I am able to work in long stretches of time
☐ I need to be online all the time	☐ I can have breaks from being online
☐ I prefer to start and complete a task in one sitting	☐ I start a task and then come back to it later
☐ I need to write things out	☐ I like to do things digitally
☐ I benefit from lots of sensory input	☐ I benefit from have quiet around me
☐ I like to work from different locations	☐ I need to always have the same workspace
☐ I need to hold a lot of calls	☐ I don't need to talk to any one during my worktime
☐ I need to be plugged in	☐ I can work on battery
☐ I can work offline	☐ I have internet access

What else do you need in order to work effectively?

_____

_____

_____

Review the areas you have just marked. What else do you notice about your workspace preferences?

_____

_____

_____

_____

What requirements does your organization or business have about where you are working?

_____

_____

_____

_____

What other considerations are there about where and how you work?

_____

_____

_____

_____

What else is important to notice?

_____

_____

_____

_____

Take time today to consider security. Are things locked up? Are devices up to speed?

_____

_____

_____

_____

WHERE TO GO

Talk to your HR and IT departments for more information.

Review what you currently have in place, what answers you need, and what changes you need to make. Don't be afraid to ask questions of your mentor and peers as well. It's never too early to improve your security.

THINGS YOU'LL SEE IN THE SPACE OF THE REMOTE WORKER

- Map
- Compass
- GPS
- Multiple devices
- Contact log
- Vision
- One-Page Plan
- Journal

NOTES AND REFLECTIONS:

DAY 6

BUILDING TRUST AND RELATIONSHIPS

"How do you have each other's backs?"
—Keith Ferrazzi

FOCUS QUESTION:
Who can support you?

WHAT?

No person is an island in the remote world. While we may work in isolation, our work is likely to be very interdependent with others. As many found in the recent "physical distancing," community and connection are essential for well-being. Relationships and relationship development form a focus here in the *90-Day Guide*.

As part of your remote work success, you will want to consider, and actively seek out, building relationships internally and externally, with key stakeholders as well as others within your industry or within similar networks.

Make a point to connect with other remote workers around topics of interest. From location-specific activities and meetups to attending annual conferences, relationship development can take many forms.

Here are some key items to help build relationships with others:

- Show genuine interest
- Offer something of value
- Ask questions to highlight their learning
- Find common ground

Great Relationship-Building Questions

Many professionals do not know where to start the question. Here are great questions to ask at any time:

- What should I know about you?

- What do you see as current priorities and trends with our work?

- What is the one place I should go for more information?

- What is the one resource you can't live without?

- What is the one habit which helps you be productive and on the mark?

SO WHAT?

You will want to put attention around a variety of key relationships, including, but not limited to these:

Relationship Circle Map

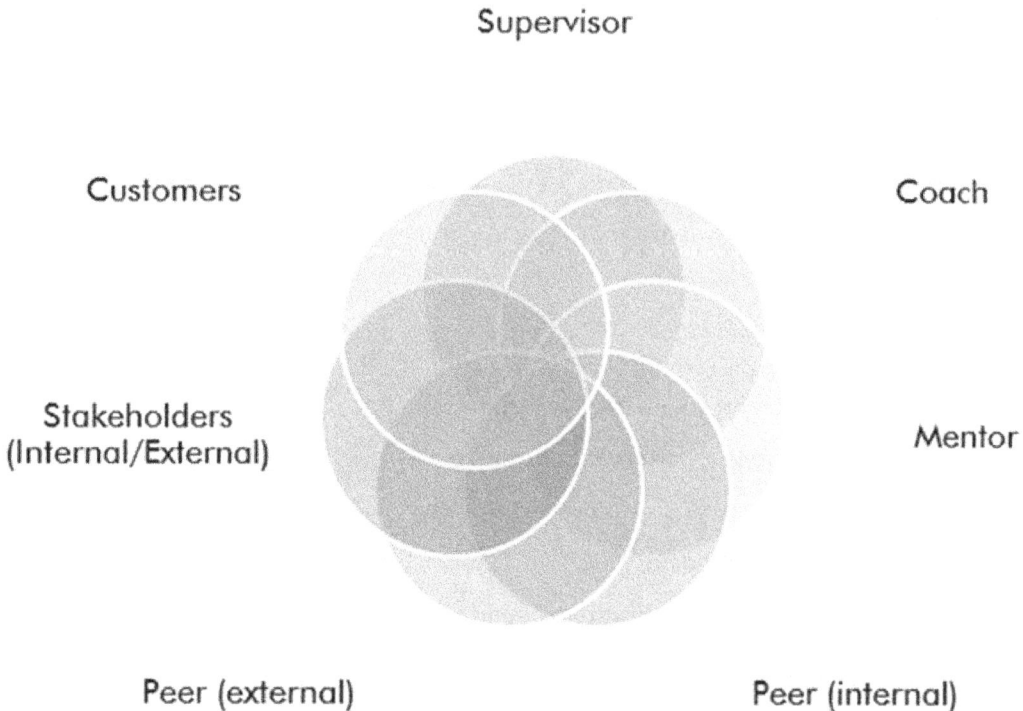

Supervisor

Customers

Coach

Stakeholders
(Internal/External)

Mentor

Peer (external)

Peer (internal)

Think about the various relationships you have. Make a list of who these people are in your network. Who else is in this network?

Who is accompanying your team?

_____

_____

_____

_____

_____

_____

Even if they are at a distance, the people and team around you can be as important as the remote worker themselves. You are likely to find yourself surrounded by:

- Catalysts
- Activators
- Advocates
- Mentors
- Academic stimulators
- Physical coaches
- Neutral sounding boards
- Those who are there to help push their mandate forward
- Community builders
- Community leaders
- Educators

As well as

- Those who can support you to do your best work;
- Those who can help you clarify your message;
- Those who help you expand your breadth and knowledge laterally;
- Those you need to collaborate with;
- Those who have resources you need to leverage (think time, skills, items, etc.)

Add these roles to the labels to the circles you have outlined above.

TYPE	WHO THEY NEED TO LINK UP TO	TOOLS WHICH ARE OF INTEREST
Solopreneur	Customers	Avatar Map
Entrepreneur	Joint venture partners, co-facilitators, or co-creators of products and programs	Partnership Mapping
Virtual facilitator	Team leader	Articulate/Kajabi/Teachable
Virtual/remote team leader	Team members, other peers	Leadership Toolkit or Team Tools
Virtual employee	Peers	Slack, Zoom, others
Project manager	Team members, stakeholders	Communication and roject management tools such as Asana, Trello, and others

Four things to keep in mind when building relationships:

1. **Be intentional.**

2. **Think about the win-win.** What is your shared ground? How are your roles interdependent? Do some tasks flow in? What is your ability to influence others?

3. **Be clear about follow-up.** Follow through, or it will erode trust. Make this visible; is there a one-pager you send out or upload to Slack in terms of commitments and who will do what? Consider what things are going to move the relationship forward.

4. **Learn more about your partner.** What are their strengths? What are their passions? What is their style? What are their aspirations? Be sure to review these and adjust your style appropriately. Consider what you want to share about how you want to be supported.

Getting the conversation started—ask these questions:

- What was your biggest challenge?
- What is the greatest opportunity for you as a remote worker?
- What do you love about your work?
- What would you trade in, if you could?
- What's the one thing you always set a priority on?

Relationships should be reciprocal. I benefit and you benefit. Another way of thinking about this is by completing the sentence:

I need ___ from you. I can offer ___ to you. Together we can _____.

You might add your new statements of request to your relationship circle map

Building solid relationships requires trust and radical candor.

Many professionals do not know where to start the conversation to develop relationships. Great questions to ask at any time:

- What should I know about you?

- What do you see as current priorities and trends with our work?

- What is the one place I should go for more information?

- What is the one resource you can't live without?

- What is the one habit which helps you be productive and on the mark?

FIELD WORK—NOW WHAT?

Be sure to complete your entire Relationship Circles Map. Look at the different layers and what's important, as well as what else you need to note. List the specific people you have surrounding you (at a distance).

Activators, Mentors, and other partners you have in your network:

_____   _____

_____   _____

_____   _____

NOTES AND REFLECTIONS:

DAY 7
TEAM EFFECTIVENESS

"Teams are an important part of the remote
world for all types of professionals."
—Lencioni

FOCUS QUESTION:
What's going to help your team do its best work?

WHAT?

Teams are an important part of the remote world for all types of professionals—entrepreneurs, project managers, leaders. In a remote environment, we do not operate in isolation; we will likely be interdependent on others. With this in mind, today's focus gets you thinking about those you work with. Teams in today's context may reflect the new normal of ongoing change and formation, also known as *teaming*. Teaming is described by Amy Edmondson as: ". . . a verb. It is a dynamic activity. Not a bounded, static entity.[32]"

Did You Know?

According to a 2016 study done by Culture Wizard, only 22% of teams at the time participated in team development activities.[33]

What do you have scheduled as a team to focus on your development?

SO WHAT?

Edmondson wrote that teams require four skills in order to participate in teaming:

1. Speaking Up
2. Collaboration
3. Experimentation
4. Reflection[34]

As you can guess, it's key that we facilitate conversations and create conditions for safety so that people feel connected and that we also raise the issues which are important.

What are you doing to foster space for skill development with each of these as a team?

Whether you are a team leader or a team member, understand the levers we have available to help teams flourish. We'll be breaking these down into what I commonly refer to as the Six Factors of High Performing Teams.

Research continues to demonstrate that teams of all kinds need certain elements to work effectively. I originally shared these areas back in 2014 in my first year of the *Teams365* blog, publishing them in 2017 in *Effective Virtual Conversations*. Here are the Six Factors:

1. **Shared purpose or mission (*Why*)**
   What is your purpose? Your mission? Why you exist? Does everyone hold the same understanding? What does this mean practically for your work? What priorities does your purpose or mission naturally create?

2. **Shared behavioral norms (*How*)**
   Behavioral norms create alignment and shared agreements about *how* you do things. What is acceptable and unacceptable on the team? What behaviors and habits exist? Which ones are supportive of exceptional performance? Which ones aren't? Shared behavioral norms are commonly known as *WOWs* (ways of working), *team agreements*, or *rules of the road*. Many studies, including Google's Project Aristotle, have found that shared behavioral norms are key for high performance. They are even more so in the remote space where people are disconnected.

3. **Shared commitment (*What*)**
   What are team members committed to? What will you get done, no matter what? Is there anything that needs to be dropped off the list?

4. **Shared performance goals (*What*)**

   In the remote context, it's important to be clear on what your goals are. Lack of alignment can quickly lead team members in divergent directions. What are key goals for the team this year? What are key individual goals? How do your goals align? Overlap? What does success look like for each member? For the entire team? Does everyone have an understanding of the key goals of others on the team and how they feed into them?

5. **Shared team practices (When)**

   Teams that work together effectively share common practices such as a Monday morning huddle, a Thursday night out or some other regular event. What practices support your relationships?

6. **Clear roles (Who)**

   Teams exist for a purpose and being clear on roles and who does what is key to remote working success. How do our roles overlap, align, and connect? What changes, if any, are needed this year around your roles giving your priorities? Holding discussions around *who* does what, and *how*, also helps to keep things on track.

Teams can find themselves in any of these several traps:

- Unclear goals

- Unclear roles

- Lack of communication

- Different styles and ways of working

- Conflict

- Lack of accountability

What areas aren't as focused for you as a team right now?

In the Spotlight—Factor #1: Clear Vision

In *Reconnecting Workspaces*, I share more detail about the Six Factors of High Performing Teams. This Spotlight digs into Factor #1: Clear Vision.

One of the precursors for high performing teams is that they are aligned around vision. Without this alignment, it's unlikely that they are focused on similar things. Gaps get magnified in the remote space.

When working with vision, be sure to:

- Check your assumptions and be sure to not second-guess what you are doing.

- Consider the aspirational vantage point of things—what things are going to help you?

- Let it go—we don't want to hold our vision too tightly. Often vision is far enough in the future to allow us to hold it aspirationally, rather than tightly, as to what we are going to do.

For more on the topic of vision, check out Day 4 on Vision.

The clearer we are on our vision, the easier it can be to be focused and intentional with what we want to create. When we are not focused, our work may be scattered and therefore less effective or productive.

FIELD WORK—NOW WHAT?

As a team, where are you with each of the Six Factors? Using the chart below rate yourself on a 1-10 (1 being low and 10 being high), and note what's working well, and what needs attention.

FACTOR	RATING (1-10)	WHAT'S WORKING WELL AND WHAT NEEDS ATTENTION
#1—Shared Vision, Purpose, or Mission		
#2—Shared Behavioral Norms		
#3—Shared Commitment		
#4—Shared Performance Goals		
#5—Shared Team Practices		
#6—Clear Roles		

What are the levers available to you as a team right now?

_____

_____

_____

What will help you thrive?

_____

_____

_____

Be sure to check out the *Remote Pathways* blog posts at www.remotepathways.com/blog/52-weeks-week-22-remote-teams-which-excel-3-of-the-6-factors and www.remotepathways.com/blog/52-weeks-week-28-6-factors-5-meetingsteam-practices and download.

NOTES AND REFLECTIONS:

THIS WEEK'S FOUNDATION THEME
WAS *TRUST*

How did your first week go? What were your accomplishments this week? List them out here:

_____ . _____ . _____ .

Connection means the following to me:

_____
_____
_____
_____
_____
_____
_____
_____

Here's where we went this week:

- Day 1—Welcome to Your Role
- Day 2—You: Areas of Focus, Getting Clear on Your Role
- Day 3—Remote Work: Similarities, Differences, Advantages
- Day 4—Vision
- Day 5—Setting Up Your Office
- Day 6—Building Trust and Relationships
- Day 7—Team Effectiveness

Questions to Consider:

What has become clear for you?

_____
_____
_____

66 | WEEK 1 REVIEW | 90-DAY GUIDE FOR SUCCESS

What do you still need support around?

_____

_____

_____

What questions do you have?

_____

_____

_____

_____

_____

_____

What needs to get carried over into future weeks?

_____

_____

_____

_____

_____

_____

END-OF-WEEK FLOW:
INTRODUCING THE DIGITAL DOZEN

THE DIGITAL DOZEN™

The Remote Pathways podcast explores the adventures of the Digital Dozen and the people, places, and pathways to remote work

Ned	Jo	Serge	Mel
New Remote Worker	Virtual Team Leader	Serial Remote Entrepreneur	Coach

Malcom	Alex	Victor	Sam
Mentor	Work From Anywhere (WFA)	Volunteer	Selling Start-up

Sujit	Sally	Mo	Jane
Project Manager	Salesperson	Creative Solopreneur	Virtual Facilitator

Many different pathways lead to remote work. Let's meet the group I call the Digital Dozen™, a varied community of different types of professionals who work and thrive in the remote space.

The Digital Dozen™ ranges from **Ned**, our new remote worker who has recently transitioned out of an office, to Serge, a seasoned remote worker building his sixth company and who has seen remote work move from the radio to satellite phone to mobile.

There are also people such as **Jo**, who leads teams across time zones.

And **Malcolm**, who is returning back as a mentor during his early retirement years.

Jane is responsible for creating and leading virtual trainings. She has found that remote workers initially need skills in areas such as prioritization, time management, influence, communication, and using the technology. Feedback and conflict management are also important areas in training and learning to work in the remote space.

There are also people like **Sam**, who scale their virtual businesses, which are eventually bought out and subsumed by others.

Victor is a remote worker in the voluntary sector. To expand their organization's talent pool, they have looked outside of their regular area and have brought on a virtual team of staff to support the volunteers across the country. They each are tasked as a project lead as well.

Sujit is in project management and is focused on leading teams across time zones, ensuring that projects are on time and within scope and budget. As a project manager, he is able to tap into resourcing across locations and industries. This may help you to really focus and move your projects forward in a way that is going to work best.

Mel is a coach who works remote and has met with her clients virtually for the last decade. While her work originally was by phone, it shifted to Skype and now Zoom.

Serge is a seasoned remotepreneur or digital entrepreneur. They are the ones carving out what remote can look like, whether it's a focus on resourcing or innovation, or a focus on something else. What can remotepreneurs do that others can't? They can see the world in all its vibrancy.

Mo is a creative solopreneur who loves the flexibility of running her business from home, while on the road, and when she is out traveling. As a creative solopreneur, Mo has the freedom and flexibility to follow what she wants. Given that her business success is about her, she does need to focus on what she is good at and/or what she is able to accomplish.

Sally is a salesperson who loves the dynamic and mobile nature of her work. She is part of the original mobile professional landscape and is used to working on the road—used to working in a mobile way. She moves from location to location, talking with businesses about the products her company offers. While her work is more virtual in nature, she's always on the move. A relationship diva at heart, she has an uncanny ability to "size people up" quickly, and she is an outstanding communicator.

Alex Works from Anywhere (WFA) and is usually seen with his laptop under his arm. He is the go-to person around all things remote and mobile. He models the best practices around remote and hybrid work naturally, including being very clear on boundaries between work and life, and exhibiting the 7 Remote Enablers™ in his work.

Who is missing with this list is **Darren**, the digital nomad. Digital nomads are a unique group in that they often weave together a love for travel and a desire to continue working. Sometimes the work they do feeds their ability to travel and work from anywhere. Sometimes, their yearning for adventure, and their need to keep the business running, provides the impetus. Some digital nomads travel by RV or by plane, locally or globally.

ARE YOU WFA OR WFH?

WFA and *WFH*: The world of acronyms exists in any industry. In the world of remote work, these are two of the common acronyms:

WFA—Work from Anywhere. Our members of the Digital Dozen are Alex, who represents the voice of the person who works from anywhere, and Sally, our salesperson. Those who work from anywhere may be traveling salespeople working out of their car, program directors who need to reach out to stakeholders and projects, or digital nomads, freelancers, and solopreneurs who run remote businesses, often in marketing, coaching, and other service-based industries.

WFAs need strong systems. They need security as they move in and out of locations and networks. They need systems so they can work from different locations and tap into different resources.

WFH—Work from Home. The tsunami of professionals moving to work from home has led to a new way of working, often blending the boundaries between personal and professional responsibilities. Check out my varied WFH posts at the *Teams365* blog. Privacy, focus, and juggling work and roles are key issues for those who work from home.

What makes remote work, work? Check out the *Remote Pathways* podcast episode 11 on this, at www.remotepathways.com/podcast/ep011-getting-up-to-speed-quickly-in-the-remote-space

_____

_____

_____

What things are going to help you as a remote worker?

_____

_____

_____

What can you think about as you move forward?

_____

_____

_____

TYPES	PROS	CONS
DIGITAL ENTREPRENEURS	• Get a lot of variety and energy from things that are new. • May need to build relationships regularly. • Great for people who are energized by newness and options.	• Don't have the time or space to build a lot of physical products. • Harder to find anchors. • Office space and security.
SOLOPRENEURS	• Freedom to carve out whatever is going to work best for them. • Have the ultimate freedom and responsibility for what they want to create.	• Time and resources to get it all done. • Prioritization. • Flow of work and resourcing. • Complete responsibility for making things happen as they are a team of one.
WORK FROM HOME	• Reduced commute time • Ability to focus productively • May support role integration for some, while creating more role dissonance for others	• Boundaries between work and life can get blurred, if not intentional • Office space at home may not be optimal.
WORK FROM ANYWHERE	• Variety and novelty created by working from different locations. • Flexibility and freedom. • Creativity sparks from working in different locations.	• May not always have the access needed to resources and materials in order to do their best work. • Lack of perceived stability and routine. • Disconnection from others in the organization and/or team
DIGITAL NOMAD	• Ability to work and travel at all times. • Freedom to work from anywhere, with no overhead. • Ongoing learning opportunities.	• Accessibility to materials, resources and people in order to do work. • Uncertainty and logistical challenges created by working in different locations. • Visibility needs to be more intentional

WEEK 1 ROUNDUP AND REVIEW

This week we looked at a variety of foundational topics, including:

- Getting Clear on Your Role

- Creating a Powerful Vision

- Getting your office set up

- Exploring key relationships in the remote space (which we'll dig deeper into next week)

- Team Effectiveness.

Grounding this work are several core philosophies of remote work: Be resourceful and innovate. Find the connection points. Simplify. Less is more. Boost learner's mindset.

- **Be resourceful and innovate**—it's not exactly like working face to face, *and* technology can be leveraged to be resourceful and innovative when needed.

- **Find the common ground** with those you are in connection with, to break down the barriers. It's easy to find differences, and as remote workers we need to explore the similarities.

- **Keep it simple. Simplify.** Simplify—being able to distill things down to their root or core is critical in the remote space. This may hold true for our communications, our call to action, and how we prioritize. What is short term? Long term?

- **Less is more—distill things down to the main points.** The complexity is in the group. Less is more—there is only so much information we can distill at one time. Aligned with the philosophy of simplify, what does "less is more" mean? Instead of sending out a long video message, can it be dripped over several days?

- **Embrace a learner's mindset**—Autonomy. Experimentation. Leading and learning are only part of the picture of remote work.

Week 1 Foundation Theme: Trust

Topics we covered this week were:

Day 1—Welcome to Your Role

Day 2—You: Areas of Focus, Getting Clear on Your Role

Day 3—Remote Work: Similarities, Differences, Advantages

Day 4—Vision

Day 5—Setting Up Your Office

Day 6—Building Trust and Relationships

Day 7—Team Effectiveness

What else is important as a remote worker? Let's look at what is important for all of us today:

- **Innovation.** From looking at BlackBerry and Apple's role in transforming HOW we communicate in the remote space with mobile phones with qwerty keyboards, to the earlier versions of calendars in our briefcases with the Palm Pilot. Many companies which are originators with innovation are no longer there as they have been acquired by larger companies. What can you do to still foster the innovative spirit?

- **Finding connection points.** A quick activity to undertake as a team is to place on your whiteboard a word such as "Community" and from there to focus on what other connection points there are.

- **Boundaries**. Things can get blurry between work and life. What are the boundaries you are going to put into place?

- **Routines.** What are you doing to make sure you are at your peak from a well-being standpoint? Are you getting exercise? Sleeping well? Eating well?

Be sure to complete the following Week 1 Review questions.

Key learning from this week's foundation themes:

_____

_____

_____

Wrap up theme:

_____

_____

_____

What are you looking forward to?

_____

_____

_____

What questions do you have? Who can help you with this?

_____

_____

_____

What routines and practices are helping you?

_____

_____

_____

What To-Dos have surfaced? (List your top 3–5)

1.

2.

3.

4.

5.

Update your tracking sheet!

_____

_____

_____

_____

_____

_____

WEEK 2 · CONNECTION

"No one can whistle a symphony. It takes an orchestra."
—H. E. Luccock

Welcome to Week 2! Our meta-theme this week is all about Connection. Connection with others. Connection with your network. Connection with your context.

This week we are going to explore the wider foundation of your work.

We're going to be exploring the following topics:

- Day 8—Goals
- Day 9—Core Skills for Success
- Day 10—Relationship Building: Your Boss
- Day 11—Relationship in Focus: Your Peers
- Day 12—Context and Navigating VUCA
- Day 13—Strengths
- Day 14—Communication

WHAT ARE YOUR TOP 3 GOALS THIS WEEK?:

1. _____

2. _____

3. _____

By the end of the week I want to be sure that . . .

_____

This week's theme is *connection*. Questions to consider around connection:

What are you noticing about the connections you are making with PEOPLE?

_____

_____

_____

With components of work?

_____

_____

_____

With *goals*?

_____

_____

_____

Write down your top 3 goals for the week and be sure to use the daily tracker to capture additional notes.

_____

_____

_____

_____

_____

_____

_____

_____

_____

FOUNDATIONAL REMOTE ELEMENT:
BUILDING CONNECTION IN THE VIRTUAL SPACE

Trust and connection are central to the thriving of teams in the remote space. Without connection, it is unlikely that team members will feel like they are part of a team.

Ways to build connection:

- Be proactive with outreach

- Schedule time for this
- Notice the common ground—and make a point of asking for what others notice about the common ground

CREATING CONNECTION AND BUILDING COMMUNITY—VIRTUALLY

Six areas to consider:

1. Find points of common connection. What is the common ground and purpose you have in your relationship?

2. What is critical for success for your work together? Discuss what is important from each perspective in terms of success, not what is similar or different.

3. Understand how people prefer to communicate. Big picture? Details? Frequent updates or summary journals? Direct? Indirect?

4. On a macro-level, who is it important for you to build relationships with?

5. Be clear on what you are after and what you are asking to connect around. Like any networking and community building, it can be important to be clear and focused on *why* you are doing it. What is your end goal? Intention?

6. Creating parameters around *how* you are going to do it is also important. Before it becomes an all-consuming activity, are you going to spend 10–15 minutes a day on social media? Are you going to dedicate one hour a month to reaching out and participating in a virtual community event? What's going to avoid scope creep around time spent?[35]

Areas to Explore

Given that remote workers learn best through observation, some of the things you will want to explore with your mentors, peers and boss include:

- How do people schedule work?

- How do people prioritize?

- What skills do they use each day?

- What do people lean into to get things done?

- What emotional intelligence skills do they need?

- What sets exceptional remote workers apart from others?

- What do you notice about the career pathways you have been on?

- What is important to notice?

- What has your biggest challenge been?

- How do you like to get feedback?

- Across the landscape of virtual options, where do you work (Remote, Hybrid, Mobile, Nomad)?

- What's the team culture you are part of?

- "We are all leaders." What does that mean to you?

What's important for you to take a look at in your connections? What are you doing to be proactive about building connections? What is still not clear to you?

ACTIVITY

Make a map of the core relationships you have with others. Who do you need to interface with on a regular basis? If you don't know yet, ask your peers, boss and mentors. What is the level of frequency of touchpoints? What is important to note about these relationships?

_____

_____

_____

_____

_____

_____

_____

_____

TRUST

As we explored a few days ago in Day 7, Trust is a foundational element. Trust plus Safety plus Connection leads to High Performance.

Check out my August 2021 TEDx talk entitled Virtual, Remote and Hybrid Checklist at https://youtu.be/BWjn_mDQa3Q.

> TRUST + SAFETY + CONNECTION = HIGH PERFORMANCE

CONNECTION—ACTIVATE THE SIX LAYERS OF CONNECTION™ IN A TEAM

Consider what you can do to connect people to:

- The topic
- Others
- You
- Content
- Context
- Platform

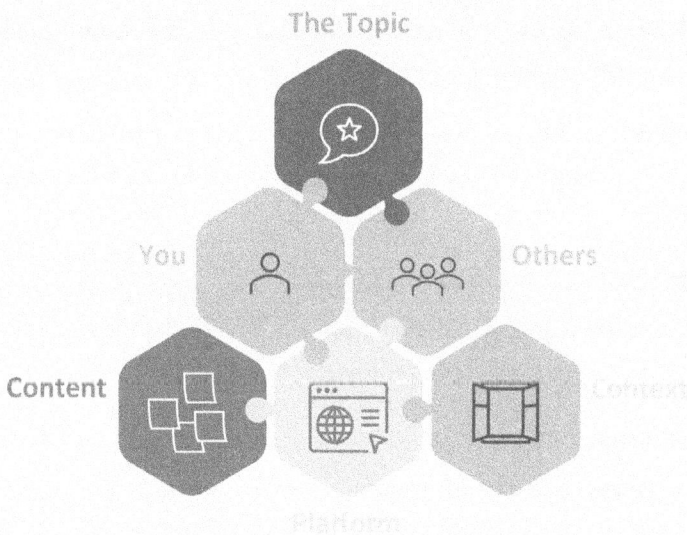

The Six Layers of Connection in Virtual Conversations

© Jennifer Britton, 2021

Along with these, we know that people are more likely to be engaged in the workplace when they can use their strengths every day.

To help people build on strengths, you may choose to undertake the Clifton Strengths Survey or have them complete the Positive Psychology Strengths VIA Survey. Dedicate a session to dialogue and sharing about who they are, what their top 5 strengths are, and how they can bring them to current projects.

Help people find the common ground—ask people to explore what the common ground is with the people they are partnered with.

What else might you do to build trust and connection?

_____

_____

_____

_____

_____

_____

BUILDING CONNECTION ACROSS THE TEAM

Trust is a required precursor for teamwork. It is also the thing that creates identity and fuses people together. Whether you are in the role of the leader or team member, what you are committed to? As a leader, you may need to stretch and go beyond to invite people to interact and connect.

Distributed teams don't just work well on the same terms as co-located teams; you have to have a basis for trust and open communication to happen.[36]

Connection in a remote team can take many forms, from weekly virtual potlucks to focused sessions when people co-work virtually together. One-on-ones can create valuable insight. Questions you might ask:

- What things should I know about your work?
- What are you working on?
- What are you focusing on?
- What things inspire you?
- How does my work connect with yours?
- What challenges are you having?
- What resources/advice/insights could I offer to help you with this?
- What opportunities do you see for our work?
- As a partner, what do you need?

KEEPING THE CONVERSATION GOING

Keeping a focus and keeping the conversation going is key in the remote space. We may be focused on a variety of different things, so what are the things that will really move us forward? Look to keeping the conversation going on this list of things.

SELF-REFLECTION QUESTIONS:
BUILDING COMMUNITY WITH YOUR TEAM

As a team member, ask yourself the following questions:

- How are you showing up?
- What are you doing to contribute?
- What are you doing to ask for support?
- What things are helping you to expand?
- What conversations need to be had?
- What are you doing to bring people together for a conversation real-time?
- What are you doing to help people learn more about each other?
- What are you doing to reward people?
- What are you doing to help people tap into their strengths?
- What are you doing to help people understand when their strengths may be overmagnified?

NOTES AND REFLECTIONS:

DAY 8

GOALS

"Begin with the end in mind."
—Stephen Covey

FOCUS QUESTION:
What major goals are you aiming for?

WHAT?

Goals are at the core of any remote worker's experience. They provide an anchor for ourselves and those we work with. Goals ground our focus, keep us motivated, and on a larger level help to ensure alignment.

Consider your work right now; and for yourself, and others you work with, what are the:

- Short-term goals
- Long-term goals
- Strategic goals
- Meta-goals (the big-picture goals—for example at the 30,000-foot view)
- Micro-goals (at the granular level)

Also, how do goals fit together across the team?

What do you notice about how goals are being achieved? What are you noticing about how your goals are getting achieved? Are there small bursts and then a big breakthrough?

In today's section, we are going to look at goals along two layers:

Making sure that goals are SMART-E. In addition to ensuring our goals are SMART-E (*Specific, Measurable, Achievable, Relevant and Timebound*), goals also need to be *exciting*. What will keep things exciting for you? What helps you focus and do your best work?

Making sure that we have enough time to meet those goals. Time estimation and figuring out just how much time it takes to get things done can be a science. Part of it may involve tracking your past results and considering just how much time it takes to get things done. Time estimation may also be assisted by exploring what others are doing with their process and how much time it takes.

Ensuring that goals are supported—What is the network that can support you in resourcing? Building in accountability partners is useful; one piece that is missing in the remote space is accountability. Accountability may be key in getting things done. It is the way to work.

As you work with goals, consider how you are going to *plan*, *do*, and *track*.

Did You Know?

SMART-E stands for Specific, Measurable, Achievable, Relevant, Timebound, and also Exciting.

S   **Specific** - What specifically do you want to achieve? What will it look like?

M   **Measurable** - How can you track progress?

A   **Achievable** - With some stretch are these achievable?

R   **Realistic** - Again, with stretch are these in range?

T   **Timebound** - What's the timeframe on this - next week, end of June, early 2015?

E   And most of all, are these goals **Exciting**? If they are not exciting, chances are they might not get done, or may get done only to get them checked off.

MOTIVATION AROUND GOALS
DIFFERENCES AND SOUNDBITES FROM THE DIGITAL DOZEN

Motivation is key for remote workers. Let's look at how different factors can influence different remote workers.

Top 5 Soundbites

Alex—Work from Anywhere *(It's all about Requirements, Results, Systems)*:

Technology has allowed us to work from anywhere. I am more productive and have learned to focus my time. I've also become really good at being clear what's required in my work, and what the end result, or success measures, are. Technology systems keep things on board and keep things flowing.

Jo—Team Leader *(It's all about being Proactive, Consistent, Clear)*:

As a remote team leader, I know how important it is to be proactive in reaching out to my team. I know how important consistency is in terms of scheduling meetings, following through, and keeping connected. I know how important clarity is—clarity around communication, processes, what's expected, what end results we are looking for.

Sujit—Project Manager *(It's all about Scope, Priorities, Negotiation, Communication)*:

As a virtual project manager, it's really key to get things moving and to ensure that they keep to *scope*, on time and on budget. The challenge in the remote space is there are so many different priorities, and scope creep can happen at any time. Negotiation is key, as is working with the entire team around prioritization. Communication needs to be ongoing and across multiple channels (email, phone, dashboards, etc.)

Mo—Creative Solopreneur *(Freedom, Community, Priorities)*:

As a creative solopreneur, I love the freedom and flexibility this affords me. I am yearning for a community I can be part of. I know it's important to bundle and focus my work. Discernment around what needs to happen is also key.

Mel—Coach *(Systems, Community)*:

As a professional coach, I want to create a pause for the people I support as clients. Remote connections allow us to focus in on their priorities. As a coach, having systems helps me scale the work I want to do and offer even more conversations.

What three soundbites from among the five above are important to you around remote work?

Establishing SMART-E Goals

SMART-E Goals Worksheet - Making Your Goals SMART-E

Original Goal Statement					
Now adapt this to become more:					
Specific	Measurable	Achievable (yes/no)	Relevant (yes/no)	Timebound Key Milestones	Exciting
Revised SMART-E Goal Statement:					

What do you need in order to be successful? Add this to your One Page Plan.

As a remote team, you may be working with goals on at least two levels—the team level, your level, and in some cases the level of goals in another part of the matrix.

Let's look at one of Ned's tasks, which is to "expand sales by 50% this quarter."

In working with goals, we want to make sure that they are SMART-E:

Specific—What specifically are you going to do? As it relates to Ned's goals, he needs to "expand sales." Specifically, what could that entail? "Expand digital sales in two program areas" is much more specific.

Measurable—The goal needs to be increased by 50%. In other words, moving from 10 sales to 20 sales this week.

Achievable—Is this achievable? If goals are not achievable, our motivation tanks. As a remote professional, motivation is everything, so it's important that we really explore the question, "What is needed to increase sales?" Hopefully, Ned is clear on what the options are in order to achieve it. This will form the basis of an upcoming conversation with Jo, his leader.

Realistic—How realistic is this? What does he need in order to do this? This might include internal and external resources, including contacts, a budget to hire some graphic designers to do some marketing copy, and linking Ned with a more seasoned mentor around this. One of the key mantras to remote work (and work in general) is "set people up for success." Ned can benefit from thinking about what he will need in order to be successful. What are the enablers? What are the derailers? Who else is going to be working on this? Does Ned know these people?

Timebound—What is the time frame on this? In looking back to the initial goal, it was to increase the sales this quarter. To get even more specific with this, what are the milestones he will need to reach each month, or each week?

Finally, how is this **Exciting**? As previously mentioned, motivation and engagement are a key part of success in the remote space. What is going to be motivational about this goal for Ned? What might he do differently to boost his motivation around it?

Let's look at the *revamped* SMART-E Goal now: "To increase sales in two digital channels by 50% over the next 3 months by focusing on *x*, *y*, and *z*."

SO WHAT?

The clearer we can get on the end result with our goal statement, the better it is for us and our team. It helps with troubleshooting, resource allocation, and networking.

Given the infrequent touchpoints and the fact that lots of people will be connecting with this goal, the clearer the goals the better.

Be sure to complete the SMART-E Goal worksheet and the related One Page Plan. The One Page Plan is an excellent resource for capturing high level details around the plan. You may also find it useful to have team members work through a SMART-E Goal worksheet each time as well. This is one of the 20 resources found in the 20 Focus Areas for Virtual and Remote Team Development at the Potentials Realized Online Store at PotentialsRealized.com.

FIELD WORK—NOW WHAT?

Work on creating a SMART-E Goal.

Have each team member complete the One Page Plan for this quarter. Bring it to your discussion with your team leader or partners. What else you do you need added?

ONE-PAGE PLAN

Goal	Description	Key Timelines	Resources (Who and What)	Enablers/Derailers

D A Y   9

CORE SKILLS FOR SUCCESS

"Skill is the unified force of experience, intellect and passion in their operation."
—John Ruskin

FOCUS QUESTION:

What skills are going to help you thrive? What are the skills you want to grow into?

WHAT?

As a remote professional, you can develop several skills to help you stand out. These are the ones I shared in *Effective Virtual Conversations* for remote leaders. As we know, everyone needs to be a leader in the remote space—these skills are critical for professionals at all levels.

SKILLS WHICH ARE IMPORTANT BEYOND THE SCREEN

It's not just technical skills that help us get ahead. In the remote space it's about focusing on the softer side of things, such as:

- Making things visual

- Team spirit

- Emotional intelligence

- Building relationships

Looking back to last week's post on the ecosystem of learning, what can you do to expand your skills in these different areas?

ACTIVITY

Listed below are 25 skills for remote and hybrid professionals. Whether you are a leader, team member, or entrepreneur, these skills will be important. For each, rate yourself on a 1–10 scale, with 1 being low and 10 being high. Note your ratings and consider what you want to do to grow in these areas you have rated low.

YOU	YOUR TEAM (WHETHER YOU ARE A LEADER OR A TEAM MEMBER)	YOUR RESULTS	OTHER
• Self-development • Influence • Collaboration • Skills • Relationship development • Emotional intelligence • Empathy • Time management • Financial management	• Styles • Support • Conflict • Communication • Relationships • Team culture	• Getting things done • Execution • Work practice • Boundaries • Reducing distractions • Online and offline work • Project management	• Disruptions • Merging your worlds and roles (worker/person; virtual and in person) • Design and making things visual

What do you need to focus on as it relates to skills in these areas? What can help you grow? What areas have you not had exposure to?

The Foundation of Remote Workers Who Thrive

Skills that remote workers need to have developed:

Coaching	Listening	Relationship building
Collaboration	Mentoring	Relationships
Conflict management	Negotiation	Social Identity
Decision making	Networking	Technology
Delegation	Planning	Time estimation
Feedback	Presentations 101	Time management
Focus	(virtual and in person)	Trouble shooting
Goal setting	Prioritization	Working across differences
Influence	Problem solving	Working across time zones
Intercultural skills	Project management	
Leadership	Questioning	

SO WHAT?

What are the things you want to make a practice of?

The benefits of remote work can be huge. In fact, one of the things I love about being a coach is the virtual or digital nature of our work. In my 2017 book, *Effective Virtual Conversations*, I explore the benefits of remote working. These range from shorter commutes to more flex-time for caregiving responsibilities (whether for the young or old) and reducing our environmental footprint.

In my former world of work, it was common to spend over a week per month traveling, touching down in five or six countries. Today, as a coach, it's not uncommon to have done that virtually by lunch time. And while working virtually is not for all coaches, it's likely that you will be working with some clients virtually—never being within touching distance.

Working remotely is getting more attention these days—from publishers like the *Harvard Business Review* to an increasing number of organizations becoming aware of the multiple benefits of remote work.

There are several skills, mindsets, and systems to consider when working in the remote and hybrid space, as someone who runs a business or works for an organization.

Just like a traditional in-person business, remote businesses thrive on a foundation of solid skills and practices. And in the remote space, many things are also magnified. So, in addition to boosting skills in certain areas, we must realize that many principles and practices underpin our work in the virtual and remote space.

Here are 15 skills, mindsets, and practices to support you in doing your best work in the remote and hybrid space:

1. **Get comfortable with the technology you use.** Becoming proficient and comfortable with the technologies you use, creates the foundation of your professionalism and remote conversations. Consider: What is your level of confidence and comfort with the technology? What could you do to increase that level of comfort?

2. **Have a process orientation for your conversations**. In a virtual conversation, there is a dynamic tension between a need for structure and leaving space for the communication. This is especially true when working virtually, as you don't have all the clues and signals you would have if you were working in person. Consider: How can you create the space needed for remote conversations? Just as in a coaching conversation, how will you take the time to co-create clarity around the process? How can you co-design expectations with your clients and partners to create safety, and the baseline for a great conversation?

3. **Build relationships with people you haven't met in person.** Remote work doesn't happen in a vacuum. Relationships are important, and even more so when working remotely. There are fewer opportunities to "chat around the water cooler" and get to know each other over a shared lunch. Make sure you build in time to proactively build relationships. Our ability

to create strong connection across distance is paramount. Consider: What are you doing to learn more about other team member, stakeholder and partner needs? How are you showing up? What presence are you bringing? What are you doing so others get to know you and what you offer? How can you build your relationships in the remote space? For example, could you have a video lunch or coffee break with someone? A regular phone check-in? What else?

4. **Grow your intercultural knowledge and global mindset.** Remote work is likely to orbit you into many different cultures geographically, and developing intercultural awareness is key. Even if you work across a continent, be aware and tune into the different ways of working, pacing, and decision making. Here's how Dr. Gary Rankin defines Global Mindset: "It is the ability to step outside one's base culture and to understand there is no universally correct way to do things."[37] Consider: How does this person/organization approach work and make decisions? How can widening your awareness and appreciation of other cultures support your work? What are you doing to grow your global mindset?

5. **Set the stage for ongoing learning.** In a remote business, adopting a growth mindset where you're always learning is important. Whether it's a new technology, new feature, new skill, new marketing method, or something else—you need to stay current. And this means that ongoing learning is essential. Consider: What do you need to learn more about? Make a list!

6. **Learn what is "good enough."** The pace of change in the remote space can be dizzying. It's helpful to learn to be okay with things being "good enough" and not perfect. In the pursuit of perfection, it's likely that the context will have changed already. Consider: Where could I go with "good enough" rather than perfect?

7. **Be observant—move beyond what you see on the screen.** When we work remotely, we see each other's worlds via the boundaries of their screen or camera. This limits our potential to get to know someone more fully and can lead to incorrect assumptions. How can you move beyond the confines of what you see via your screen? For example, some teams intentionally call in from different locations within an office to provide more of a complete picture of what things are like at a remote location. Consider: What are you noticing? What are you not seeing? What do you need to learn more about or be curious about?

8. **Use the skill of questioning.** The art of questioning continues to be a backbone of the coaching conversation. Ask questions to explore your clients' and partners' broader context. Consider: What things would it be useful to inquire about? What do you need to bust assumptions around?

9. **Use visual anchor points.** A picture speaks a thousand words. When working remotely, there are so many pieces and types of information to manage. Images can help us communicate faster and with more depth. Consider: What are the images and metaphors that will communicate your message quicker and more visually?

10. **Less is more.** Less is more in the world of the remote worker; we are all so busy these days. Working remotely means dealing with more information and trying to figure out more things alone. So, learning to focus on what's really important is essential. Consider: What are the imperative things to communicate? What needs to be prioritized?

11. **Maintain your visibility.** Don't let "out of sight" lead to "out of mind." Be proactive in building relationships, communicating, and addressing issues. Just as quickly as your world changes, so do your partners. Visibility can take many forms—emails, video calls, instant messages, etc. Consider: How can you maintain visibility with your important partnerships and relationships?

12. **Check your assumptions.** The coaching skills of observation, asking questions and listening is key in checking our assumptions. We all bring our own experiential and 'cultural lens' to the work we do. So, an important practice of coaches working in the remote space is to examine your biases on a regular basis. Consider: What's important to note and become curious around? What is your intuition telling you to listen to? What biases do you need to explore for yourself?

13. **Make it meaningful—and clear.** Engage and connect people to their WIIFM—What's in it for me? Rushing from one call to another all day can leave people wondering, "Who did I speak with?" and "What did we talk about?" Make it a practice to share, summarize, and highlight next steps, commitments and accountabilities. Consider: How can I bring more meaning and purpose to my relationships and meetings? How can I ensure clarity?

14. **Follow-through.** Trust takes longer to build and is more fragile in the virtual and remote space. Issues can easily get magnified. So be sure to follow through with any commitments you've made. Trust quickly gets eroded when there is no follow-through. Consider: How can I ensure that I follow through and don't miss deadlines?

15. **People are people are people.** Finding common ground is key to partnering in the remote space. Many times, if we look, we find that we are more similar than different. Consider: What goals and values do we share? What can I do to bring attention to our similarities?

As you reflect on these 15 mindsets, skills, and practices which can help professionals thrive in the remote space, ask yourself:

- Which of these mindsets and practices are important for me to notice in my work, conversations, and relationships?

- Which of these skills are already well developed for you?

- What are the things you want to become better at?

- Where could you enhance your skills?

FIELD WORK—NOW WHAT?

Review the 15 mindsets core skills and related questions as listed above.

What is important to note?

1. _____

2. _____

3. _____

4. _____

5. _____

6. _____

7. _____

8. _____

9. _____

10. _____

11. _____

12. _____

13. _____

14. _____

15. _____

NOTES AND REFLECTIONS:

RELATIONSHIP BUILDING: YOUR BOSS

"Any supervisor worth [their] salt would rather deal with people who attempt too much than with those who try too little."
—Lee Iacocca

FOCUS QUESTION:

What things are going to make your relationship with your boss thrive?

WHAT?

Unless you are a solopreneur and work for yourself, it's likely that you are part of a bigger organizational framework and that one of your most important relationships will be with your boss.

If you are working remote, it's likely that you will be the one responsible for moving this forward, so it's always best to be proactive from the start.

Questions to consider:

- What are the preferences of your boss?

- What are the objectives they want to achieve?

- What are their main goals? In support of what their goals are, how can you help them?

If you do need to raise issues, be sure to check with your boss early on in your tenure as to:

- How they would like you to flag issues—are there status report meetings, reports?

- Consider what solutions you can come up with for the issue, rather than just stating the problem.

94 | DAY 10 | 90-DAY GUIDE FOR SUCCESS

- Work to solve the issue or provide various options with potential costs (time, resources, money) and benefits.

10 Areas to Consider as You Get Started with Your Role

Many professionals new to remote work are curious about what they want to add to their toolbox. These are areas you will want to check out with your boss.

These may include such things as:

1. **Systems to keep you focused.** Systems may range from financial systems (budget, expenses) to communication systems (voice, text, email, instant messaging) and knowledge management systems (where you get information, how you share it, and how you file and access it for others across the team).

2. **Team development tools.** Having a variety of team development tools to help the team connect, get to know each other, and focus in on the work and results you want.

3. **Relationship management tools.** What is going to help you build relationships with both internal and external stakeholders? If you are part of a remote team, it's likely that you are also navigating matrix relationships, and are part of multiple teams. Ask your boss who you should connect with, and how frequently.

4. **Planning tools.** As a team, what are your key goals? What do you need to focus on?

5. **Planning tools as an individual.** As professionals, we likely all have different preferences for planning. Some remote workers want to keep it all in the cloud; whereas, others want an analog, paper-based planning tool. In addition to the daily plans, are you taking time to focus on the quarterly and annual plans in your work or business? This is what I designed the *PlanDoTrack* planner for. It's an analog (i.e., paper-based) workbook and planner to help you and other team members get clear on what's important along planning, personal productivity, and skills levels.

6. **Getting organized.** Key to success is having a well-set-up office which functions; what's going to help you feel organized. "There's a place for everything, and everything in its place." In a future section in this guide we will explore some of the foundational elements you will want to have in place.

7. **Performance tools.** Business is about getting results, and it's important that the team is clear on what needs to get done and what success will look like. What is the current state of performance on a team and individual level? What conversations need to take place?

8. **Coaching tools.** Going hand in hand with performance tools are tools to have great conversations. A range of different conversations needs to take place on the team level, from performance conversations (what's working well and what isn't) to project reviews, stand-ups, team meeting, and ongoing feedback. What coaching and other conversational tools will support you?

9. **Project management tools.** In your work as a remote professional, it's likely that you are regularly navigating projects. What is important to note about your project management skills and tools? Considering the projects you are navigating, how are they going along in terms of *scope*, *time*, and *budget*? What needs attention? Who can help you with this?

10. **A focus on team culture and identity.** While it might seem out of the norm to include this, team culture and identity are critical in today's workspace. Our culture is *Who* We are, *How* We Do Things, and What We *Value*. When was the last time you spent time having a discussion around your team identity and how you do things? If you have team agreements around how you do things, when did you last explore these? If you don't have them, is it time to create them?

SO WHAT?

It's good practice to be proactive in setting up regular meetings with your boss. Consider the best cadence and rhythm.

Areas to explore with your first meeting with your boss:

- What are your priorities as my boss?
- What should I know about you?
- Do you prefer text, phone . . . ?
- What types of issues should be communicated along the different channels?
- How does my work fit into the bigger part of the team?
- What are the reporting elements I need to be submitting?
- How often will we be meeting?
- Where can I go for more information?
- What else should I know about?

Five types of conversations you need to have with your boss:

- Situational diagnosis—how your boss sees the portfolio and what's needed. Michael Watkins framework of STARS—start-up, turnaround, accelerated growth, realignment, and sustaining success—can help to frame the conversation. Listen in to his discussion with HBR about this, at https://hbr.org/2009/01/picking-the-right-transition-strategy.
- Expectations
- Resources
- Styles

- Personal development—how you are doing and where you need to focus (what will happen as you move into the role)

Expectations of remote team members:

- Ask for what you need
- Be proactive in scheduling meetings—the expectation is that beyond the weekly reporting, there would be a weekly one-on-one coaching
- Be clear about your priorities and context and where you are going
- Being able to focus in on what's important
- Being comfortable with uncertainty

FIRST MEETING BETWEEN NED AND JO

The first meeting between a leader and their team member is foundational. During their first meeting Jo and Ned explored these areas:

- What Ned needs from Jo as his leader
- What Jo needs from Ned
- What Jo should know about Ned; more about his preferences and styles
- Providing Ned with the opportunity to focus in on what is truly important
- Inviting Ned to co-design working sessions
- Ned's focusing in on learning experiences and taking on special projects
- Apprising Ned of things that are most challenging for new remote staff
- Getting to know people—making a point to proactively reach out to someone new
- Taking advantage of mentoring opportunities and peer partners
- Knowing where to go
- Becoming comfortable with follow-up and outreach to others outside the team, and even within the organization
- Self-motivation
- Creating boundaries
- Clearly asking questions but also having a solution

- Things Jo loves about her work—being a support for team members, getting to learn about a lot of different things, not leading in the traditional sense, and helping others do their best work
- Ned's expectations of her
- Reporting requirements' being key, as Jo needs to know what Ned needs and what he is focusing on

FIELD WORK—NOW WHAT?

Make a list of questions you want to explore with your boss during your next meeting.

_____

_____

_____

_____

_____

What else is important to note?

_____

_____

_____

_____

NOTES AND REFLECTIONS:

RELATIONSHIP IN FOCUS: YOUR PEERS

"If you are building a culture where honest expectations are communicated and peer accountability is the norm, then the group will address poor performance and attitudes."
—Henry Cloud

FOCUS QUESTION:
Who are your peers?

WHAT?

Unless you are a solopreneur, it's likely that you will need to work with others and develop solid working relationships with them.

In order to do this, we want to make sure that we are focused on building trust. Building trust in the remote space often entails two things:

- **Consistency**—consistency around your messaging, consistency around your communication.
- **Follow-through**—how are you following through with others?

As a remote professional, it's important to have a set of people you can reach out to, internally and externally.

Peer relationships are some of the most important business relationships we can have. Who are the people who can support you with your work? What are the types of supports you want to have in place? What's going to work best for you?

Here are some examples of different types of peer networks:

- One group gets together for meetings on Friday afternoons to get things done. This is a last sprint for their week, helping them get everything done.

- Accountability groups may meet at the start and end of the week. These focus on what their top 3–5 goals are.

- Masterminds—groups that gather periodically to tackle challenges and problems together, asking and offering advice, making helpful connections, etc.

- Professional associations, LinkedIn groups/membership. (Word of caution: note when you are becoming too diluted; relationships may be more important when it is quality over quantity.)

- Common interest groups, meeting around hobbies. For example, as part of multiple writing groups—including Muskoka Novel Marathon and NaNoWriMo—I've met many inspirational people.

- Circles which meet to discuss and explore common issues of interest.

In Focus: Listening

Listening can be a key skill for remote and hybrid workers, made even more complicated when we are not able to see each other.

Notice your listening next time you meet. Are you listening for what they are saying, or are you rushing to say something?

What do you notice about the other person's pace, pitch, and body language?

SO WHAT?

It's not uncommon to reach out to peers on a regular basis for advice, best practices, resources, or connections.

Peer relationships are reciprocal. They're a give and take. What do you bring to the table?

_____

_____

_____

_____

What do they bring?

_____

_____

_____

_____

What's valuable for both of you?

_____

_____

_____

_____

If you have a copy of *Effective Virtual Conversations*, work through the questions in Chapter 12 on Collaboration.

FIELD WORK—NOW WHAT?

Identify a type of peer network you want to explore or join. What is your commitment around the amount of time you will spend on this?

_____

_____

_____

_____

QUESTIONS TO BE EXPLORING WITH PEERS.

- What are your priorities?
- What should I know about you?
- Do you prefer text, phone, . . . ?
- What types of issues should be communicated along the different channels?
- How does my work connect into your work?
- How often would you like to meet?
- What are your recommendations?
- Where can I go for more information?
- What else should I know?

DAY 12

CONTEXT AND NAVIGATING VUCA

"Today's VUCA context is Volatile, Uncertain, Complex and Ambiguous.
It's a context where things are changing radically and rapidly,
and 'good enough' has become a mantra."
—Jennifer Britton, *PlanDoTrack*

FOCUS QUESTION:
What context are you operating within?

WHAT?

What's happening beyond your screen? We don't operate in a vacuum. The context in which we operate is dynamic and ever changing. The events of the pandemic have radically shifted the way people work. What are you noticing about the context in which you operate?

The Seven Layers of Context

One of the challenges for today's remote worker is that they are often more closely connected to the context in which they are operating. Their context may also be different from that of their colleagues.

Let's take a look at each one, as there are several layers to context:

1. Global and meta-level
2. Industry layer
3. Organizational layer
4. Leadership layer

5. The team level of your world—matrix teams

6. The micro-context of your world—your office space, your focus, your motivation

7. Your self—your focus, your motivation, well-being (social, environmental, etc.)

SO WHAT?

Let's explore each of these seven layers, starting with the largest and moving to the smallest.

The global/meta-level—connects into such key trends as VUCA, disruption, AI, globalization, Brexit, and geographic invisible boundaries.

VUCA is an acronym which is currently being used to describe the business context as:

> **Volatility**—ever changing. Things that once were stable are now changing. In your organization, role or industry, what does volatility mean? How are things changing rapidly? Broadly?

> **Uncertainty**—what's happening today may not happen tomorrow. What do you notice about the level of uncertainty in your work? Where does uncertainty show up?

> **Complexity**—complexity is being created by many forces, from changes in technology to changes in the way we do things. What once were distinct disciplines are now becoming more interconnected. In what ways is your work becoming more complex? What do you notice about your approach to complexity?

> **Ambiguity**—refers to how things are not always clear. Related to things becoming more connected, it may be harder to discern things. Things may have more "gray areas" rather than being discretely black and white. What are you noticing about ambiguity? What does that mean in your context?

Industry level—what is happening at your industry level; is it an industry of growth? Of decline? Of competition? Of innovation? Tapping into others in your industry and related industries can be an important resource for remote workers. Sometimes, given location, our industry connections may provide more of a direct influence than our organization, especially if the organization is located half a world away. What resources are you able to tap into in your industry? What are the current trends?

GLOBAL/META
INDUSTRY
ORGANIZATIONAL
LEADERSHIP
TEAM
MICRO
PERSONAL

Organizational level—the organization you are attached to will also have an influence on *how* things are completed. What are the current strategic priorities? What are the expectations of all remote workers? What support is available to you? What activities and events can you connect into? Hybrid and remote work often lead to changes in the way the organization works.

Leadership level—your leader also will have an influence on your work. As a remote worker, you are likely managed by one or more leaders. What are their priorities? What are their preferences in terms of communication? On a regular basis, be sure to reach out and schedule one-on-ones and ask for feedback. Leaders provide direction and resources. (More on feedback and one-on-ones to come.) When are you scheduling meetings with them?

If you are your own boss, how would you describe your leadership? What areas can you grow in?

Team level of your world—matrix teams. Most remote workers will have a variety of peers they can connect into, from one or more teams. What type of support do you want from your peers? How are you connecting in with them?

If you are a solopreneur, operating on your own, what is your vision for a team? Will you ever grow your own team of full-time or part-time workers? Might you expand the scale of your work by bringing on subcontractors?

Micro-context of your world—your office space, your focus, your motivation. Your day-to-day context includes your office space, your technical systems, and your virtual connection with others. What is the state of this context? Is everything organized and working for you? What needs attention? Things that might be perceived as small by family members, such as a slower internet connection or poor lighting can become a big issue for remote professionals. More on setting up your office and how that can help you thrive is found in Day 5.

Your self—Your focus, your motivation, and your well-being (social, environmental, etc.).

Finally, you also have created a context for yourself. Your focus, your motivation, your values, and your mindsets are worth exploring. Many of these are included in the Iceberg analogy I originally introduced in *PlanDoTrack* and *Coaching Business Builder*. We'll be exploring these as we go, in this guide as well.

Before moving on, ask yourself, what needs attention? What areas are really clear for you? Which ones aren't? What questions do you need to ask? Of whom; who can you reach out to?

FIELD WORK—NOW WHAT?

The 7 Layers of Context. Take a look at the context in which you operate. Identify the key elements in your 7 layers of context. What is important to note? What levels do you want to focus on?

GLOBAL/META	
INDUSTRY	
ORGANIZATIONAL	
LEADERSHIP	
TEAM	
MICRO	
YOUR SELF	
OTHER	

DAY 13
STRENGTHS

*"Sometimes you don't realize your own strength until you come
face to face with your greatest weakness."*
—Susan Gale

FOCUS QUESTION:
What helps you thrive?

WHAT?

Strengths are the things we want to make sure we leverage as a remote worker.

Here's what the research shows from Gallup Strengths Center:

- Individuals and teams that are able to lead more by strengths, are:

    o 6x more engaged

    o 3x more likely to report having excellent quality of life

    o 8.9% more profitable

- Teams which focus on strengths have 12.5% greater productivity

It's a fallacy that we may be able to work with our strengths for every minute of every day, *but* we will want to make sure that we are leveraging them as much as possible. Because our strengths are so much a part of who we are and how we see the world, they can seem almost invisible. It's often when people say "of course, that's what you do . . ." when you are working with others.

If you have not yet undertaken a strengths assessment, it may be interesting for you to check out one of the many available. This could include:

- Positive Psychology's VIA Strengths Survey
- CliftonStrengths Assessment (formerly known as Gallup's StrengthsFinder 2.0)

Undertake one of these and see what your strengths are. What are they? How are they magnified in the remote space? How can these be considered superpowers for you to lean into? What happens when your strengths are overmagnified?

Did You Know?

Some useful strengths to have include:

- Connection
- Community
- Learning
- Experimentation
- Exposure (to new ideas, ways of doing things, other perspectives, feedback)

Ways to use strengths every day:

- Special projects
- Your projects
- Hobbies

SUPERPOWERS

Superpowers for each of the Digital Dozen:

- Ned, the new remote worker—likes smores and Flexibility.
- Malcolm, the mentor—the sage; loves Teaching.
- Serge, the serial entrepreneur—has Persistence.
- Mo, the creative solopreneur—has Creative Spark, Innovation; is great at creating in the moment.
- Jo, the virtual team leader—engages in Ongoing Learning.

- Alex, the voluntary sector professional—Enrolling Others; helping people connect with what is.

- Jane, the virtual facilitator—has great Design Techniques

- Darren, the digital nomad—Networking and Relationship Building; meets people in every location.

- Mel, the coach—is great at Communication, especially asking questions which help to explore action and evoke awareness.

- Sujit, the project manager—focuses on Estimation; it's his way to make sure that project stays on target, on track.

- Alex, who works from anywhere—is skilled at Focusing.

Make sure *you* are using strengths every day in your work.

As much as the Digital Dozen know, it's also important to ensure that they do not overmagnify their strengths. It is important that the underbelly of strengths is not present. While strengths create a unique fingerprint for us, they are likely to get overmagnified in times of stress.

Strengths Days for Teams. Many team leaders ask us to facilitate a strengths day for them. Teams excel when they are clear on their results and they are also clear on the relationships and connections that they have.

Components of a strengths day may include:

- A focus on relationships. This is about getting to know each other. Who each person is. What their strengths are. How they intersect.

- A focus on results. This is about what people do, what their role is, what goals they are responsible for.

One of the activities you may want to undertake as a team is mapping your team strengths according to what their top 5 activities are. Overlay the framework of *Strengths-based Leadership* to explore what the team looks like in terms of their focus on the four strengths areas—Strategic, Execution, Influence and Relationship Building. Each one of these has advantages. How do they align with your strategic goals?

SO WHAT?

What are the things you want to focus in on?

What's going to magnify what you are good at, or your superpowers? Or how can you do more of what you are good at?

Together with your collaborators, what will help you excel?

FIELD WORK—NOW WHAT?

Working in your strengths. Outline your top 5 strengths. What are you doing every day to use these?

STRENGTH	WHAT IT LOOKS LIKE TO ME	WHEN I OVERUSE IT . . .	WHAT I NEED TO BE AWARE OF	BECAUSE OF THIS, I MAY ALSO WANT TO PARTNER WITH . . .

BONUS: Working in the Margins

What are you doing to create time, space, and focus for the important items? Working in the margins is really quite important in terms of finding space and time to get things done.

_____

_____

_____

_____

Where do you need to stretch a bit more?

_____

_____

_____

_____

What extra edge do you have that can help you get ahead?

_____

_____

_____

_____

Are you embracing your natural talents?

_____

_____

_____

_____

Are you trying to minimize them, or are they coming to the forefront?

_____

_____

_____

_____

Be sure to link to strengths!

NOTES AND REFLECTIONS:

COMMUNICATION

"Good communication is the bridge between confusion and clarity."
—Nat Turner

FOCUS QUESTION:
What is important to note around communication?

WHAT?

Communication is one of the cornerstones of exceptional remote work. What can you do to boost your communication skills in service to your clients?

Communication can take many forms in remote working—from texting to instant messaging to voice mails left in Voxer to messages in Slack.

Part of the challenge of remote work is using the right communication channel for the right type of message. Sending an important message to your boss for discussion is likely to be better done by phone or email than IM. Sharing a quick tip with a co-worker who needs a response *now* is probably better done in a quick IM than in a full-blown email.

Did You Know?

In the remote space we lose a huge amount of the visual cues we have in face-to-face business contexts—that of visual cues. It is often said that in F2F environments we get 55% of our message from body language, and only 8% from the words which are used.

Where to Go? Communication tools—spell check. Grammarly.

SO WHAT?

Basic components for communication:

There are two parts to communication—the message and how it's interpreted. What are you doing to check in that your message was received as it was intended?

- Be clear with your request—What are you asking people to take action on?
- Check for understanding—Is what you said, what's being interpreted?

What are you listening for?

What lens or perspective are you listening through? What role does context play? Consider going back to the 7 Layers of Context at the end of Day 12.

It's also critical to be clear on what our bias is.

Writing—writing skills are critical for remote workers, as this is one of our main channels. Are we using words which are understood by all in the same way?

Also, is there a call-to-action? Is this specified in the request? For example, "I need you to" or "as a next step" or "respond by [date]."

Check subject lines and formatting. Use bold for emphasis. Does something need to be supported with a drawing, a video, or other?

FIELD WORK—NOW WHAT?

What key issues around communication are important to you right now?

_____
_____
_____
_____

This week, check for understanding. Consider what your major forms of communication are:

_____
_____
_____
_____

Writing—This week be clearer in your writing. Is there a call to action? Are you making a request? Is there a timeline?

Make a list of 10 questions you want to use in your conversations.

1. _____

2. _____

3. _____

4. _____

5. _____

6. _____

7. _____

8. _____

9. _____

10. _____

Asking Powerful Questions

What type of questions are going to open up space for great communication? Keep these principles in mind:

1. Starting a question with WHAT makes questions open ended.

2. Make sure your questions are short and to the point. 5-7 words can be a good length to aim for.

3. Consider what types of questions you want to ask. Is it to help the other person:

    - Generate ideas?

    - Explore options?

    - Focus?

    - Prioritize?

    - Make decisions?

THIS WEEK'S FOUNDATION THEME WAS
CONNECTION

Congrats! You are now through the first two weeks of your role.
What was it like? Describe it here in three words:

_____ · _____ · _____

Connection means the following to me:

_____

_____

_____

_____

What's important about the 7 Layers of Context right now?

_____

_____

_____

_____

Topics we covered this week were:

- Day 8—Goals
- Day 9—Core Skills for Success
- Day 10—Relationship Building: Your Boss
- Day 11—Relationship in Focus: Your Peers
- Day 12—Context and Navigating VUCA
- Day 13—Strengths
- Day 14—Communication

Key learning this week:

_____

_____

_____

_____

_____

_____

Wrap up theme:

_____

_____

_____

_____

What are you looking forward to?

_____

_____

_____

_____

What questions do you have? Who can help you?

_____

_____

_____

_____

_____

_____

What To-Dos have surfaced? (List your top 3–5)

1. _____

2. _____

3. _____

4. _____

5. _____

Update your tracking sheet!

WEEK 3 · CLARITY

"You must first clearly see a thing in your mind before you can do it."
—Alex Morrison

Welcome to Week 3!

This week we are going to explore Clarity—clarity of goals, process, message, purpose, and expectations.

We're going to be exploring the following topics:

- Day 15—Systems for Working Remote
- Day 16—Planning
- Day 17—Personal Brand
- Day 18—Time Management and Staying at Peak
- Day 19—Motivation
- Day 20—Prioritization
- Day 21—Teams in Focus: Types of Teams

WHAT ARE YOUR TOP 3 GOALS THIS WEEK?:

1. _____

2. _____

3. _____

By the end of the week I want to be sure that . . .

_____

What are you noticing about things that are clear (goals, process, message (instructions, communication, etc.), purpose, and expectations?

What is unclear?

What conversations are important to have?

Tip: The 7 Remote Enablers

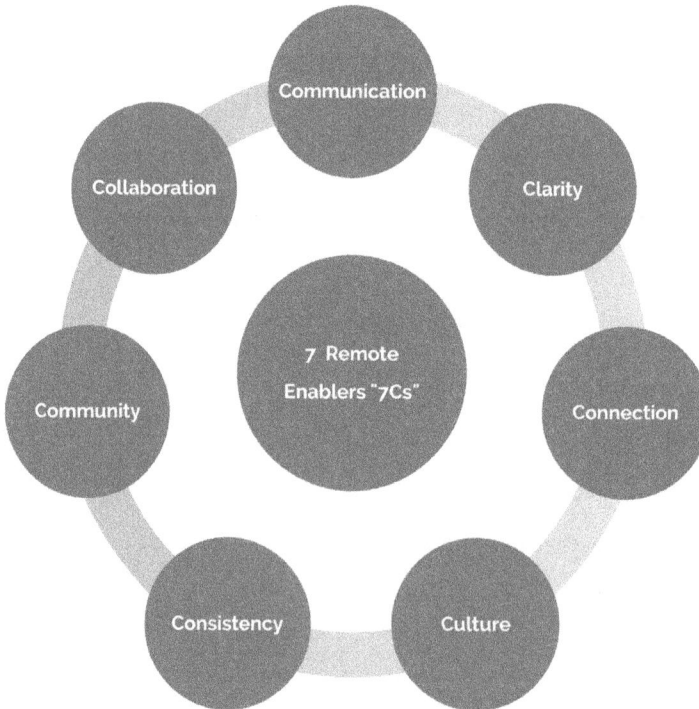

In my writing, including *Reconnecting Workspaces*, I share the 7 Remote Enablers. These are all levers which can be used to create an organization that thrives. This week we are dipping into three of the seven Cs of remote work:

- **Clarity** around communication, process, end results, successes, measures and touchpoints. At the team level, this will also include clarity about roles and how people are interconnected.

- **Communication** includes communication in all its forms. Are we using the right channel for the right message? Is this the right way to communicate for the right person's system?

- **Consistency** also is an enabler as it helps people know what to expect and when to expect it. If we know that we always meet on Friday at 6 a.m., that creates consistency. I can plan around it. Even if it's not a convenient time, it may be better than if there is no plan at all.

What are you doing to ensure that there is *clarity*, *consistency*, and *communication*?

Linked to the tip that perception does not equal reality, clarity is paramount in today's remote workspace.

Prior to COVID-19, the average worker would send 121 emails a day, and it has been estimated that they send 50% more now.[38]

General rules of thumb with remote communication—Make the implicit, explicit. Spell things out and be clear. Demonstrate where possible; show it via video if you can. Ask clearly for what you need from people.

In practice, it is important to be clear on multiple levels:

- Purpose—what is important about this? Why are we doing it? Who will it help? What is this connected to?

- Process—what do people need to do? How are things connected?

- Communication—regardless of communication vehicle (spoken, text, email, phone), clarity involves ensuring that:

    o Your message is clear

    o It's been received (did it reach the person)

    o It's been interpreted in the way you want

Check for understanding where you can, and/or be sure to follow up in case things are not clear and take someone in a different tangent.

Clarify Expectations

Clear expectations are one of the most important ingredients for remote work success.

What are the team expectations around the following?

- Showing up for meetings
- Focus at meetings
- Being prepared
- Being punctual
- Quality of work
- Surfacing issues
- Addressing difficult conversations
- Manner of interaction with each other
- Sharing information

- Connecting with others outside of the organization
- Participating in ongoing learning

In a remote team, we may be part of multiple matrix relationships, which makes it even more important for us to be clear on our expectations about *how things are done.*

Teams can benefit from taking time to create Ways of Working or Team Agreements about how they will operate together.

Each one of the items found in the text box could spark a conversation around multiple factors.

When expectations are not clear, we run the risk of doing things differently, having varied output, and, most importantly, creating assumptions that might not be well founded. These can have the most detrimental impact in the long run.

As a team, what expectations do you want to make clear?

DAY 15

SYSTEMS FOR WORKING REMOTE

"Let systems run the business and people run the systems. People come and go but the systems remain constant."
—Michael E. Gerber, *The E-Myth Revisited*

FOCUS QUESTION:

What systems are going to help you scale and be consistent?

WHAT?

Systems allow us to scale our work and are an important part of ensuring consistency across a remote workforce. Systems also allow us to share information and build off one another. For most remote workers today, you'll likely look to establish systems in areas including:

- Project management
- Learning
- Communication
- Knowledge management
- Relationship building
- Finance
- Administration
- Reporting

Systems are at the heart of most remote workspaces. When we are working alone, it may feel like we are doing it all on our own, but we usually aren't.

If we are part of an organization, we are linking in with others, and likely with others in different time zones. While I may be working on a project in the morning of my day, my colleague may need to pick that up 12 hours later when they start their work the next day. Systems are essential in allowing for the overlap of items.

If you are working as a solopreneur or a remotepreneur, you are a one-person show—at this moment at least. Many new solopreneurs don't think about what happens when their business grows, and their capacity gets stretched. What do you do as your work scales?

Follow the system. Systems are key to remote work success. They help us scale our work so that we are not always doing things that can be automated. They also ensure consistency across sites. This is particularly important when we are part of a team.

When it comes to systems on a team, it's important not to innovate. Systems are there for a reason. If you do see another way of doing things, bring it to the team, build a business case, and implement it as a team.

What are you in compliance around? What are you not?

We can be learning many different things as we go. I did this myself as a remote worker and young leader . . . sometimes we learn the most from the things we did not do well. What do you want to make sure you can do more effectively?

Systems can take many different forms. According to vocabulary.com/dictionary/system, there are nine of them:

1. Group of independent but interrelated elements comprising a unified whole
2. Instrumentality that combines interrelated interacting artifacts designed to work as a coherent entity (like a stereo system)
3. The living body considered as made up of interdependent components forming a unified whole
4. A group of physiologically or anatomically related organs or parts
5. A sample of matter in which substances in different phases are in equilibrium (physical chemistry)
6. An ordered manner; orderliness by virtue of being methodical and well organized
7. A complex of methods or rules governing behavior
8. An organized structure for arranging or classifying
9. A procedure or process for attaining an objective

Did You Know?

Systems to Create:

- Customer
- Team (feedback, coaching…)
- Reporting
- Financial
- Project management
- Learning
- Meetings
- Administration

What else?

SO WHAT?

Here are systems questions to consider regarding learning, communication, and project management:

- What systems do you have in place already?

_____

_____

_____

- What are the things which are going to help you as a team be consistent?

_____

_____

_____

- What are the systems which are going to help you scale your work?

_____

_____

_____

For resources to consider, take a look at Section 3 of *PlanDoTrack*.

FIELD WORK—NOW WHAT?

Take some time to identify your systems. What is working? What is not?

SYSTEM	WHAT WORKS	WHAT DOESN'T	HOW DOES IT ENSURE CONSISTENCY? SCALING?

Bonus: For 10 Systems to Focus on, check out the *Remote Pathways* podcast episode #32.

NOTES AND REFLECTIONS:

PLANNING

"Having a strategy suggests an ability to look up from the short term and the trivial to view the long term and the essential, to address causes rather than symptoms, to see woods rather than trees."
—Lawrence Freedman

FOCUS QUESTION:

What type of planning are you undertaking?
How much time are you dedicating to it?

WHAT?

Planning is an essential everyday activity for work in the remote space. With team members working at a distance, it's not easy to "wing it," as we could have in person. Work is interdependent when you are part of a team, and making sure that everyone is clear on what you need to do *when* and *how*, and *what success* will look like, is critical.

Planning takes place at multiple levels—Daily, Weekly, Monthly, and Quarterly—as well as short term, long term, contingency planning, and strategic planning.

Strategic issues help us look at things from the big picture. Strategic issues may be the focus of our work "down the road" or the 3–5-year view.

Being aware of the strategic issues helps us retain a focus on this. While it may not appear that strategic issues are important in the short term because things are happening so quickly, they do serve as an anchor for us through the ups and downs.

In the remote-space part of the challenge is identifying strategic issues at the macro level.

Each staff, and each location, may have a different focus. What would you indicate as the strategic issues of importance?

Strategic Issues Mapping is one visual tool which can be undertaken as a team.

Questions to ask in identifying strategic issues:

- What issues are important for **me** right now? 1 year from now? 5 years?
- What issues will be important for **my team** right now? 1 year from now? 5 years?
- What issues are being flagged by **our stakeholders/customers** right now? 1 year from now? 5 years?

Key issues for remote workers around planning can also include:

- **Building in a pause.** Taking time regularly (think *every day*) to do 10 minutes of planning from the next day. The common adage is that 10 minutes of planning can save 60 minutes of unfocussed effort.
- **Prioritizing.** What are the top 3–5 items you want to focus on today?
- **Quick wins.** Consider what are the easy things you can get off your list; what is going to create some momentum?
- **Tracking things.** We don't always remember things like they happen. Leading by objectives, or with a results-focus is key in the remote space. Knowing your data is important. Consider tracking, on a regular basis, key items, such as walking, revenue in, TV time, time spent as a family on fun things, etc. Consider what you want to track around your top 3-5 goals

Did You Know?

There are multitude of levels on which we can plan. Planning types you might explore are:

- Trackers
- Daily planners
- Weekly planners
- Content planners
- Quarterly plans
- Annual plans

SO WHAT?

The Strategic Issues Mapping Tool can be useful in facilitating and mapping key issues facing the team/organization at a number of levels, such as duration (short term, medium term, long term) or geography (local, national, international). Each circle can be assigned an appropriate label. Have team members brainstorm the factors facing the team at each one of these levels.

You will likely have a wide number of issues at each level. In order to work with them, you will also want to prioritize them and/or identify which ones you can control.

You can facilitate this conversation through preparation, instructions, and discussion.

Preparation. Prepare a blank slide with the Strategic Issues Map on it (see next page). Determine what the different layers for focus are. Is it short-term, medium-term, long-term? *Or* local, national, global? *Or* other?

Instructions. First ask each individual team member to reflect and create a list of the top 3–10 strategic issues they see at their location.

Collect these on one screen, either by having everyone share one at a time or by having them annotate their list in a specific spot on a blank slide. Take a screen shot and/or save this.

Next, get people to identify whether the issue is short-term, medium-term, or long-term. Decide as a team what those time frames are, i.e., is short-term the next quarter or the next year?

Next, transfer the items from their strategic issues list to the round map (see graphic on the following page).

Go around and group common issues. Get comments on what issues are showing up.

Finally, vote on which ones in each area are priorities. Provide each person with one or two dots for voting on their priorities.

Discussion. What is a priority? Who is going to take on the task of moving these issues forward? What are the next steps? When will we check in?

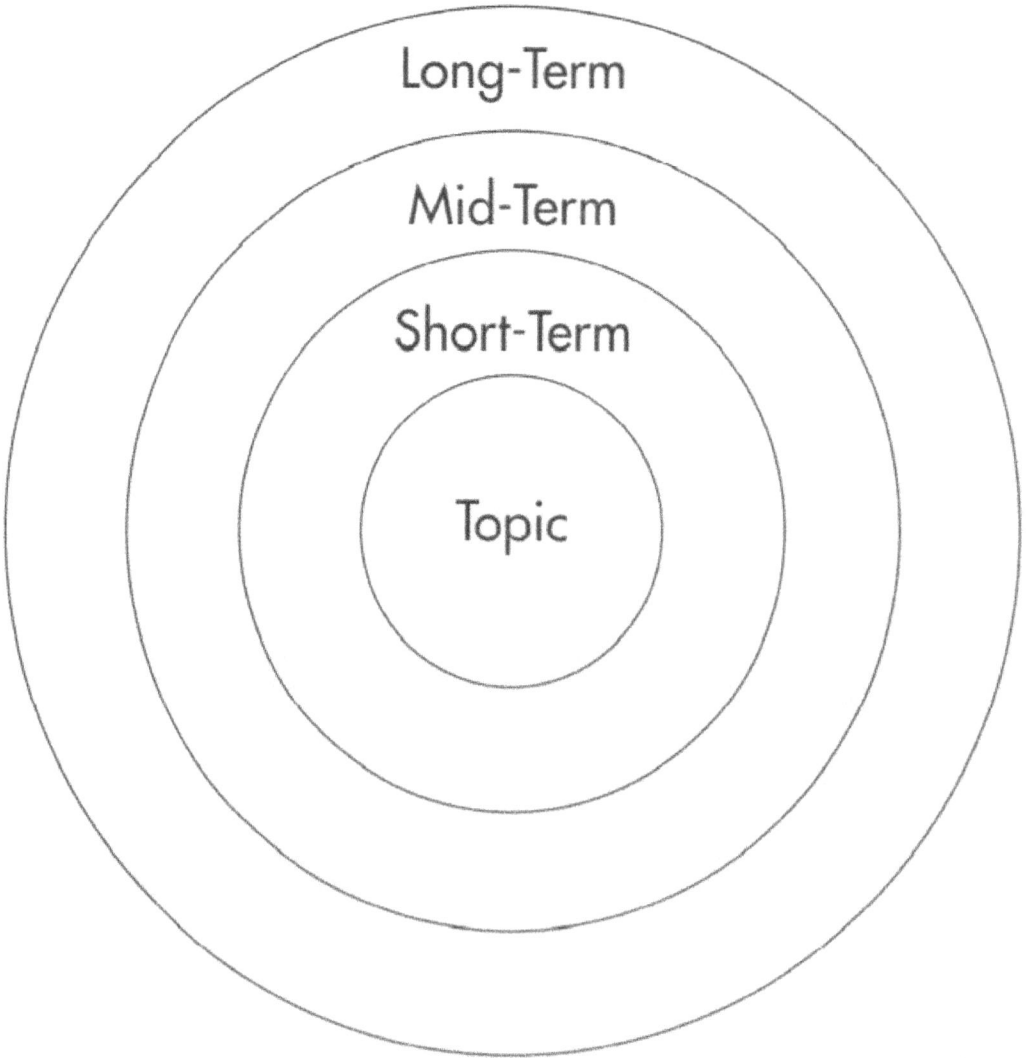

Long-Term

Mid-Term

Short-Term

Topic

FIELD WORK—NOW WHAT?

Complete a strategic issues map of your work right now (that could include your portfolio—what you do and the areas you cover).

What are your primary focus areas?

_____

_____

_____

Share it with others. What do you notice? What is the meta focus for everyone?

_____

_____

_____

_____

_____

_____

_____

_____

_____

_____

If you have a copy of my *PlanDo Track Workbook and Planner*, check out a copy of the more extended description in Section 4.

NOTES AND REFLECTIONS:

DAY 17
PERSONAL BRAND

"People don't buy what you do, they buy why you do it."
—Simon Sinek

FOCUS QUESTION:
What are the elements of a personal brand?

WHAT?

A brand includes the elements of colors, taglines, movement, sounds, and images. It is grounded in your values as a business and communicates succinctly what you provide to the world. It is an external representation of who you are as a professional, and what you take a stand for.

Your brand can be signaled through your signature, how you are dressed, and/or what you communicate. It is closely related to your reputation. Given that people see us for only short windows at a time, your brand is key.

Who are you? What do you take a stand for? What is your reputation?

While branding used to be something only businesses thought about, the concept of a personal brand has become an important topic for professionals of all types.

This might seem like an out-of-place topic if you are working for a large organization and are not a remotepreneur; but in fact, personal brand is an important topic for all remote workers to consider. How do you want to be known? We have 8 seconds to make a first impression. What are the three adjectives which you want people to connect in with you around this topic?

What do you need to create?

In my work as a business coach, the focus on this last part, or the benefits you provide, can be the missing link.

What are the icons and elements you think describe your brand? What makes you unique?

What are the values you take a stand for?

Did You Know?

Branding is not always about how you look. It can also be about what you say; getting to the core of your unique message. Fill in the blanks:

I am a _____

who works with _____

by providing _____

in order to _____.

SO WHAT?

Our brand and reputation may carry wider than we could even imagine. A brand consists of several different elements, including:

- Colors
- Words
- Metaphors/Images
- Taglines

Where to go? Branding is a large topic that you may want to learn more about. It may take you into the landscape of learning more about colors (check out Gretchen Rubin), words, or even marketing. Even if we work in a non-profit, learning more about brand and marketing can be of service. As someone who spent the bulk of the first half of my career working in the voluntary sector, I learned marketing can take many forms. The ability to build a business case and position your message can be as important in building a vision for a new community project as it is in selling a product.

What role do marketing and branding have in your world?

On a personal level, what do you want to be known for?

FIELD WORK—NOW WHAT?

Spend some time today thinking about the brand you want to create or own, and the reputation you want to develop in your work.

Take a few minutes reading through the following list, picking out the top 5–10 words that describe the brand you want to create for yourself, your work, or your business.

- Antique
- Artsy
- Balanced
- Bold
- Cartoon
- Clean
- Elaborate
- Fancy

- Fun
- Historic
- Hip
- Innovative
- Modern
- Minimal
- Natural
- Refined

- Simple
- Sophisticated
- Strong
- Striking
- Refined
- Vintage

WHAT IS IMPORTANT ABOUT MY BRAND

- Colors:_____

- Graphics and images to note:_____

- Motto:_____

- Tagline:_____

DAY 18
TIME MANAGEMENT AND STAYING AT PEAK

*"Do the biggest, most important thing in the morning
and the rest won't feel so bad."*
—Tony Crabbe

FOCUS QUESTION:
Where do you spend your time?

WHAT?

Time management and personal productivity is a primary concern for many remote workers.

Key issues in time management include:

- Boundaries
- Renewal
- Doing your best work or staying at your peak performance
- Deciding what to do, and what not to do
- Remembering: "What doesn't get scheduled, doesn't get done"
- Questioning: "Am I being productive or busy?"
- Prioritization
- Focus
- Simplification

Time management is an even more important focus for team members, given that they are the ones needing to manage different relationships, time zones, and relationships.

THE GREAT DEBATE: PRODUCTIVITY IN THE REMOTE AND HYBRID SPACE

A lot has been written about remote work and productivity. For more on this topic, check out Laura Vanderkam's book, *168 Hours*.

In his article "Remote Work Improves Productivity,"[39] author Sammi Caramela asserts:

- "Remote workers take longer breaks on average, but they remain productive for an additional 10 minutes per day.

- Remote employees work 1.4 more days per month than their office-based counterparts, resulting in more than three additional weeks of work per year.

- 29% of remote employees said they struggle with work-life balance, and 31% said they have needed to take a day off for their mental health.

A 2021 survey found that "**On average, those who work from home spend 10 minutes less a day being unproductive, work one more day a week, and are 47% more productive.**"[40]

According to Tess Hanna, 70% of Nintex remote-working respondents found their experiences working from home to be better and more productive than they initially projected, citing more family time, no commute, fewer interruptions, and improved work-life balance.[41]

FACTOIDS AROUND TIME MANAGEMENT

According to Tony Crabbe, "Switching regularly between tasks makes you 40% slower, even if it makes you feel productive."[42]

David Allen shares the 2-minute rule: "If you can do it in 2 minutes—do it!"

Tony Crabbe asserts that there needs to be a "balance of focus and recovery...52 minutes of focus and 17 minutes away from the desk"[43]

Amy Cuddy's "famous" power stance showed increases in testosterone of 10%, associated with confidence and decrease of cortisol by 25%.[44] Additional studies have supported and refuted the claims around postural feedback hypothesis. Check out these related research studies at https://docs.google.com/spreadsheets/d/1VZQxTNGncn-x7nz9OsNXmkz9rFkhdYEjzNXN7vqrYKA/pubhtml?gid=1181532305&single=true

According to David Myer, it's more productive to reduce switching between tasks. When we try to multitask it can increase overall time needed to complete a task by 40%.[45]

As to big chunking, according to the research of Teresa Ambile and Easel Bryant Ford at Harvard Business School, in a 9,000-person study there was more of a productivity breakthrough when they were able to work on a single project for the entire day.[46]

Note that dopamine is released when we switch tasks, which is why it can feel so good.

According to the research of Jonathan Spira, chief analyst at Basex, a business research firm, "Increasing inefficiency and ineffectiveness of multi-tasking is wasting 28 billion hours of knowledge workers' time in the US."[47] He further indicates that the estimated cost of interruptions to the American economy is nearly $650 billion a year.[48]

Did You Know?

"I find that I am moving from project to project to project. I am not getting a break. What should I do?" It's important to stay at your peak.

Factors for peak performance in the virtual space include:

- Boundaries
- Incorporating a variety of approaches
- Signaling when you are off
- Mindfulness
- Tools for getting things done virtually will include the following:
- Prioritization—including the four tools covered in this guide - The SWOT, Strategic Issues Mapping, the Prioritization Matrix, and Stephen Covey's Urgent/Important Framework.
- Delegation—The is/is not Tool
- Influence
- Time management
- Doing more with less—how to prioritize, how to use the resources you have
- Asking for help
- Collaboration

SO WHAT?

Where does a remote worker's time go?

Notice where your time is going. The following could be signals that something needs attention:

- Forgetting topics—signals need for system around time management, planning, workflow
- Working too many hours
- Not getting everything done
- Getting organized
- Stopping to find information
- Ongoing meetings

Things that remote workers can make a practice of doing:

- Scheduling time—good apps for this include Toggl, Trello, Workflow
- Exploring what is important for each stakeholder
- Clarifying and re-clarifying job expectations
- Focusing in on the high-leverage work—getting this out of the way
- Noticing what distractions exist and what needs to happen to keep things moving
- Building relationships with those who can _____ (fill in the blank with what you need)
- Asking questions around requirements and expectations
- Asking for feedback regularly to ensure _____ (fill in the blank with what you need)
- Being visible to keep on top of people's minds

What are the things you want to make a practice of?

TIME TRACKING: HOW TO KEEP PRODUCTIVE AS A REMOTE WORKER

As remote workers, we work in isolation. Keeping motivated and focused are fundamental to our productivity. Without this focus, it's unlikely that we will be able to get moving on the things that are important. Review the earlier focus on Motivation, and also consider the following elements which will support you in keeping productive as a remote worker:

- Being clear on what you have to do
- Knowing the end result and what it's going to take to get there
- Having a plan

HOW TO KEEP HEALTHY AS A REMOTE WORKER

What gets you sick? In remote working, your lifestyle choices may be good, but life can become sedentary. What do you need to do to keep yourself at your prime?

- Are you working out?
- Are you connecting with others?
- Are you creating a release valve?
- Are you focusing in on things that add value?
- Are you creating community across a group?
- What is your reaction to chaos?
- What is your reaction when you get disconnected?

TIME MANAGEMENT

Tasks expand to the amount of time we give them—Parkinson's Rule. Think about it—if we give something a few hours, chances are we will likely take several hours.

What can you do to ensure that what is important gets scheduled? You may want to be ruthless in scheduling right away. Block-off time windows in half-hour-or-greater increments so you can do some deep thinking. Consider how to adjust your working hours so you can do so.

Track your time. While you might not have commuting time as a major time sucker, what things *are* taking up the bulk of your time in the remote space?

FIELD WORK—NOW WHAT?

Track your time for a week or more:

What do you notice about your most productive times?

_____

_____

_____

_____

What is going to help support you with your work?

_____

_____

_____

_____

Use the following tracker on the next page to track your time for a week or more.

Time Tracker – Where Does Your Time Go?

For the period of a week, on a daily basis, track where your time does. Categorize the blocks by time used. At the end of the week, note how much time you have spent in each category.

POTENTIALS REALIZED

	Monday	Tuesday	Wednesday	Thursday	Friday	Saturday	Sunday
Before 6 am							
6:00 - 6:15							
6:15 - 6:30							
6:30 - 6:45							
6:45 - 7:00							
7:00 - 7:15							
7:15 - 7:30							
7:30 - 7:45							
7:45 - 8:00							
8:00 - 8:15							
8:15 - 8:30							
8:30 - 8:45							
8:45 - 9:00							
9:00 - 9:15							
9:15 - 9:30							
9:30 - 9:45							
9:45 - 10:00							
10:00 - 10:15							
10:15 - 10:30							
10:30 - 10:45							
10:45 - 11:00							
11:00 - 11:15							
11:15 - 11:30							
11:30 - 11:45							
11:45 - 12:00							
12:00 - 12:15							
12:15 - 12:30							
12:30 - 12:45							
12:45 - 1:00							
1:00 - 1:15							
1:15 - 1:30							
1:30 - 1:45							
1:45 - 2:00							
2:00 - 2:15							
2:15 - 2:30							
2:30 - 2:45							
2:45 - 3:00							
3:00 - 3:15							
3:15 - 3:30							
3:30 - 3:45							
3:45 - 4:00							
4:00 - 4:15							
4: 15 - 4:30							
4:30 - 4:45							
4:45 - 5:00							
5:00 - 5:15							
5:15 - 5:30							
5:30 - 5:45							
5:45 - 6:00							
6:00 - 6:15							
6:15 - 6:30							
6:30 - 6:45							
6:45 - 7:00							
7:00 - 7:15							
7:15 - 7:30							
7:30 - 7:45							
7:45 - 8:00							
8:00 - 8:15							
8:15 - 8:30							
8:30 - 8:45							
8:45 - 9:00							
9:00 - 9:15							
9:15 - 9:30							
9:30 - 9:45							
9:45 - 10:00							
After 10 pm							
Other							

What is important to note?

D A Y   1 9

MOTIVATION

"With an enthusiastic team, you can achieve almost anything"
—Tahir Shah

FOCUS QUESTION:
What motivates you?

WHAT?

What elements are going to keep you moving forward with your work? Motivation has several components—internal and external factors. Ultimately motivation is about:

- What's going to get you out of bed in the morning?
- What's going to keep you moving?
- What gets you excited about your work?

Self-motivation can be critical for remote workers, given that we are working in isolation and many issues get magnified.

What inspires you? What helps you go "above and beyond"? When do you know it's time to stop?

Motivation is an even more important topic for the remote and hybrid workspace, compared to an in-person environment. Our own internal motivation is often our oxygen. It's what helps us move forward, as well as arrests us. What would you say your motivational factors are?

We often talk about the Big Five in motivation. They are remembered by the acronym OCEAN (openness, conscientiousness, extraversion, agreeableness, and neuroticism).

Other motivational frameworks include Daniel Pink's framework of being motivated by Autonomy, Mastery, and Purpose. What things motivate you as a remote professional?

Did You Know?

What makes you feel like you belong or don't belong?

- Sense of purpose
- Sense of mission
- Sense of connection to others
- Clarity about your work—what you need to do, how you need to do it
- How your work impacts others
- What contribution you are making to others
- How you are learning and growing—as a remote worker, professional, and human being

SO WHAT?

Two layers of motivation around remote and hybrid work include our *Why* and the *How*:

Motivation of *why* we want to work remote. There are many "drivers" or reasons why people want to work remote, including:

- Flexibility, ability to juggle multiple projects or clients
- Wanting to avoid the commute

Take time to identify what your *Why* factors are. Why do you love remote work? What motivates you in the remote space? Make a list of motivators, as well as de-motivators such as loneliness, less visibility, etc.

Motivation for how to do work. Knowing the latter helps us when our well runs dry and we need to find ways to get ourselves out of a slump. According to the approaches identified in a 2017 study by Grenny and Maxfield of more than 1,100 remote workers, the following elements were found to provide more support for remote workers.[49] This included:

- More frequent 1-1 time
- Explicit expectations
- More face-to-face or voice-to-voice time
- Prioritizing relationships
- Being available

Motivation and goals. Motivation is a key issue for remote workers. It also links back to the topic of SMART-E Goals we explored in Day 8. In my writing, I talk about the importance of creating SMART-E Goals; in addition to SMART-E goals, we want to make sure our goals are exciting (the "-E" part). If they are not exciting, it's unlikely that we are going to follow through and work on them.

What can we do to make sure our goals are exciting?

- Go to the big picture—a year from now, how can this help move your career forward?
- Think about how it will help you learn, grow, change.
- Consider what is important in terms of the bigger picture, our legacy or our impact.

Red flags around motivation. Note when these things are happening. They may be a signal that something is afoot:

- Procrastination
- Lack of focus
- Missing deadlines
- Not getting all the details/requirements around a project
- Withdrawal and changes to your schedule

Motivational issues are critical to address and/or discuss with your leader and/or mentor. It is important to do so as early as possible, given the self-directed nature of the remote worker's world.

THE CLAIMS MODEL TO MOTIVATION™

In my work as a leader and coach of remote and hybrid teams, I have always found motivation to be one of the most important issues. Over the years I have developed a framework around it called the CLAIMS Model to Motivation. Consider which of these are your primary and secondary "drivers" or motivators in the remote and hybrid space.

C—Community. We want to be part of a bigger whole. Some call this belonging. In this work, it's about relationship development, communication, and strong team culture.

L—Learning. Ongoing learning is critical for success within the remote workspace, particularly as teams today are fluid and ever changing. What are the different ways you want to learn? To contribute?

A—Autonomy. Remote work is not short on autonomy. When clarity exists, remote workers can focus in on what's important.

I—Impact. What's the impact you want to make? As remote workers, we often measure our impact through our output (what results we get). Don't forget that it can also be measured through the influence we have over others, and how we build a sense of community and team.

M—Money. Monetarily, what's important?

S—Status. What is our role? Learn more about status and think about how it fits in the remote space.

Consider both the internal and external motivating factors.

FIELD WORK—NOW WHAT?

Consider the CLAIMS model. What motivates you?

C:_____

L:_____

A:_____

I:_____

M:_____

S:_____

What motivates others around you?

_____

_____

_____

_____

What can you do with others, that is not possible by yourself? This will connect into *Community* and *Collaboration*.

_____

_____

_____

_____

What are you proud of? What are you not proud of?

_____

_____

_____

_____

How do you recover from a mistake?

_____

_____

_____

_____

How do you recover from a fall?

_____

_____

_____

_____

NOTES AND REFLECTIONS:

PRIORITIZATION

"It is not a daily increase, but a daily decrease. Hack away at the inessentials."
—Bruce Lee

FOCUS QUESTION:

What's going to help you prioritize the most important tasks in your work?

WHAT?

There are many competing priorities in remote work. Given our geographic range, what I am prioritizing today may not be the things my boss wants me to prioritize. What are the things you want to focus on today? This week?

As remote workers, we are unlikely ever to complete our To-Do list. We can overwork ourselves to the point of burnout. Time is a non-renewable resource. Once we use it, we can't get it back. Therefore, it's important to be clear on what tasks and items we focus on.

For virtual and remote professionals, the issue of prioritization takes on immense significance, given that we are likely to be part of multiple teams, working across different time zones, with each team and leader having different priorities. Having to work more autonomously we also can benefit from prioritizing what's important from the "bigger picture" of what's on our desk at any given moment.

In *Coaching Business Builder* and *PlanDoTrack*, I share four different prioritization tools to help you identify your focus:

- Strategic Issues Mapping
- The SWOT

- Covey's Urgent/Important Matrix
- Likelihood/Impact Matrix

The Cycle of Fives

Have you ever noticed how workflow occurs in different timeframes? What is your cycle of preference? How might you be able to focus more fully on different activities? In my work, there are often cycles of fives:

- Five-year cycles in terms of my workflow

- Five-year cycles in terms of my home flow

- Five-year cycles in terms of my project flows

- What's your cycle of five?

SO WHAT?

Activity. Make a list of all the things you need to do today. Look at mapping them out using one of these tools—possibly the Urgent Important Matrix. We covered Strategic Issues Mapping earlier, as we did with Covey's Urgent/Important Matrix, in our focus on Time Management (Day 18).

If you are doing some longer-term planning, refer to the SWOT and/or Strategic Issues Mapping (Day 17).

If you are feeling overwhelmed, feeling stuck, or working on immediate priorities, consider using the other prioritization tools. The one I want to focus on here as the Urgency/Importance Matrix.

First, make a list of all the things you have to do. Then plot them out according to how *urgent* each is, and the likelihood that it will have impact. The resulting scattershot you see will help you determine which ones you want to start off with first. It may also give you an indication of what can be delegated or outsourced.

TO-DO LIST

_____   _____

_____   _____

_____   _____

_____   _____

High

Impact

Low ─────────────────────┼──────────────────────► High

Likelihood

Low

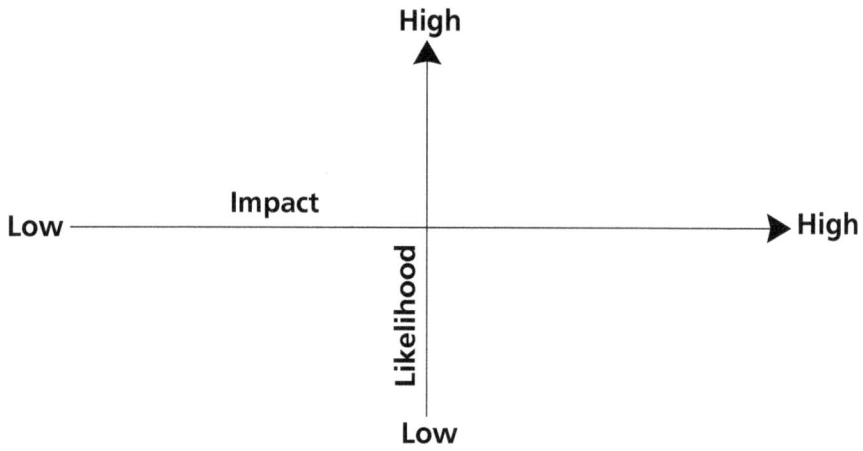

FIELD WORK—NOW WHAT?

In your To-Do list, what do you notice about your work and how each activity has the possibility for *Impact* and *Likelihood*?

_____

_____

_____

_____

What could you look to focus on more?

_____

_____

_____

_____

What is going to have the most impact?

_____

_____

_____

_____

NOTES AND REFLECTIONS:

DAY 21
TEAMS IN FOCUS: TYPES OF TEAMS

"It takes two flints to make a fire."
—Louisa May Alcott

FOCUS QUESTION:
What types of teams do you belong to?

WHAT?

As a remote professional, you are likely to be part of many different types of teams.

In a remote or virtual team, the concept of *team* is an interesting one. Given the remote nature of our work, it may be easier to focus on "our stuff" rather than focus in on being part of a team. Likely, our work is interdependent with others. Over the next few days, we'll be exploring the concept of teams. Today's focus is more about the foundations of remote teams.

7 TEAM FOUNDATIONS

1. **Five key dynamics.** The Aristotle Project from Google found that teams which excel have five key dynamics, which lead to questions the team can answer.[50] Let's look at these five areas and their related questions:

   - *Psychological safety.* Can we take risks together?

   - *Dependability.* Can we count on each other?

   - *Structure and clarity.* Do we have clarity around our goals, roles, plans, and communications?

   - *Meaning of work.* How is our work personally important?

- *Impact of work.* Do we believe that what we are doing matters?

2. **The strength of teams is its diversity.** Everyone is different on a team, and a key part of working together is getting to be able to work together.

3. **Teams are like elephants.** They move slowly and can feel unwieldy. What is going to help them to move forward?

4. **Results and relationships.** Teams which excel have both solid relationships and clarity on the results they are aiming for. Being clear on results includes understanding what we are doing, how we are doing it, and what success is going to look like. It is also linked into the team leadership and vision of our work. Being clear about our relationships means that we know who each person is, what skills they bring, and how each one of us uniquely contributes.

5. **Core Ingredients.** A reminder of the Six Factors of High Performing Teams which help teams thrive. Refer to Day 5 for more on the Six Factors.

6. **Team identity and culture.** Creating a robust team culture is critical for helping people feel part of, and aligned with, the team. Team Identity and Culture is further explored in Day 35. Don't be among the 78% who don't focus on team development. A 2016 Culture Wizard survey found that only 22% of remote teams focused on their team development.

7. **Great teams don't just happen.** They're part of a process of growth and skill development. What are the core skills and strengths for you as a team? How are you at *trust*? Working across differences? Collaboration also fits into this area.

The elements required by teams are woven throughout the book.

OTHER REMOTE TEAM TIPS

Make it visual. Our brains process images more quickly than text. While the research roots of this are harder to pinpoint, it has been estimated that we process 42% more effectively with visual cues. For example, when goals are written down, we are 42% more likely to achieve them.[51] Given that there may be multiple languages at play across a global team, you may want to consider how you can incorporate more visuals via icons or images versus written word.

- What key messages could be incorporated?
- What elements need textual elements?

Overcommunicate in varied ways. Think before you email. Use CC sparingly; who else needs to know?

Agile In Focus

Agile teams are one type of team which have become increasingly common. Common Practices of Agile Small Teams include the following:

- Work in small batches
- Five to nine small, cross-functional teams
- Limited work in process
- Autonomous teams
- Getting to "Done"
- Work without interruption
- Daily standups
- Radical transparency
- Customer feedback each cycle
- Retrospective views[52]

SO WHAT?

Remote team myths. A number of team myths operate for remote teams, including the following:

- What's important for me, is important to everyone else
- No person is an island
- Out of sight equals out of mind

In order to get around some of these more common pitfalls, consider these four areas:

1. **Creating shared expectations.** Given that your staff member will be managed by two or more sets of people, creating shared expectations among the three (or more) of you is key. Who do you report to on what? What does success look like to all the parties involved? What are everyone's various expectations and priorities? How do these align? Conflict?

2. **Clarity.** Clarity around roles and responsibilities, reporting relationships, goals and who does what is key in successful matrix management. Taking time to be extremely clear is key to success. Having a plan and process in place to address lack-of-clarity issues can also be important.

3. **Checking assumptions.** Given that matrix management relationships often occur at a distance, it is important to check the various assumptions. Assumptions about priorities, flow, pace, quality may be a starting point for discussion on a regular basis.

4. **Encouraging frequent touch points and adjustments.** Regular and frequent touch points among the three parties can be very useful, along with an understanding that regular adjustments will need to be made. In my former world of work, I usually tried to aim for quarterly or semi-annual three-way meetings (both supervisors and employee). While this took some planning time, it was often identified as a critical success factor.[53]

REMOTE TEAM TOOLS IN YOUR TOOLBOX

Teams, and members of teams, can thrive when they have the right tools in their toolbox. Team tools which you may want to tap into—DiSC, StrengthsFinder. In our remote professional toolkit, we will want to have a number of resources. Let's explore each one of these in turn.

Prioritization—matrix. Part of the challenge of being part of a matrix is the fact that you are often part of many different teams, with competing priorities. Two potentially useful prioritization tools are the Urgent/Important Matrix (Eisenhower principle) and the Is/Is Not Table. These will be explored later in the book.

Planning tools—individual planning. On a personal planning level, you will want to consider what the best level of planning is. Do you have a quarterly One Page Plan where you can keep your high-level goals over the period of a week?

Project management planning. Planning within your top 3–5 goals can be important for you in terms of identifying core elements to keep an eye on. Whether these items get attention first, or you schedule out blocks for them, you will want to experiment with them.

Team planning tools. On a team planning level, bringing people together regularly—i.e., bi-weekly or weekly, along with a focus on this quarterly and annually will help keep your teams aligned. You will also want to make sure you are updating systems regularly. What needs to get updated and shared across the team?

Communication tools. These can vary dramatically. Look at the communication area. In brief, team members will want to make sure they are focused on items including email, instant messaging, text etc. What are the preferences and what are the BOUNDARIES?

Presentation tools—Zoom, Skype, Teams. Presentation can be an art form and is covered in Day 48.

Day 56 will address the topic of Tools in Your Toolbox further.

FIELD WORK—NOW WHAT?

Consider which of the remote team myths you might fall into?

_____

_____

_____

Which of the 7 core areas are important to explore?

_____

_____

_____

_____

_____

Which team tools are important to note?

_____

_____

_____

NOTES AND REFLECTIONS:

THIS WEEK'S FOUNDATION THEME WAS
CLARITY

Congratulations—you are now through the first three weeks of your role. What was it like? Describe it here in three words:

_____ . _____ . _____

It used to be said that new habits took only 21 days to create. We now know that it may take longer than this; research is pointing to a range of 18 to 254 days, with an average of 66 days.[54]

What are you noticing about your workflow?

_____

_____

_____

_____

Topics we covered this week were:

- Day 15—Systems for Working Remote

- Day 16—Planning

- Day 17—Personal Brand

- Day 18—Time Management and Staying at Peak

- Day 19—Motivation

- Day 20—Prioritization

- Day 21—Teams in Focus: Types of Teams

Wrap up theme:

_____

_____

_____

_____

What are you looking forward to?

_____

_____

_____

_____

What questions do you have?

_____

_____

_____

_____

_____

What To-Dos have surfaced? (List your top 3–5)

1.

2.

3.

4.

5.

Update your tracking sheet!

WEEK 4 · LEARNING BY DOING

"I have been impressed with the urgency of doing. Knowing is not enough; we must apply. Being willing is not enough; we must do.
—Leonardo da Vinci

Welcome to Week 4! Here is what we'll be covering:

- Day 22—Styles

- Day 23—Metrics Matter

- Day 24—Project Management

- Day 25—Networking

- Day 26—Personal Productivity

- Day 27—Focus (and Attention)

- Day 28—Teams in Focus: Matrix Teams

WHAT ARE YOUR TOP 3 GOALS THIS WEEK?:

1. _____

2. _____

3. _____

By the end of the week I want to be sure that . . .

_____

The notion of experiential learning is that we learn by doing. This likely goes back to the days of Ancient Greece. Aristotle wrote "for the things we have to learn before we can do them, we learn by doing them."

What are the things you have learned by doing?

As a remote worker, getting into the practice of asking a series of questions along the lines of *What? So What? Now What?* Can be a valuable way to coach yourself through challenges and also through everyday events.

If you have picked up a copy of the *Reconnecting Workspaces: Pathways to Thrive in the Virtual, Remote, and Hybrid World*, you will note that this framework is woven throughout the 90 Days of tips.

Let's break this down into smaller components:

WHAT? What are you doing? What are you learning? What's working? What's not?

SO WHAT? Take some time to review and reflect on what's important about what's happening. What's important about the fact that every time you go to do a task that has been earmarked by your boss as important, that it doesn't get done?

NOW WHAT? Now what are you learning from the process of this learning? What are you going to do about it? What steps are you going to take?

Building in this reflective practice is critical for work and engagement. What are you noticing about your opportunities to self-coach? What are you doing to break things down into more manageable chunks?

Enjoy the conversation and the reflection!

DIGITAL DOZEN SPOTLIGHT
LEARNING CAN LEAD TO ACTION

Some of the accomplishments of the Digital Dozen:

Sam's biggest accomplishment is, of course, selling her start-up. While it's every start-up's dream to sell or be acquired, it doesn't always happen. Sam attributes it to great timing, a great product, and a great team who was able to executive on their innovative idea.

Victor in the voluntary sector has won many awards for innovation and community building. He has a knack in begin able to bring people together to collaborate and work effectively.

Alex works from anywhere. He is able to focus his attention to the task at hand and has spent time this year writing from a number of very interesting locations including extended spurts in his hometown, at a cabin he rented and also at his relative's condo. He finds that he gets productive when he can have a change of scenery every few months. This worked well in pandemic times.

Sally is a salesperson who is very seasoned at working remote. Some consider mobile sales force as the originators. With Sally's world, it's about connecting need with profit. This year she has been very successful in closing her own deals and also supporting newer sales folk coming on board.

Mo, the creative solopreneur, is celebrating a milestone of a new workshop for her work. She is able to rest on the experience of bringing people together to focus and create together.

Jane is a virtual facilitator and has brought forward a range of programs in the current year. She is most productive working with a remote team which spanned all continents (except for Antarctica) and who moved a line of business forward.

Jo is the virtual team leader and she also has been able to indicate her success in onboarding a whole secondary team, which is a special project for the organization she is attached to. Her skill set has been recognized with several new projects, and she is enjoying the landscape of the matrix workplace.

Mel is a coach and has been engaged this year by several different organizations to help with their remote team development and productivity.

Sujit is a project manager and he has enjoyed embracing Agile methodologies. Most of the projects he has worked on this year have come in on time, on scope, and on budget.

Of course, Ned has focused on the advancement of the new remote worker. He's pleased that he's been able to move forward with the remote work that he's been doing.

Serge is a seasoned remotepreneur. Having started and sold multiple businesses, he is continuing to explore what work can look like for him in his next business iteration.

Malcolm is a mentor and this year he's proud of the accomplishments his mentees have achieved. He's been involved in group mentoring and has several of the digital dozen in attendance. He is keen on expanding the number of people he will mentor next year with some additions to the group.

Ode to the Remote Professional

R—Remote, Real, Ready

E—Energetic, Engaged

M—Micro and Macro

O—Open

T—Technology, Themes

E—Experimental

P—Planning, Perseverance, Persistence

R—Relational, Results

O—Optimistic, Original

F—Flexible, Focused

E—Excellence

S—Straightforward

S—Stability

I—Inspired, Ingenious

O—Opportunities

N—Nomad

A—Awareness, Agile, Additive

L—Leverage

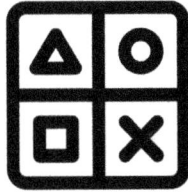

STYLES

"Remember, the point of doing this [personality inquiry] is not to pigeonhole yourself with a four-letter type but to get clear on important aspects of your makeup—your personal blueprint. Use this inquiry as a mirror to see yourself more clearly. Don't accept the results as truth. Use them to find clues."
—Nicholas Lore's The Pathfinder: How to Choose or Change Your Career for a Lifetime of Satisfaction and Success

FOCUS QUESTION:

What is your style, and how does that connect with others?

WHAT?

Part of the greatest challenge and opportunity in teams is their diversity. Research continues to show that teams that thrive are well balanced, rather than necessarily being all the same. Today's complex and uncertain environment requires that we look at things in different ways, leveraging different skill sets and being able to work with, and foster, diverse perspectives.

The HBR article by Alison Reynolds and David Lewis, "The Two Traits of the Best Problem-Solving Teams," delves into this topic.

Amy Edmondson's book, with Jean-Francois Harvey, *Extreme Teaming: Lessons in Complex, Cross-Sector Leadership*, also feeds into this conversation with teams (and leaders).

Our styles are an inherent part of us.

We all have different preferences in terms of how we approach work. This may be shaped by our socialization, professional orientation, and simply who we are. Learning more about ourselves and our preferences is key in the remote space, as it can help us understand what we will find easy and what may be challenging. That information can signal tasks which might be better done with support or collaboration, versus things we can do on our own.

A deep well of information and knowledge is available in this area. One framework which has been iterated on is the research done by Marston in which he identified four types of styles—Dominance (D), Influence (I), Steadiness (S), and Conscientiousness (C). In essence, people vary across two continua: Task versus People, and Fast-Paced versus Moderate-Paced. Our styles influence our decisions, our communication, what we prioritize, and what we find stressful.

Teams and Styles

When we are part of a team, it's important to think about how you are showing up.

Consider these questions:

- What are my preferred ways of working?
- Under times of pressure and stress, what gets magnified?
- What is important to communicate to others who are working with me?
- What do I need to consider about the people I work with? Think through what each person values and needs in a working relationship.
- What's your style?

Just like a cocktail party, each one of us brings our own unique identity. We have about 8 seconds to make a first impression. Therefore:

- What's the impression you want to make?
- How do you want to be remembered?
- How are you being seen?
- Are you the one dressed up with the tails and top hat?
- Are you fashionably late?
- Are you always showing up with a partner, or do you go solo?
- Are you approachable?
- Are you the one looking to close a deal?
- Are you the lone wolf?
- Do you need to reach another shore?

- Are you giving the queen's wave?

- Are you the silent observer?

- Are you curling up with a good book, or are you ready to engage in deeper discussion, in learning?

Also, a part of the cocktail scene is opening the conversation. What are you going to do to put the other person at ease? What will you say to open the dialogue and exchange? What can you ask to engage? What do you want them to explain?

Use the following chart to think through who you might be meeting and what they are focusing on, and listening for:

NAME	DETAILS	TASK	PEOPLE	FAST	MODERATE	OTHER

SO WHAT?

Key to becoming more effective in working with different styles in a team are the following:

1. Know your own style and strengths. We each have a unique style, and there are many great assessments on the marketplace today—MBTI, DiSC, or the series of strengths-based work through such assessments as VIA Character Strengths, or StrengthsFinder2.0. What do you know about your style and strengths? How does that help you? Hinder you in your work?

2. Understand the limitations of your own style. With strengths come limitations, particularly if we are over-utilizing or focusing on them. When others have to work with you as a detail-oriented person, what is that like? If you are constantly driving for results, how is that for others who have to work with you? How do your strengths and styles help you? Help the team? Get in the way?

3. Understand what happens to your style when you are under pressure. Pressure in today's context is a daily occurrence for many. Whether it's working with limited resources or getting a project done in half the time it needs, pressure is constant. What typically happens when we are under pressure—time, resource pressure or stress—is that our styles can get magnified. Our strengths become a blind spot. So, our attention to detail becomes over magnified, or our penchant for strategy becomes over-utilized without a focus on the practicality of what can and needs to get done.

What happens to your style when you are under pressure? The focus on ourselves is one part of the equation. The other part is to explore what happens across the team and how strengths and styles overlap and connect. There may also be gaps. Have you as a team created space to talk about strengths/styles? Where are you aligned? Where are you in contradiction or opposition to each other? What gaps exist?

Finally, with these ideas in mind, we also need to think about how we "dial up" and "dial down" our strengths. When do they become over magnified? When are they not enough? When do we become entrenched with them?[55]

OBJECTIVES AND KEY RESULTS (OKRS) AND REMOTE WORK OUTCOMES

It has been noted as more people move to remote work how important results and outcomes become in terms of leadership and getting things done.

As Brigid Schulte wrote, "The best workplaces recognize that working in a new way requires new skills and not assuming people automatically just know how to work with flexibility. Employees are trained to understand their work style." She continued, "Managers are trained to measure performance, not hours. The mission of the company and the scope and quality of the work expected from each employee are clearly defined and communicated—none of the 'we'll know it when we see it' ambiguity that organizational psychologists have found is the biggest workplace stressor."[56] .

While KPIs, or Key Performance Indicators, often framed work in person, many organizations lead by OKRs—Objectives and Key Results. This is an iteration of how I grew up as a young leader, focusing on Management by Objectives (MBO).

Schulte poses three questions to help with focus:

- How much is enough?
- When is it good enough?
- How will I know?

FIELD WORK—NOW WHAT?

Beyond considering your styles and the questions included here, think about these questions in terms of what lies ahead of you:

Questions to consider—as an individual and as a team:

What challenges and opportunities are we facing this quarter?

_____

_____

_____

_____

How will they necessitate that we look at things in a different way?

_____

_____

_____

_____

What diverse skill sets can we leverage across our team?

_____

_____

_____

_____

What diverse vantage points can we leverage across our team?

_____

_____

_____

_____

What aren't we thinking about, or considering?

_____

_____

_____

_____

What else?

_____

_____

_____

_____

If we were to look at things in a totally different way, what would that be?[57]

_____

_____

_____

_____

NOTES AND REFLECTIONS:

DAY 23
METRICS MATTER

"What's measured, improves."
—Peter Drucker

FOCUS QUESTION:
What are you measuring?

WHAT?

Metrics matter when capturing data,

Metrics are at the heart of any business. Some professionals will not be well versed with what metrics are available to them. With your boss and peers, consider what metrics are available and need to be tracked. Be sure to have quantifiable metrics that you are working towards.

Sales	Speaking engagements
Website visits	Page Likes
Downloads	Numbers of clients
Revenue	Hours billed
Page Reads	Net profit
Number of prospective client conversations (i.e., Discovery calls, sample sessions, etc.)	Number of visitors on your social feeds
	Number of books sold
Products developed	Operating revenue

If you are an entrepreneur, here's a quick list of some of the metrics you may want to track: What else do you have metrics around? What else might you want to note?

If you are a remote worker attached to a team, here are some others metrics to track:

- Key meetings held
- Proposals created
- Presentations given
- Number of funds raised
- One-on-one time with boss/peers/others
- Team meetings
- Networking
- Learning/Professional Development

SO WHAT?

Metrics are important for a variety of reasons:

- **They anchor.** While we may be a Jack or Jill of all trades, it can be important to bring "Experts" on board as well.

- **They provide data.** This data helps with decision making. If we are a business or team, the data can help us when offering a variety of engagement types in determining the best mix of products and services.

- **They help us scale.** Scaling and business growth is a key part of remote and hybrid work. Metrics will provide clues to the best way to grow.

- **They help us know where we are going.** Metrics will provide data on what's working and what's not, helping us to prioritize and make decisions around where we are going.

- **They help us allocate resources.** Metrics and data can also support decisions around resource allocation.

Data can also provide new insights, inspiring the expansion of new ideas and avenues in business, whether they are new products, services, or offers. And offering a variety of engagement types can allow you to expand your reach and geographic impact.

Metrics help keep your work fresh, so that you are working around similar issues but in different formats.

FIELD WORK—NOW WHAT?

Consider the metrics you want to track. What are they?

_____

_____

_____

_____

Is there a particular type of tracker you want to use?

_____

_____

Check out the following:

- Monthly Trackers in *Coaching Business Builder* and *PlanDo Track*
- The Content Trackers as well
- If you are undertaking a 30-day sprint around a topic, note your metrics and/or action steps using the 30-Day Challenge resource

_____

_____

_____

_____

_____

_____

NOTES AND REFLECTIONS:

PROJECT MANAGEMENT

"Those who plan do better than those who do not plan,
even though they rarely stick to their plan."
—Winston Churchill

FOCUS QUESTION:

What projects are you leading? What's important to note about the outcome?

WHAT?

What project management fundamentals should I be aware of?

In project management we always talk about the Triple Constraint—Time, Scope, and Budget. In order to "balance" things, we need to have these three elements. So, if the time window shortens, to compensate we may need to reduce our scope (what's entailed in the project) or what's in the budget.

Are you doing a waterfall project (where tasks are laid out like today's graphic), or is this an Agile project?

Key to project management reporting:

- Make it easy, make it regular.
- Flag issues before they become a bigger thing.
- Note how much time things are really taking, for reference when estimating time on future projects.

PROJECT MANAGEMENT: IS IT REALLY A PROJECT?

Answer the following questions:

1. Can you complete the activity in one sitting? If you can, it's likely not a project.

2. Can you do the activity without anyone else's help?

3. Can you complete the activity in less than four hours?

4. Has the activity been on your to-do list for less than one month?

5. Can you clearly define how you will measure when the task is done?[58] (Topics related to project management include:

   - Prioritization
   - Influence
   - Negotiation

Did You Know?

Check out these different project management tools which many remote professionals and teams use to keep on track, and to share information and project components:

- Monday.com
- Asana
- Trello
- Basecamp
- Other

SO WHAT?

Several core skills are needed for project management, including skills in relationship building, project requirements, time estimation, negotiation, and monitoring and evaluation. In today's So What? consider how you are boosting these skills.

Refer back to Days 10 and 11 for more on Relationship Building. The topic of negotiation is covered in Day 62, Core Skills for Project Management.

TIME ESTIMATES

One of the biggest questions a remote worker may have is "How much time will this take?" When determining this, we can:

- Base it on past experience
- Reach out to people we know
- Do some research

Most time-estimate models are similar in suggesting that the major steps required in doing a time estimate include:

1. Determining the tasks and activities which make up the project, and
2. Breaking it down into discrete parts (think about chunks that you could actually put time around).

MONITORING AND EVALUATION

Keeping a "finger on the pulse" of projects is a critical part of project success. The process of monitoring and evaluation runs across the entire project cycle and will include such activities as project kickoff, mid-point evaluations, and end-of-project debriefs. It will likely involve weekly status reports and regular huddles, especially for shorter projects.

What questions are you asking to note where the project stands? This might include:

- What's working well? What's not?
- What have we achieved?
- What lessons have been learned?
- What do we need to carry forward?

One of the recent shifts in meetings is the introduction of Agile practices including scrums and stand-up meetings. Stand-up questions from scrum may include:

- What did you do yesterday?
- What are you going to do today?
- What obstacles stand in your way?

FIELD WORK—NOW WHAT?

Consider a project you are working on:

What do you notice about the Triple Constraint?

_____

_____

_____

_____

What do you notice about Time Estimation?

_____

_____

_____

_____

What else is important to note around project management?

_____

_____

_____

_____

NOTES AND REFLECTIONS:

DAY 25

NETWORKING

"Networking is the No. 1 unwritten rule of success in business."
—Sallie Krawcheck

FOCUS QUESTION:

What networks do you want to create?

WHAT?

Relationships are a key component of working remotely and successfully. Networking is an important activity to build in, to stand out, and to be visible in your organization and your industry.

Today's focus is on networking. What are you doing to expand your network?

Note that today's topic also connects with mentoring and other topics.

You are invited to a networking event—what's it like? Meetups have become a significant meeting place for remote workers. Every hour you could attend a different event. Before attending, ask yourself these questions:

- What's the purpose of attending an event? Take a few minutes before attending an event to consider what you want to get out of the experience. Is it for finding a resource, for learning something, or for some other reason?

- What do you want to contribute? Networking is about establishing and building a conversation. Conversations take two people. What is it that you want to contribute to the conversation of the group you are connecting with?

- What do you want to get out of the conversation? As to the dual nature of conversation, what are you hoping to walk away from the conversation with?

- What do you want to leave people with? Is it a business card, a brochure, a post card, or something else? Moo.com and Vistaprint.com both offer some creative marketing materials.

Did You Know?

How many connections are enough?

The Dunbar Number asserts that there is a "cognitive limit to the number of people with whom any individual can maintain table social relationships—relationship in which the individual knows who each person is and how each person relates to every other person."

The commonly used value is 150. If there are more than 150 people, we need hierarchical rules and norms to maintain a stable, cohesive group.

Is it more important for you to develop more relationships or reduce the number of relationships you have?

SO WHAT?

So when we get to the networking event, what do we do?

There's a skill in introductions:

- Hello—I am _____. My work is currently focusing on _____. I think we may have an intersect in the following area. (adjust according to what you know of the person)
- I wanted to set up this meeting so I could learn more about you and learn about how our work may connect and interface.
- What should I know about your work?
- Tell me a little about what you do?
- What do you enjoy as a remote worker yourself?
- What do you find the most challenging?
- How did you relate with/interface with my predecessor?
- What piece of advice would you commend to me, based on what you know of my work and network?
- What resources would you recommend I tap into?
- What other tips do you have from your years of experience?
- What are the characteristics you have seen remote workers thrive with?
- What else?

IN THE SPOTLIGHT
DIGITAL DOZEN:

Ned noticed Serge's quiet self-confidence and his ability to seemingly take in everything—he seemed to be sizing it up.

Serge quickly took hold of the meeting—asking him questions with laser like precision—almost knocking Ned off his feet. Ned was happy that he had prepared for this and had a list of questions he was able to pull out.

Here are some of Serge's favorite networking questions:

- What changes have you seen in the remote space in the last few years?
- What makes people successful in this space?
- What internal/external relationships do you think are important for me to invest in?
- What else is important to note?
- What are the things you have seen derail people's focus?
- What do you think is the biggest challenge for remote workers?
- What else is important to explore?
- What makes people excel in this space?
- What resources would you recommend I tap into?
- What skills should I develop?
- What can I do to manage up?
- Who else should I look to for advice?
- Where else should I look to invest my time and focus?
- What one piece of advice would you give?
- What associations or professional groups would you recommend I connect with?

Someone had warned Ned that Serge was lightning fast in both his speech and thinking. It's no wonder that he had founded, scaled, and sold multiple businesses over time.

Note the questions you would want to include in your meetings.

FIELD WORK—NOW WHAT?

Consider an upcoming networking opportunity:

What's important to note about networking for you?

Write down your *purpose* for attending:

_____

_____

_____

_____

Write down your *intention* for attending:

_____

_____

_____

_____

Write down the specific *goals* you have for attending:

_____

_____

_____

_____

Make a list of questions you might ask at a networking event:

1.

2.

3.

4.

5.

DAY 26
PERSONAL PRODUCTIVITY

"Productivity is never an accident. It is always the result of a commitment to excellence, intelligent planning, and focused effort."
—Paul J. Meyer

FOCUS QUESTION:
What's going to help you be most productive?

WHAT?

Personal Productivity is a wide category, including such issues as focus, motivation, time management, boundaries, and prioritization. These have all emerged as key issues during the pandemic. What does personal productivity mean for you?

In today's installment, we are looking at myths around time management, circadian rhythms, and getting things done.

This week's solopreneur myth on time management is that Time Spent = Efficiency.

Not all of the time spent on projects and tasks is the most efficient use of our time. Think about your own scheduling—when are you at your prime? When can you complete tasks quickly and with focus, minus interruptions?

It may be useful to track your own efficiency over the course of a few days or weeks to notice what patterns emerge.

While the notion of circadian rhythms has been around for decades, the field of chronobiology is expanding its data set to help us understand our natural rhythms.

Some of us are early birds, others night owls. In my own work, I find it much easier to get writing projects completed first thing in the morning, before I open email or get distracted with other projects. My weekly writing while in one of my local libraries usually is more focused and plentiful than writing done from my office later in the day.

Did You Know? – Fear and Overwhelm

"Overwhelm can shrink the thinking brain."—Yale Stress Center

Research has continued to demonstrate the importance of the "power of the pause." Neuroscientists at Harvard found that after eight weeks of meditation, yoga, or noticing their bodies for a minimum of 27 minutes a day, there was a growth in grey matter.

Studies "found increased gray-matter density in the hippocampus, known to be important for learning and memory, and in structures associated with self-awareness, compassion, and introspection."[59]

SO WHAT?

Another component of personal productivity that can be useful is *chunking*. In chunking, we bundle "like" tasks together in blocks. So I could earmark half a day to accounting, reporting, and paperwork. That would be different than the focus and brain activity I would need for working on a creative project. Chunking also helps when we have role switching—like when I wear the hat of entrepreneur versus mother.

As Terry Monaghan writes, "Your brain can stay focused on anything, even an unpleasant task, if it knows it will only last thirty minutes."

Two other areas to consider are:

- Get it done! As Doris Lessing writes, "Whatever you are meant to do, do it now. The conditions are always impossible."

- For those who are entrepreneurs, many "kick themselves" for not starting projects earlier. *Start today.* Schedule in 15 minutes a day, or do it first thing in the morning so you know it will get done. As I write in *PlanDoTrack*, "Daily Steps + Consistent Action = Momentum."

Boundaries: "My work and life seem to be blurred. What can I do?"

Sometimes overwhelm or fear can get in the way of getting things done. Check out more in the text box.

FIELD WORK—NOW WHAT?

Think about some of the recent tasks you have completed. What do you notice about speed? Quality? Efficiency?

_____

_____

_____

_____

Consider tracking your work output for several days in several locations and/or at different times of the day. This will work if your tasks are similar but may be harder if they are not. As you look at your work output and time spent, what do you notice?

_____

_____

_____

_____

For more on this, refer to section 5 of the _PlanDoTrack_ workbook and planner, using the different productivity tips there, including—

- The Monthly Daily Tracker
- The Monthly To-Do List

You will also want to check out the Solopreneur myth – Time Spent = Efficiency at the Coaching Business Builder blog at www.coachingbusinessbuilder.com/blog/solopreneur-myth-time-spent-efficiency

NOTES AND REFLECTIONS:

DAY 27

FOCUS (AND ATTENTION)

*"What you focus on grows, what you think about expands,
and what you dwell upon determines your destiny."*
—Robin Sharma

FOCUS QUESTION:
What are you focused on?

WHAT?

Focus and attention are two areas which are in high demand and short supply for remote workers.

In the remote space, getting *the* important things done is key. Navigating competing priorities is the norm, especially when juggling different projects, partners, and/or matrix teams.

What are the projects you need to move forward? How do you build in space to ensure that these important things are getting done?

What gets through the filter? (Think Reticular Articulating System.) What doesn't get attention? Sometimes the things we don't pay attention to are the things that can get us in the most amount of trouble. What are the things you want to make sure you are getting off your action list?

Need to Know:

Even though recent research is finding that remote workers are more productive, don't rest on those laurels. FOCUS and interruptions abound. Dr. Gloria Mark found that it can take upwards of 22 minutes to regain your focus when interrupted.

Techniques for supporting focus:

Turn off all distractions (this may include IM, Pings, and other things that distract you)

Take it outside of the office

Take a break (see the text box)

Go for a walk (check out this and other ways to create attention and focus—https://ideas.ted.com/4-simple-exercises-to-strengthen-your-attention-and-reduce-distractibility/)

Did You Know?

A 2019 Airtasker study found that remote employees "worked 1.4 more days every month, or 16.8 more days every year" https://www.businessnewsdaily.com/15259-working-from-home-more-productive.html

37% of remote workers say the best way to boost productivity is to take regular breaks—https://review42.com/remote-work-statistics/

SO WHAT?

Here are several practical things you can do to create more focus:

- Reduce the distractions. Turn off notifications for a time window. This may need to be done across the team as well, so that no one is feeling like they are left behind.
- Zoom into, or focus on, what really needs to get done.
- Practice simplification and explore what is absolutely necessary—MVP and also simplify.
- Work in bursts. Short windows of time create urgency, just like we have seen with the 21 for 21 Sprint Series.
- Chunk it down.
- Think about your body rhythm and where things may work best for you.

What practices are going to help you focus?

What the research says about focus—what do we need? Link to circadian rhythm.

Several different frameworks can support you with focus in the remote space. Consider these:

- Get it Done afternoons
- Pomodoro technique

Refer to the Time Management section for tips and hacks on building in time so you have the margin to get work done.

THE 21 FOR 21 SPRINT SERIES

From messy spaces to minimalist environments. From corporate co-working spaces to beachside retreats. These are the varied locations for remote professionals today. What office space is going to work best for you?

In early 2021 I started hosting the 21 for 21 Sprint series of virtual co-working. This program included 21 days of consecutive virtual co-working meetings where participants joined me to tackle their most important projects. Participants found that they were able to create a focus and momentum from the daily process of deep work around one project over these quick 21 minutes of uninterrupted work.

What is going to help you focus?

The science of attention. While you may not have the same interruptions faced in the in-person space, it can be a challenge for people to maintain focus when:

- New notifications come in
- Stretches of work go on for too long

Antidotes to chaos and antidotes to lack of focus. What creates chaos on a virtual or remote team? When everyone is on different pages. This can happen when the goal is not clear, or the pathway has not been defined. It's also possible that the performance measures have not been articulated or spelled out.

Our reaction to chaos, and lack of focus, is often the amygdala hijack, where we may go into *fight*, *freeze*, or *flee*. Watch what happens to you when you work in a chaotic environment. Strategies to avoid these might include:

- Returning back to your values as a reminder of what's important.
- Knowing when it is "good enough" can be important to ensure that you keep moving work forward. Go back to the project or task requirements. What does success look like? What does the *Is/Is Not* exercise say about this task or activity?
- Having a peer partner, coach, or other accountability structure which can help you explore these blocks and keep moving.

What do you need in order to move it forward?

Where do you go?

- For more on the Pomodoro technique, check out more resources from its creator, Francesco Cirillo.
- For more on Get it Done Days, contact me by email. I'm happy to host these action-focused, accountability-rich afternoons for you in-house.
- Take a look at these books for more information: *Productivity Habit*, by Chris, and *Science of Attention*, by Robert Biswas-Diener

Consider:

- What do you need to have with you for tasks?
- What things need to be done in a secure environment?
- What will stimulate creative tasks?
- What is the best rhythm of work for you?

FIELD WORK—NOW WHAT?

Make a list of all the important things that need to get done today. This week. How much time will they take? (Look at this in conjunction with time estimation, time tracking, and scheduling. Consider how much is enough, or what is commonly referred to as the Minimal Viable Product.) Schedule these things in.

_____

_____

_____

_____

_____

_____

_____

_____

_____

_____

If you need to move between in-person and virtual meetings, think about how you may chunk it. The friction of trying to merge both worlds can be exhausting; and while it may be needed, be sensitive to your scheduling.

When thinking of _focus_, also keep in mind your Circadian Rhythm:

When are you at your best?

_____

_____

_____

_____

What is the best time of day to do different tasks?

_____

_____

_____

_____

_____

_____

Consider: What will help you work with focus?

_____

_____

_____

_____

What interruptions are there?

_____

_____

_____

_____

NOTES AND REFLECTIONS:

TEAMS IN FOCUS: MATRIX TEAMS

"If you are not willing to risk the usual, you will have to settle for the ordinary."
—Jim Rohn

FOCUS QUESTION:
I have multiple matrix relationships.
What can I do to say no? I have too much work!

WHAT?

In most remote workplaces, professionals will be part of multiple matrix teams, reporting to several managers and working with a wide variety of people under those. For example, I may be part of a team that focuses on talent development issues, but given that I am based out of Toronto, I may also interlink with the Toronto-based team. In my talent work, I connect much more frequently with my colleagues globally in the US, London, and Shanghai.

In remote work, matrix relationships are more the norm than the exception. They provide the challenge of being part of multiple teams and projects. Each team may have its own culture.

CHALLENGES FOR MATRIX TEAMS

There are several challenges for matrix teams—not knowing your teams, not being clear on roles, goals, etc.

Other pitfalls to matrix management include:

- Being part of multiple teams, which can have competing priorities
- Lack of communication

- Different time zones and work demands

- Different work cultures in each location

- Different team cultures or how we do things

- Different context

What do you see as some of the pitfalls in matrix management?

MATRIX MANAGEMENT—TO DOS

When we think of working in a matrix environment, it can be important to get clear on what the goals are.

If you do lead matrix teams, be sure to incorporate the following on a regular basis:

- Understand the team identity. Know how it operates.

- Ensure that you are regularly facilitating a three-way meeting between your different partners. This might involve reviewing what the key priorities are, focusing on lessons learned and how to do it.

Some other key tips when working with those in a matrix relationship: Focus in on what your to-dos are. Consider how work interfaces with each other. Clarify assumptions.

Did You Know?

There can be a lack of clarity of priorities when you are part of matrix teams. Be proactive in making sure you are asking clarifying questions like these:

- What needs to be done?

- By when?

- How much time do you anticipate this will take?

- What other projects rely on this?

- What else should I know about the program?

SO WHAT?

In the matrix environment, we are often juggling competing demands. Asking questions like those you saw in today's text box can help you prioritize if two items need attention at the same time.

There may also be instances when demands compete with each other. Facilitating a three-way meeting with both leaders may be necessary to confirm what needs to happen when.

Open communication is key. What needs to be shared when, how, and with whom?

Unspoken assumptions can be problematic. While assumptions "are the kiss of death" for a team, in a matrix environment they can obscure many different elements. What are the things you want to clarify?

Knowing the team can support your efforts to prioritize and complete your work. Given that you may be part of two or more teams, how do you get to know them?

Understanding the context of operations is important. While remote workers in general may not know the context or culture you are operating in, this understanding can be augmented with others.

Understand the team identity and know how it operates. Team culture is a key part of the experience of teams. It's what shapes us and makes us who we are. Refer to Days 35 and 42 on Team Identity and Culture.

IN THE SPOTLIGHT: MAKING THE MATRIX WORK

Here are four keys to making matrix management work:

- **Creating shared expectations.** Given that your staff member will be managed by two or more sets of people, creating shared expectations among the three (or more) of you is key. Whom do you report to on what? What does success look like to all the parties involved? What are everyone's various expectations and priorities? How do these align? Create conflict?

- **Maintaining clarity.** Clarity around roles and responsibilities, reporting relationships, goals, and who does what is key in successful matrix management. Having a plan and process in place to address unclear issues can also be important.

- **Checking assumptions.** Given that matrix management relationships occur at a distance, it is important to check the various assumptions. Assumptions about priorities, flow, pace, and quality may be a starting point for discussion on a regular basis.

- **Invoking frequent touch points and adjustments.** Regular and frequent touch points among the three parties can be very useful, along with an understanding that regular adjustments will need to be made. In my former world of work, I usually tried to aim for quarterly or semi-annual three-way meetings (both supervisors and employee). While this took some planning time, it was often identified as a critical success factor.[60]

FIELD WORK—NOW WHAT?

Consider the conversations you need to have, using the following prompts to help you explore your context, and the matrix teams you are part of:

QUESTIONS TO CONSIDER	MATRIX TEAM 1	MATRIX TEAM 2	MATRIX TEAM 3
WHAT IS THE TEAM CULTURE?			
WHO IS PART OF THE TEAM?			
WHAT'S ACCEPTABLE? WHAT'S NOT?			

What are you doing to create shared expectations?

_____

_____

What are you doing to maintain clarity?

_____

_____

What are you doing to check assumptions?

_____

_____

What are you doing to create frequent touch points and adjustments?

_____

_____

THIS WEEK'S FOUNDATION THEME WAS
LEARNING BY DOING

Congrats you are now through four weeks of your role. What was the last month like?
Describe it here in three words:

_____ . _____ . _____

Topics we covered this week were:

- Day 22—Styles
- Day 23—Metrics Matter
- Day 24—Project Management
- Day 25—Networking
- Day 26—Personal Productivity
- Day 27—Focus (and Attention)
- Day 28—Teams in Focus: Matrix Teams

Wrap up theme for this week:

_____

_____

_____

_____

What are you looking forward to?

_____

_____

_____

_____

What questions do you have?

_____

_____

_____

_____

_____

_____

What To-Dos have surfaced? (List your top 3–5)

1.

2.

3.

4.

5.

Update your tracking sheet!

WEEK 5 · RESILIENCE AND CHANGE

"The oak fought the wind and was broken,
the willow bent when it must and survived."
—Robert Jordan

Welcome to Week 5. This week's theme is all about resilience and change. This is an ongoing theme for those who work remotely, whether it's in times of a pandemic or any other time.

As Daniel Goleman shared in Focus, "Problems of such complexity and urgency require an approach to problem-solving that integrates our self-awareness and how we act, and our empathy and compassion, with a nuanced understanding of the systems at play."[61]

Change is the only option for remote workers. Flexibility is key. As Ray Wang wrote, "Digital Darwinism is unkind to those who wait."

WEEKLY FOCUS

Topics we are covering this week are:

- Day 29—The Iceberg: Introduction and Values
- Month One Check-In
- Day 30—Mentoring
- Day 31—Obstacles and Challenges
- Day 32—Troubleshooting and Decision Making
- Day 33—Getting Unstuck
- Day 34—Coaching
- Day 35—Teams in Focus: Team Identity and Culture

1. _____

2. _____

3. _____

By the end of the week I want to be sure that . . .

_____

IN FOCUS: CHANGE, RESILIENCE, AND FLOW

Resilience—We are our own support network many times in the remote space and it can be very important to become well versed in knowing what's going to get you down, and what's going to pick you up. Self-management and the ability to experience the range of emotion that occurs in the span of a day, by yourself, can be important. What do you notice about resilience?

What books would you recommend? Podcasts? Other resources?

How to strengthen adaptability and resilience:

- Actively seek out novelty
- Work in jobs where learning is encouraged
- Acquire new skills
- Be ready to let go of approaches that worked before

WORKING WITH CHANGE

Elena Lytkina Botelho, Kim Rosenkoetter Powell, Stephen Kincaid, and Dina Wang studied more than 2000 leaders and found the following four CEO genome behaviors that led to exceptional results. These leaders had skills which allowed them to:

- Decide
- Engage for Impact
- Ruthless Reliability
- Adapt Boldly

What are you doing to build these skills?

The data behind why this is important is vast. Consider these factoids:

- "Adapt or perish, now as ever it's today's inexorable impetus." —HG wells paraphrase
- Average life span of companies has shifted from 65 to 23 years.
- "CEOs who adapt boldly are roughly seven times more likely to be successful than those who wait for change to be comfortable."[62]
- "The best leaders have systems awareness, helping them answer the constant query, 'Where should we head?'[63]

FLOW-IN FOCUS—A COUNTERBALANCE TO CHANGE

Change is ongoing and inevitable in the remote space. *Flow* can be an antidote, which renews remote professionals. In my three decades of experience with remote work, I have seen that part of success in remote work is about being an ongoing learner, as well as finding moments of flow.

As Goleman shared in *Focus: The Hidden Driver of Excellence*,

"Only about 20 percent of people have flow moments at least once a day. Around 15 percent of people never enter a flow state during a typical day."

According to Mike Oppland, Csikszentmihalyi describes eight characteristics of flow:

1. Complete concentration on the task;
2. Clarity of goals and reward in mind and immediate feedback;
3. Transformation of time (speeding up/slowing down);
4. An intrinsically rewarding experience;
5. Effortlessness and ease;
6. A balance between challenge and skills;
7. Merging of actions and awareness—a loss of self-conscious rumination;
8. A feeling of control over the task.[64]

"One key to more flow in life comes when we align what we do with what we enjoy . . . . High achievers in any field . . . have hit on this combination."[65]

What flags might signal that you are in lower levels of motivation?

_____

_____

What elements can signal that you are in flow?

_____

_____

Consider which of these areas are important for you. Is it about exploring flow, decisions, speed?

_____

_____

_____

THE ICEBERG: INTRODUCTION AND VALUES

"Your beliefs become your thoughts, your thoughts become your words, your words become your actions, your actions become your habits, your habits become your values, your values become your destiny."
—Gandhi

FOCUS QUESTION:

What elements of what's important to you are visible to others?
What elements are not visible?

WHAT?

In the remote and hybrid world, at an individual and on a team level, it is important to explore the things that we can see, but also to go "below the waterline." Think about the work you see, or don't see, your colleagues do every day.

Part of the value of coaching is making what's below the waterline and often invisible, visible, connecting it to the behaviors and results we get. Above the waterline are results and behaviors. Below the waterline we have mindsets, habits, perspectives, assumptions, beliefs, and values.

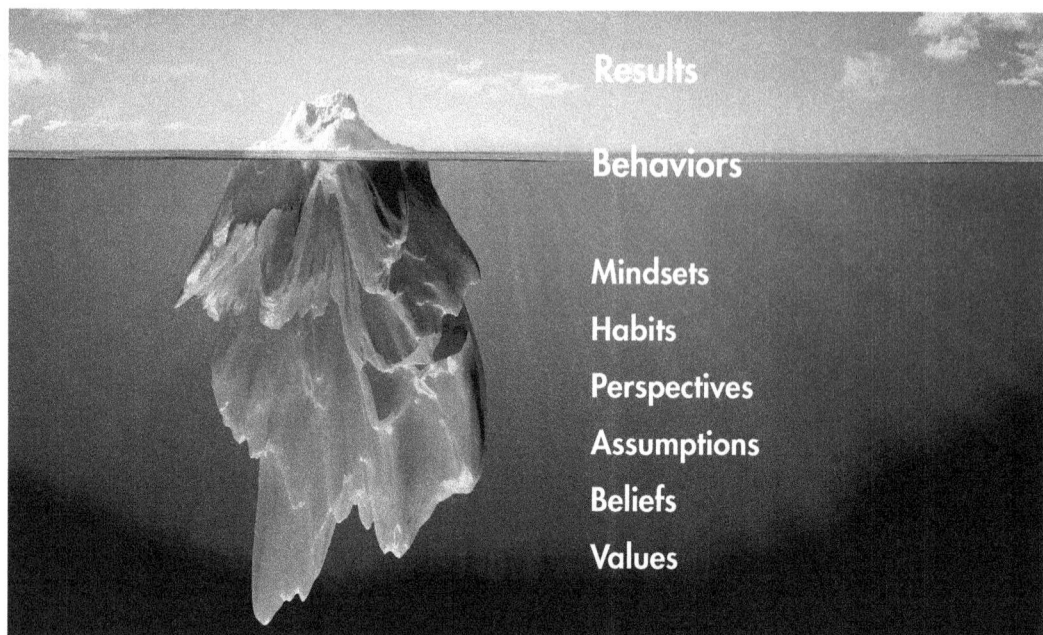

In business, we see people's results. If we work in person, we can see their behaviors. In contrast, if we work remote or hybrid, a lot goes on in getting results, which is either unseen or unclear.

An important metaphor to explore what's above and below the waterline is the iceberg. This is a concept I expand upon in Section 1 of *PlanDoTrack* and the *Coaching Business Builder*.

Remember, only about 10% of an iceberg is above the waterline. The rest lies beneath the surface, obscured from view. One of the major concepts we'll be exploring throughout this guide is "what's above and what's below the waterline."

WHAT'S ABOVE AND BELOW THE WATERLINE

Above the waterline exist all the things we can see or hear. It's our behavior while on screen. It's our symbols and the language we use. It's also about our *results*.

At the waterline are our norms and the patterns of behaviors.

Below the waterline are multiple unseen layers. These are experienced during the time we are together in the virtual space. They include our fundamental values and assumptions which shape the results we get.

When working on a remote or hybrid team, given our different locations, it is critical to check in around the assumptions you are making, especially when your context is different.

The iceberg concept is explored in greater depth in both *Reconnecting Workspaces* and *PlanDoTrack*.

Settling In

For more on the topic of the Iceberg, check out Sections 1 and 4 of *PlanDoTrack* and or Chapter 3 of *Reconnecting Workspaces*. Section 1 gets you to explore what behaviors flow out of your values. Again, if you have a value of freedom, what behaviors does it lead to? How can that help and/or hinder your work and relationships with others in the remote space?

SO WHAT?

As you can see, above the waterline we can see behaviors, which then lead to results. It's actually what's below the waterline—our mindsets, habits, perspectives, assumptions, beliefs, and values—that shape *what* we do and what we choose to focus on. This is an important topic, as it shapes our relationships with others.

There are multiple layers to the waterline. In today's installment we are going to explore three areas—values, perspectives, and assumptions. Routines and beliefs are covered in Day 36. Mindsets are also covered later.

VALUES

Our values act as anchors and help us with decision making and prioritization. When we act in alignment with our values, professionals may find a higher degree of satisfaction. For example, if I hold a value of freedom, I may thrive in a workplace where I have the freedom to determine *how* I do the work, *when* I do the work. While I still may be responsible for end results, being in control of what I do and don't do may be invaluable.

When part of a remote team, it is important to explore values on several levels:

1. **Our personal values.** What's important to you? What things do you need in order to function most effectively? How do your values translate onto others?

2. **Our team values.** Our team, even if we are stretched across four time zones, has values as well. Our values shape our behaviors. If we are a team that values quality, we will each make sure that we review things before sending them off. If we value collaboration, we will work together or involve others. We may even hold more meetings or practices.

3. **Our organizational values.** What are the values of the organization we are part of? How do those vary from what we are doing? From what we take a stand for? How can our organizational values align us as a team?

Values are in part what make you stand out.

Standing out in today's remote space is key. What are you known for? How does your reputation precede you? Are you known for your follow through? Your reliability? Your energy?

Take some time this week finding out from your peers, or your boss, how you are seen. This can be an important feedback mechanism in terms of learning how you are envisioned and what people expect from you, even before you get going.

If things are unclear, what do you need to do in order to clarify?

Related to values are perspectives and assumptions, two additional layers to consider with the Iceberg.

PERSPECTIVES

There are many different ways we can look at issues. Perspectives are linked into our point of view, our mindset, and our context.

Each one of us can look at the same photo and have multiple interpretations.

Consider this drawing[66].

What do you see? To some, the duck is visible. To others, the rabbit is visible.

Perspectives act like lenses in a pair of glasses. They impact how we see items.

ASSUMPTIONS

Henry Winkler wrote, "Assumptions are the termites of any relationship."

In the remote space, assumptions abound. This may be because we haven't taken the time to understand our colleagues, understand their context, and/or looked at what is possible.

What's important for you? What are your anchors?

FIELD WORK—NOW WHAT?

Take a look at the following list. Check the values you hold true.

☐ Achievement	☐ Freedom
☐ Adventure	☐ Friendship
☐ Appreciation	☐ Gratitude
☐ Awareness	☐ Hard work
☐ Awe	☐ Integrity
☐ Balance	☐ Leadership
☐ Beauty	☐ Recognition
☐ Benevolence	☐ Risk
☐ Creativity	☐ Satisfaction
☐ Elegance	☐ Security
☐ Equity	☐ Service
☐ Fairness	☐ Speed
☐ Fame	☐ Stability

Note the connection between the Personal Brand, Values, Team Values, and Organizational Values.

As you review your top 5 values, which ones are non-negotiable?

_____

_____

_____

_____

What can you do to adjust your work and flow in order to live more by your values?

_____

_____

_____

_____

Focusing on your values, which of these are important to you?

_____

_____

_____

_____

What things are really important to you as a professional? Sometimes we find our values when they are absent or are stepped upon. A powerful rush of emotion, or a lift of the eyebrow, may be a signal that a value is not present.

_____

_____

_____

_____

Assumptions—What assumptions are you making in your work?

_____

_____

_____

Perspectives—What perspectives are you holding with this?

_____

_____

_____

_____

NOTES AND REFLECTIONS:

DAY 30

MENTORING

"Tell me and I forget, teach me and I may remember, involve me and I learn."
—Benjamin Franklin

WHAT?

At all stages of our careers, mentoring is an important activity for remote work success. Mentors are able to provide a birds-eye view of their work, usually via their stories. This is critical for remote work, as we know that the best remote workers have seen best practices modeled by others. Historically, mentoring has involved the more junior person being mentored by a senior person. Today reverse mentoring is becoming even more popular and focuses on having the mentee or protégé also sharing their insights. Mentoring is a reciprocal relationship, with both parties receiving some value from the relationship.

Working with a mentor can have multiple benefits, including:

- Helping you understand the unspoken currents in an industry or organization.
- Helping you diplomatically navigate the hidden political currents in an organization or industry.
- Helping you navigate through opportunities.
- Helping you focus and explore alternative angles around current challenges.
- Bringing a historical piece of the puzzle.
- Benefiting from someone else's experience.
- Shedding light on trends and what is happening "under the waterline" of work.
- Opening the door to new ideas, resources, and/or networks.
- Receiving insights/perspectives from someone who has been there already.

Given how fast the business context is changing today, one note of caution: It can be valuable *not* to compare your experience to anyone else's. Mentoring provides you with the *mentor's* perspective; and their truth, perspectives, and experience may be very different from yours.

Key pitfalls with mentoring include:

- A lack of clarity of what and why you are connecting, and discussion around the roles and responsibilities.

- Not taking it seriously enough.

- Not providing a formal start and end to the process.

Mentoring is an important modality of learning. Whether we engage a mentor informally or join a formal mentoring program as part of our organization or industry, mentors can play a key role in helping you understand the context of an organization, and learn how to navigate it. Mentors become an even more important role when things are ever changing.

Critical Success Measures

Critical success factors for making mentoring work:

- Make conversations consistent.
- Build trust and connection with your mentor.
- Keep meeting spots neutral.
- Consider who's responsible for what.
- Remember that mentoring is a relationship, with conversations occurring over time.

What makes mentoring work:

- Clear goals
- Shared expectations
- Being clear on purpose—what's the purpose?
- Being clear on outcome—what do I want to get out of it?
- Understanding what's expected of me
- Clarifying roles and responsibilities
- Knowing who is taking the lead on what (i.e., setting meetings, creating the agenda, etc.)
- Building relationships "with purpose"

What things are going to make this a valuable relationship for you both? Have you discussed:

- What each of you is bringing to the mentoring relationship?

- What you want out of the experience?
- What are the core activities which to help you keep a focus on mentoring as you move forward?

Derailers with mentoring:

- Lack of clarity around roles
- Not scheduling meetings in advance
- Not indicating and agreeing to the type of support needed
- Not being specific with goals
- When and where you are meeting—making it easy and equitable
- Agreements
- What else?

Before you select a mentor, consider these questions:

- What am I looking for in a mentor?
- What are my expectations around this process?
- What check points are we going to build in around this work?

What to Do

Activities you might consider undertaking as a mentoring pair:

- Reading books
- Listening to podcasts
- Peer partners
- Exploring strengths
- Attending events together

SO WHAT?

Sage words of advice from mentors and mentees:

- Have a focus.
- Make it regular.
- Surface issues that need to be discussed.
- Have a start and end to the entire process. Many mentoring relationships last only six to nine months.

- Consider what the optimum length of time will be.

- Create evaluation touchpoints throughout. Consider what's working, what's not, what's giving traction, what could accelerate results.

- Mentors should be attuned to what's adding value from their experience.

- Mentees can enhance the experience for themselves by being prepared.

Questions to Consider Asking Your Mentor:

1. What have been the greatest lessons learned during your role/career?

2. What's the one thing you wish you had learned earlier?

3. What did your mentor do with or for you that was so valuable?

4. What do you think is important to understand?

5. What are the items I might not be aware of?

6. Where do you see the industry going?

7. What can we do to ensure that this mentoring is of value to you?

For more on mentoring, check out these resources—MentorRoadmap.com or Mentor.org.

Mentors can benefit from growing skills in these areas:

1. Listening

2. Feedback

3. Creating powerful questions (powerful questions rarely start with *Why*; they are open ended and often start with *What*)

4. Accountability, acknowledging, celebrating, and encouraging

5. Expanding our insights about what professional experience can look like in an industry

SO WHAT?

As you get started with mentoring, consider these questions:

- What insights would you want to gain from mentoring?

- What is the role you would like a mentor to play?

- What are the insights you hope to learn?

- What are the goals of the mentoring relationship?

- What else are you hoping to gain out of the mentoring process?

Mentoring Meetings 101—as you go to meet, consider incorporating these questions:

- What are the main goals/objectives for this meeting?
- What are the topics we want to focus on?
- What do we want to accomplish?
- What outcomes do we want?
- What do I need in order to be prepared for the meeting?
- What agenda will give us the results we are looking for?
- What takeaways are there?
- What should we do differently next time?

FIELD WORK—NOW WHAT?

Questions to consider:

How might you benefit from a mentoring relationship?

_____
_____
_____
_____

What skills or experiences would you like to learn more about?

_____
_____
_____
_____
_____
_____

What mentoring opportunities are available? Consider any professional associations you belong to.

_____
_____
_____
_____
_____
_____

What would be on your list of goals for the mentoring partnership?

_____

_____

_____

_____

_____

IN THE SPOTLIGHT—DIGITAL DOZEN:
THE MENTORING CONVERSATION

Here is how the mentoring conversation plays out in the world of the Digital Dozen.

Malcolm and Ned—our new remote worker, Ned, is paired with his mentor, Malcolm. Ned recognizes that mentoring is an important relationship for new remote workers. He is eager to make mentoring work virtually and recalls what Malcolm had shared with him; that just like in-person meetings, virtual mentoring meetings benefit from:

- Having a focus on who is responsible—the mentee or mentor?
- Clear agreements on each other's roles

Malcolm and Ned also talked about some of the pitfalls and what ultimately Ned wanted to get out of the mentoring experience.

In their first meeting, Malcolm assigned field work—for Ned to map out a topic for each of the sessions and to come into each session with a list of 3–4 questions they could discuss.

They agreed on the following roles and responsibilities of the mentor:

- To share their stories and insights around their own experience
- To provide a list of recommended resources, activities and locations
- To encourage Ned as the mentee/protégé to undertake some specific fieldwork steps between sessions

Then they agreed on the following roles and responsibilities of the mentee:

- To come prepared with a topic for each call; this would be confirmed at the end of the previous session
- To ask for what they need and to provide feedback real-time
- To follow through on commitments

They avoided some of the pitfalls which had been highlighted by:

- Ensuring the dates were securely etched in their work
- Focusing on the tangible outcomes
- Identifying a reading selection they both could work on

They also highlighted their fourth meeting, which would be the mid-point, as a time when they would evaluate using these questions:

- What worked well?
- What are you (the mentee) taking away?
- What should we do differently next time?

NOTES AND REFLECTIONS:

MONTH ONE CHECK-IN

"We are constantly reviewing our processes to
identify areas where we can learn and improve."
—Tricia Griffith, CEO & President of Progressive

WHAT?

Let's build in some time for a micro-pause for reflection.

Every month I will be including a pause to undertake a quarterly checkpoint. In addition to weekly and monthly planning, it can be valuable to spend time undertaking quarterly planning. Looking at your goals and achievements over a three-month period can provide a different perspective.

Building in micro-pauses can be critical for learning. Without taking time to pause, we may be too focused on other events. What are the pauses you can create in your work? It might involve having a journey to capture your top-3 learning each day, or space in a notebook to capture your learning using *PlanDoTrack*'s One Line a Day.

What are the micro-pauses you can incorporate into your work?

SO WHAT?

As we know from learning theory, learning doesn't just happen. It occurs via a series of different successive activities, including reflection.

In 1984, David Kolb wrote, "Learning is the process whereby knowledge is created through the transformation of experience." Kolb's model of education involved four stages of the learning cycle: concrete experience, reflective observation, abstract conceptualization, and active experimentation. He abbreviated these to ERGA (Experience, Reflection, Generalize, Application).

It can be important for you, as a remote worker, to keep these in mind as you go about your daily work. What are you doing to build in each piece? Let's look at them in turn:

Experience—We have an experience. For example, I move through a great writing session.

Upon ***Reflection***, or a pause, I realize that I am a better writer than I have given myself credit for, but that I am best at this during a certain time of day.

Generalize—I wonder how I might have a similar experience in a different setting. In generalizing, it is important for me to think about other situations where this might be of use.

Application—The final stage of learning is application. This is key in the remote space, as we don't have time to wait. What can I do to apply this in other areas?

FIELD WORK—NOW WHAT?

Activity:

Create a micro-pause (30 minutes or so) to undertake your Monthly Check-In.

Note the following, this month:

What have you accomplished?

_____

_____

_____

_____

What things still need to get done?

_____

_____

_____

_____

What has been your key learning over time?

_____

_____

_____

_____

Over the last month consider:

What patterns are you noticing?

_____

_____

_____

_____

What has shifted?

_____

_____

_____

_____

What has stayed the same?

_____

_____

_____

_____

What are you surprised about?

_____

_____

_____

_____

What are you doing to leverage your strengths?

_____

_____

_____

_____

What strengths are becoming overmagnified?

_____

_____

_____

_____

What habits are helping you?

_____

_____

_____

_____

What habits do you want to put more attention around?

_____

_____

_____

_____

Note your programming and/or services delivered. Ask yourself:

Where have you been spending your time?

_____

_____

_____

_____

What have you prioritized?

_____

_____

_____

_____

What's working and what's not?

_____

_____

_____

_____

_____

_____

_____

_____

What volume of work have you been completing?

_____

_____

_____

_____

What metrics do you want to note?

_____

_____

_____

_____

Anything else?

_____

_____

_____

_____

NOTES AND REFLECTIONS:

OBSTACLES AND CHALLENGES

"Problems are not stop signs; they are guidelines."
—Robert Schuller

FOCUS QUESTION:
What challenges and obstacles are you facing right now?

WHAT?

For remote workers, troubles, challenges, and obstacles can take many forms—from lack of resources to not knowing where to go. Today we are going to explore overcoming obstacles and getting unstuck.

Key obstacles you might face:

- Technical issues
- Conflict issues
- Resourcing issues
- Communication issues
- Relationship issues
- Goal and results issues
- Systems issues
- Team Issues
- What else?

Another huge category of obstacles for remote workers is that of *not knowing*. Not knowing what to do and not being paralyzed by it.

When Teams Get Stuck

Teams can also get stuck. When this happens, it can be useful to bring people back to the main page and help them focus:

- What is our purpose?
- What are we all committed to?
- What happens when we don't do it?
- What happens when we do?
- What is the collaborative payoff?
- What happens when we focus?
- What are we able to deliver when we are on point?

SO WHAT?

The good news with tricky issues is that many of them can be mitigated or improved when we have stronger levels of trust, safety, and connection. Without these levels of trust, it's hard to move forward.

When things don't go well, there are a number of things you can do when facing obstacles, including the following areas:

- Take stock of what's working.
- Reassess.
- Sleep on it. Practice the 24-hour rule—never respond in the heat of the moment. Sleep on it and reply in the morning.
- Be gentle with yourself.
- Let go—readjust our goals, or reframe what's possible.
- Get into action—start to build your confidence again by taking regular steps.
- Easy wins—What things are going to help you get your mojo back?
- Have a release valve. This may mean leaving the office and doing something else and coming back to it at a later date. When you are triggered—an amygdala hijack can occur and—you need to take a break. It can take 15–20 minutes for your body to return back to homeostasis.
- Things get magnified when you are in the remote space—talk with others.

Reach out to others:

- Ask for more feedback.

- See it modeled well by others.

- Ask for more input or examples of best practice.

- Take it to your mentor or other person who can support you.

Getting up after a fall. It's unlikely that everything will go smoothly in the first 90-day cycle. Keeping good humor about what's not working and soldiering on can be very important. Same as easing back in. Recovery is just as important as everything's going well. It can reinforce what you enjoy and what you don't.

Are you waiting for things to get moving again?

CHALLENGES FOR REMOTE WORKERS	HOW TO GET AROUND THE CHALLENGES
Too many priorities	Have regular one-on-ones with team leaders and partners
Unclear on output	Always ensure discussion in team or new project meetings, asking the questions, "What will success look like?" and "What end results are we looking for?"
Unable to see people	Relationships are still key—use one of the trust builders covered in week 1 (Refer to Week 1)

IN THE SPOTLIGHT—THE DIGITAL DOZEN:
LEARNING FROM OBSTACLES AND GETTING UP AGAIN

Learning from failure and getting up again is a key success factor for remote workers. It's about being able to focus on what is important and being able to reactivate.

In the virtual space, many things can go wrong, from small items to big things, including:

- Not getting a project right

- Mixing up time zones

- Being culturally illiterate

- Not knowing who to go to

- Not understanding how an organizational structure works

- Passing out incorrect information or sending an email to the wrong person

- Focusing on the wrong goals—not prioritizing things correctly

- Creating conflict in the remote space

Let's take a look at each of the Digital Dozen. What's the area which has been their biggest mistake?

Ned—Ned, the new remote worker, notes that his biggest mistake has been not taking time to observe what was going on and not asking questions because he thought they were too small. As his mentor, Malcolm, always says, "There's never a silly question!"

Jo—as a virtual team leader, Jo noted that her biggest issue was when she took over the team she was tempted to jump in and make changes right away, but she heard her mentor's voice in her head and slowed down the pace. Originally, she felt that she did not do enough one-on-ones with people.

Malcolm—Not thinking early enough in his career about ongoing learning. The workforce continues to change—breadth can be as important as depth.

Jane—In her own role as a virtual facilitator, she has focused too much on talking *at* people, rather than engaging them. She took a great course and learned how to do it right.

Victor's biggest mistake was not thinking enough about the drivers of experience. On helping people focus on, and ask for, what motivates them. Given that he works with volunteers, the E of SMART- E goals, or tapping into the Excitement factor—is critical.

What other things are helpful to review?

Mo—Not trusting her own abilities. Not being as self-disciplined as she would like to have been.

Sally—Not reaching out enough to organizations that she partners with—taking the relationship for granted.

Sujit—Allowing scope creep to happen. Not being confident enough to articulate this and re-negotiate it back.

Mel—Not promoting her services enough.

Sam—Not thinking earlier about her selling of the business.

Part of recovery after a mistake is ensuring that you are focused on what's important.

FIELD WORK—NOW WHAT?

For the next 3 days, pick a real-time topic (obstacle or challenge) you are struggling with and use it for the daily field work.

Today's question is:

_____

Identify the obstacle.

_____
_____
_____
_____

What's important about this?

_____
_____
_____
_____

What's the cost of this? Why does it need to change?

_____
_____
_____
_____

What's at the core of this?

_____
_____
_____
_____

What would a member of the Digital Dozen say about it?

_____
_____

_____

_____

Up tomorrow is troubleshooting and decision making—so stay tuned!

NOTES AND REFLECTIONS:

DAY 32

TROUBLESHOOTING AND DECISION MAKING

"Whenever you see a successful business,
someone once made a courageous decision."
—Peter F. Drucker

FOCUS QUESTION:

What needs troubleshooting? What decisions do you need to make?

WHAT?

Yesterday we explored obstacles and challenges. Today we look at troubleshooting and decision making. Let's build onto yesterday's focus on obstacles. Today we work to troubleshoot and make decisions around those topics.

Decision making is a skill *all* remote professionals need to have. This includes skills in the area of problem solving. Along with decision making, we need to ensure that our team also has the authority to get things done.

Things that can really get in the way of remote work:

- **Mindset**—our mental health is important to note. When things are getting stressful, what are your release valves? (Check out Day 81 Renewal/Release Valve/Well-Being)

- **Getting yourself out of a pit.** We all face days where it is really challenging, when things are not going well, or you may have made a mistake.

When mistakes happen:

- Take ownership of the problem.
- Note what steps you need to rectify it.

- Apologize.
- Be proactive in discussing what needs to change on a process level next time. (For example, do you need more check points or do you need to do things differently?)

What's going to help you and others with this process?

Remote Tool—Is/Is Not

To ensure that work does get done, be sure to follow these ideas:
- Be sure that people have the tools and the responsibility to get the work done.
- Build in frequent checkpoints for update. Be sure to review the work.
- Provide good examples of what success can look like.
- Work with the *Is/Is Not Tool*. (Read more about this on Day 41.)

SO WHAT?

Troubleshooting may involve working through a decision-making tree of what you need to do and when.

Questions to ask:
- What's the issue?
- What are the factors contributing to it?
- What are some possible solutions?
- Which one do I start with?

NEXT STEPS—CHOICES AND THE DECISION TREE

Given that we are often on our own, it can be challenging to make choices. What do we do to make choices?

Decision trees are also useful in helping the team think through and make decisions. Follow the decision tree from the following example.

Decision trees prompt remote or hybrid teams to think through the questions in a similar fashion. What is important for you to note?

What to do when?
The Performance Analysis Flow Diagram

What's the Problem?
Does the Performance Concern You? → Yes → Describe Discrepancy → Is It Worth Solving? → Worth Pursuing? (What's the cost?) → No → Done

Can We Apply Fast Fixes?
Expectations Clear?
- No → Clarify Expectations → No → Provide Resources → No → Provide Feedback? → Yes → Done
- Yes → Resources Adequate? → Yes → Performance Quality Visible → Yes → Problem Sufficiently Solved?

Other Factors
Is the Environment Supportive?
- No → What Gets Rewarded? → No → What Other Issues Are Impacting → No → Identify
- Yes → Address Situational Issues → Yes → Identity Behavior → Yes → Problem Sufficiently Solved?

Do They Already Know How?
Genuine Skill Deficiency? → Yes Not Sure → Did It in the Past?
- Yes Used Often → No → Provide Feedback
- No → Yes → Provide Practice

Are There More Clues?
Can Task Be Made Easier?
- No → Any Other Obstacles? → No → Person Has Potential to Change → Yes → Train
- Yes → Simplify Task → Yes → Remove Obstacles → No → Replace Person

Select and Implement Solutions
Select Best Solution(s) → Draft Action Plan → Implement and Monitor → Done

Adapted from The Center for Effective Performance, © 1997

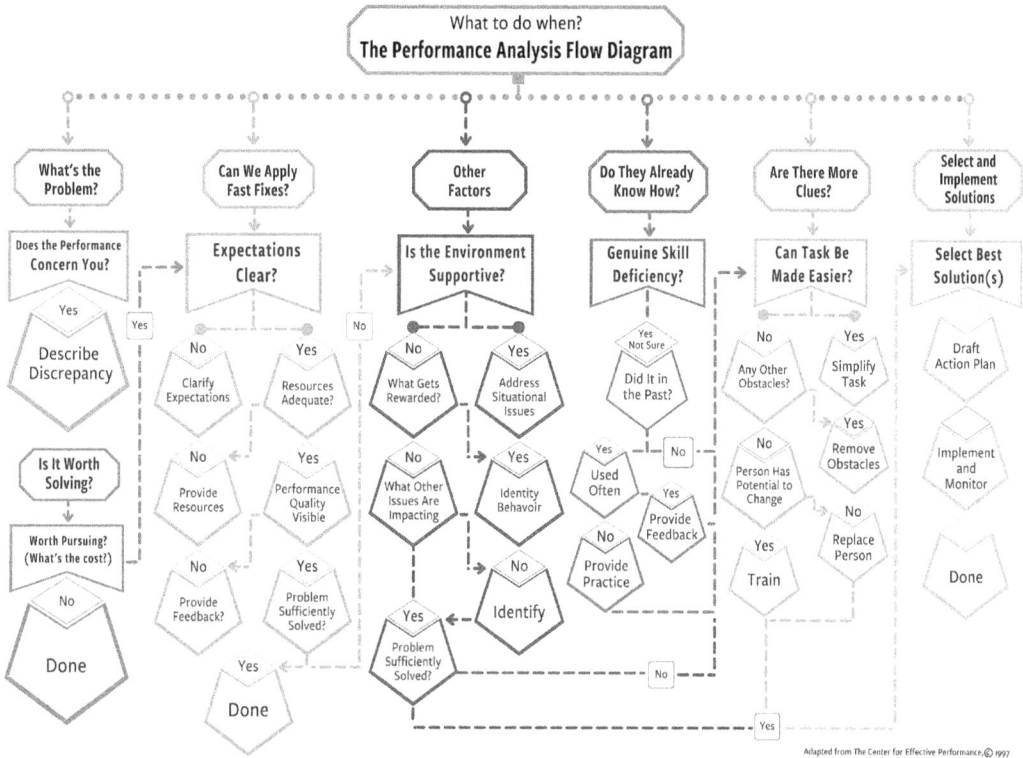

Choices and checklists you need to make:

- What are the choice points for remote workers?
- What are the inflection points in business? (For a remote worker—who do you surround yourself with?)

FIELD WORK—NOW WHAT?

Work through the Decision Tree for a current challenge you are facing. Read this in tandem with Day 34.

Consider these things as you work through the Decision Tree:

- Identify the main challenges you think you may face in your work.
- Identify what the decision tree is.
- Who do you go to at different times?
- What might you take to your boss rather than to your mentor?
- What might you reach out to your peers around first?

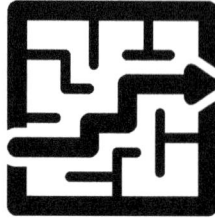

DAY 33
GETTING UNSTUCK

"We cannot solve our problems with the same thinking we used when we created them."
—Albert Einstein

FOCUS QUESTION:
What's going to help you get unstuck?

WHAT?

Over the last few days, we've looked at Obstacles and Challenges (Day 31), then Troubleshooting and Decision Making (Day 32). Today it's all about Getting Unstuck.

Even after making decisions, it's easy to feel stuck. When this is the case, consider asking these questions:

- What's the issue?
- What are the factors contributing to it?
- What are some possible solutions?
- Which one do I start with?

NEED TO KNOW: GETTING UNSTUCK

When you feel stuck, there may be days when you are not feeling at your peak and you need to get things done. Use some of these prompts to get you moving and creating some traction:

- Take 5 minutes to plan and/or review. What do you notice? What things are going to help you?

- Set a timer and work to that. If you've given yourself 15 minutes, this may create some urgency for you. It may help you identify what you do know and what you don't. Reach out to a team member, your mentor, or someone else for words or advice. There's likely to be someone who can help.

- Refer to the web and see what you find there as well.

- Mind-map—get all your ideas down on paper.

- Put it aside for a few minutes and go for a walk. Einstein said that we often have our greatest moments when we are thinking about something else.

- Get a change of scenery—sometimes we do need a different perspective. Would it be useful to take your work to a local library or a café? This may spur some ideas.

- Work through the block—there may be times when you just need to work through it.

- Leave it and come back to it with fresh eyes and mindset. Sometimes we really need to leave it be and come back to it in the morning. Put it away and switch to another task. Come back to it. Let your brain breathe and go to work out. As many creatives assert, insights and aha moments happen when we are thinking about something else.

- What else might you do to help you over a period of stuckness?

OVERCOMING OBSTACLES

What do you think will be impossible?

Overcoming the impossible. Here are some typical concerns for Day 1 of your work:

- I won't be able to get to know everyone.

- I'm going to be lost.

- I won't know what to do.

- No one is going to see me struggle.

Did You Know?

Where it's easy to feel adrift as a remote professional. You might ask yourself:

- Where am I going?

- What impact is my work having?

- What quality is my work, and how does it compare to that of others?

- What will this lead to?

- How does this fit into the bigger picture?

- What else is important to note about all of this?
- It may be valuable to share your thoughts around these questions with a mentor, a peer, or a coach.

SO WHAT?

To help you overcome challenges, use your network—Put it out there. Focus in on what's really at the core.

Ask yourself about the mindset you are in. In a fixed mindset, we see situations and instances as static. The reality of today's work context is that it's anything but! Growth mindset helps us recognize that we are always learning, and it encourages us to keep on trying. We just can't do something *yet*.

Take a break. Get out and see things from another perspective. Get creative. Talk it through with someone . Write it out. Look at it in a different way. Take up a new hobby. Look out to the horizon—what can you see from the horizon perspective?

Set up accountability partners to support you in what you need to do. We know that the action of accountability makes a significant inroad.

QUESTIONS TO CONSIDER—GETTING UNSTUCK

When getting unstuck or taking a new perspective around an issue, ask yourself:

- What's at the core?
- What's another possibility?
- What's the flip side of this?
- What would the protagonist do?
- What is the long-term view?
- What can be erased?
- What do you see/consider when you look to the horizon—what next steps are needed?
- What would your wisest collaborator say?
- In the long term, what's most important?
- With the resources you have, what's an option?
- Where can you learn from someone completely different?
- What new skills do you need to take on?
- What's the shadow view?

- What would it be like to take on the most advanced path – also known as the double diamond trail in skiing?

- What's unique about this place? When have you seen something different?

- What are you surrounded by?

- Who's in the school of fish with you?

- What makes this unique?

- What is a unique perspective about this?

- What unique signals are there around this issue?

- What patterns can you see?

- What patterns can you discern?

- What are you ignorant to?

- What haven't you considered?

- What can be activated?

- What's underwater?

It's quite common for remote workers to feel adrift or lost in the woods, not quite sure where they need to go. When this happens:

Focus on what you need to do. Think about the bigger picture. What is important about this task?

Review the requirements again. Is there a sample you can learn from or use as a prompt? Is there some past work you have completed that could be used to inform or inspire this?

When you think you can't go any more—review, make a plan, and start afresh the next day.

What are the elements of momentum? Daily steps + Consistent Action = Momentum

What might you be undecided for—Where to go? What to prioritize?

It can be helpful to create a structure—put boundaries around it. When things are too broad, we may not focus as much as we could. Putting some frame around it can help us focus on what's important.

Here are more questions to ask:

- What things will help you the most in your work?

- What else can you do to get anchored when feedback is not positive?

- What can you repurpose here? It's not always about creating but also repurposing—that might involve exploring another way of presenting the information. Getting it out to a new community—getting it in front of new eyes.

Here are more suggestions to consider:

- Consider best practice examples.

- Get some coaching around it.

- Focus on the high-level overview of what's important.

- Go to the opposite or negative of it. What's not being said? What are we not exploring? What's the focus element for others?

- Put a time window around it. What do you need to know in order to do it?

- Do some research—what are others doing around it?

- Mix it up—would it be useful to undertake another task in the process?

- How much do you know about what's getting in focus from others?

- Consider where you are with the Dip process (check out Day 39 Changes and the Dip)

- Bring on other team members. This may be the thing you need—we can't always do it alone or by ourselves. We too need support.

FIELD WORK—NOW WHAT?

Continue working with your current challenge to get unstuck. Identify the strategies you can activate to help you get unstuck. List out 3-5 you can experiment with.

_____

_____

_____

_____

_____

_____

_____

NOTES AND REFLECTIONS:

DAY 34
COACHING

"I absolutely believe that people, unless coached,
never reach their maximum capabilities."
—Bob Nardelli

FOCUS QUESTION:

Where could you benefit with thought partnership for more active awareness?

WHAT?

Coaching is a conversation with intent. At the heart of the coaching conversation is helping someone step into *What's possible?* Coaching conversations take many forms. At the core, they are about clarifying and working towards goals, holding accountability around this, supporting them into action, and supporting them to develop new awareness around the topic.

Coaching is a conversation you can have with a peer or your boss. When coaching, it's about deep listening, as well as asking powerful questions to enhance insights, gain traction, and identify and experiment with new responses.

Coaching is a critical skill set in the remote space, given that we need to work through people and empower them. Coaching skills benefit all employees at all levels—not only leaders. Coaching skills help with peer problem solving, motivation, and encouragement. Team leaders may hold formal and informal coaching conversations with the team—individually and collectively. A third common type of coaching is peer coaching, where peers become thought partners for each other.

There are several key components for any coaching conversation. As I share in *Reconnecting Workspaces* there is the Arc of the Coaching Conversation:

THE ARC OF THE COACHING CONVERSATION

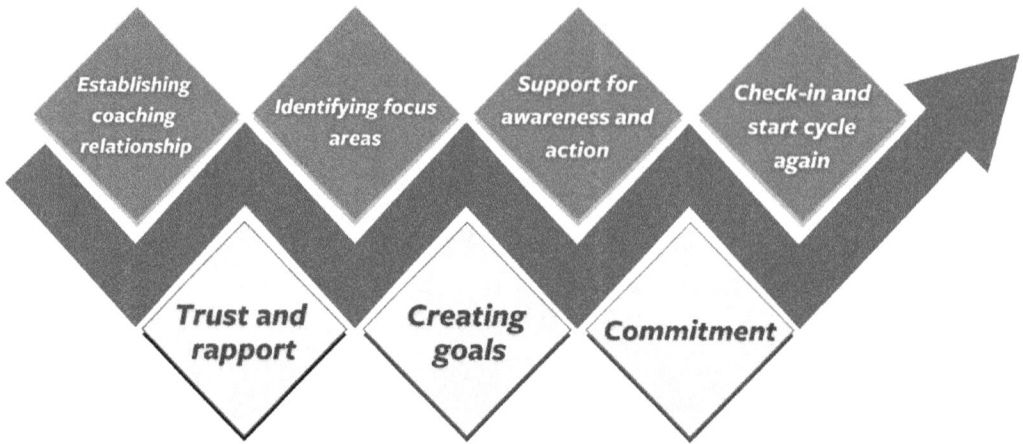

The International Coaching Federation has established a series of core competencies underpinning any coaching model. These include the following eight competencies:

- Demonstrates ethical practice

- Embodies a coaching mindset including reflective practice, awareness, self-management, and regulation

- Establishes and maintains agreements—it's a designed partnership, like mentoring, and any remote or hybrid relationships should be planned out

- Cultivates trust and safety

- Maintains presence

- Listens actively

- Evokes awareness

- Facilitates client growth

The foundations of coaching are grounded in a belief that the person being coached (the coachee or client) is capable of making the changes they want.

The coachee/client takes the lead in shaping the coaching conversation. They play the primary role in identifying their goals, and use coaching as a partnership to explore issues, identify options and explore topics from different perspectives. The coaching process is often as much about gaining awareness as it is about taking action.

Did You Know?

Questions serve as the backbone to great conversations. Questions either open up, or shut down conversations. Here are Coach Mel's favorite coaching questions:

- What's another way of looking at this?
- Where are you now?
- Where do you want to go?
- What will success look like at the end of this process?
- If you had no boundaries/limitations, what would you do?
- What's important?
- What else?
- What could you do differently?
- What might get in the way?
- What's the cost of not doing that?
- What will success look like?
- What perspectives are you holding around this?
- What beliefs do you have?
- What assumptions are you making?

SO WHAT?

The International Coaching Federation has listed a number of benefits of coaching, including both results and relationship elements. On the results front, coaching has been found to lead to improved work performance, improved business management, improved time management, and improved team effectiveness (Global Coaching Client Survey from International Coach Federation, 2009).

On the personal and relationship front, coaching has been found to lead to improved self-confidence, improved relationships, improved communication skills, and improved work-life balance.

The top three barriers to building a coaching culture in an organization were identified in the 2020 Global Coaching Client Survey[67] as:

- Limited support from senior leaders (50%).
- Inability to measure impact of coaching (42%).
- Lack of budget for coaching activities (38%).

FIELD WORK—NOW WHAT?

What are the topics you want to explore via coaching?

_____

_____

_____

_____

What is important about each topic?

_____

_____

_____

_____

What will success look like for each topic/

_____

_____

_____

_____

Identify 5-7 coaching questions which you might explore in the conversation.

_____

_____

_____

_____

_____

DAY 35

TEAMS IN FOCUS: TEAM CULTURE

"Culture = Values + Behavior"
—Simon Sinek

FOCUS QUESTION:
What's the culture you want to create?

WHAT?

What's the team culture you are part of? What is the culture of your work context?

Our team culture is **how** we do things. It consists of our brand, how we are known, and how we focus on messaging. It also includes our mascots, our sayings, and our taglines. Our culture shapes our identity and signals in the remote and hybrid space what we are a part of.

What three adjectives describe your team identity and culture?

As Simon Sinek writes in his book, *The Infinite Game*, "To build a culture based on trust takes a lot of work. It starts by creating a space in which people feel safe and comfortable to be themselves."[68]

TEAM CULTURE

Developing a strong team identity and team culture is even more important in a virtual space, given that we may be members of several different groups at any given time. Without the virtual cues around us, team culture in the remote space needs to be made explicit.

Our team culture can take many shapes and may include:

- Sayings

- Graphics
- Slogans
- Acronyms
- Mascots

Strong team culture is an important part of belonging and connection.

Team culture is "how we do things here." Identity is knowing that you are part of a bigger entity.

In developing your team culture, consider the following:

- What's important to us?
- What are the things we hold to be "true"?
- What three adjectives describe us?
- How do others describe us?
- What are the things we value?
- Who do we aspire to be?
- What is taboo on this team?
- What is non-negotiable?
- What is not ever complete on this team?
- What doesn't get attention?
- Where do I begin in my workflow?

The flip side or underbelly of a strong team culture is that it leads to silos and a fractioning. When our team culture is strong, it may be impermeable to others, and thus creates a wall. Teams will want to be sure that they are open enough that team culture is not a barrier, but rather a signal of expectations and agreements.

Questions: Consider the icons and images which surround your team. What does it say about your culture?

_____

_____

_____

What are the elements which describe who you are?

_____

_____

_____

Our Focus at Potentials Realized

Underneath the umbrella of remote, hybrid, and virtual work, there are several streams of programs, products, and services including:

- **A focus on coaching many in the remote space.** Whether you are designing and delivering group coaching or coaching teams, being able to scale the coaching conversation to many can be an integral part of the coaching conversation.

- **A focus on the dozen different ways we may find ourselves working in the remote space.** From remotepreneurs to coaches to project managers, remote work is increasingly varied and diverse.

- **A focus on facilitating great conversations.** In my work, the *Virtual Facilitation Essentials* program provides a vehicle for focusing on moving the conversation forward in the virtual space, while the *Group and Coaching Essentials* and *Team Coaching Essentials* programs focus on expanding the coaching conversation to many.

- **Supporting those who are stepping into the leadership and teamwork realm.** Anyone part of remote and virtual teams can benefit from remote leadership skills today. We all can benefit from emotional intelligence, communication, decision making, and prioritization skills.

Together these form a suite of services, specifically geared for those in the virtual, remote, and hybrid space.

SO WHAT?

Here are some questions to consider, relating to team culture:

- As a team, how do you do things?
- What's important for you?
- What is the team mantra?
- What is the team warrior call?
- What values do you have emblazoned on your sleeve?
- What photos represent who you are at your best?
- What do you have emblazoned?
- Are there a series of icons that capture yourselves as a team?
- Whom do you want to influence?

Team culture usually has three components—*who we are*, *how do we do things*, and *what is important to us*. Each area has a different focus. Let's explore all three.

Who we are. Virtual teams which excel know each other. They have strong relationships across the team, which allows them to call on others, and "have each other's backs." To strengthen your connection, consider these activities:

- Have the team brainstorm a list of words/adjectives which describe who you are as a team. Shape these into a word cloud which can be shared and used as a screensaver or logo.

- Discuss the question "Who are we when we are at our best?" Again, use the words to create a graphic about who you are.

- At your next team meeting, have each person share one thing others may not know about them.

- At your next team meeting, have each person share something that is unique to their location. (This works especially well if you have a global team.)

- In your next meeting, share your screen, which includes a variety of photos or icons. Have each person select the photo or icon which represents what they bring to the team.

How we do things. Each team will have its own unique practices and ways of doing things. This will vary from team to team. Spending time discussing how you do things, and what the expectations are, creates clarity and builds trust, boosting both performance and results.

To explore this topic further consider:

- Discussing "how we do things" (communicate, make decisions, work across differences, address conflict). It can be a series of different discussions and activities. It might include a Rules of the Road, which everyone has signed off on.

- What makes you unique and distinct in terms of how you do things?

- Another tool is to look at the *Is/Is Not* table. **What is important to us.** Clarity around priorities and goals for the entire team helps with alignment, prioritization, and decision making. Spending time on a regular basis, discussing what is important to us, may also involve:

- A list visible to the entire team (i.e., Think Intranet or other social network; have each team member post their:

    - Top 5 Goals for the month

    - Top 5 Priorities for the week

    - Top 5 Priorities for the quarter

- Enshrining your Team Agreements or Ways of Working into something that is visible. Some teams have enshrined this into a plaque or a screen saver, for example.

WHERE TO GO?

Refer to Chapters 3 and 4 of Reconnecting Workspaces for an in-depth view of remote and hybrid team culture and how to build it. For more on these topics, and a demonstration of what some of these can look like, take a look at my January 2019 Virtual Team Builders call, which I did as part of the Effective Virtual Conversations series. You can check it out here: www.potentialsrealized.com/teams-365-blog/teams365-2048-flashback-friday-articulating-your-virtual-team-culture

FIELD WORK—NOW WHAT?

Identify the main components of your team culture – *who* you are, *how* you do things, and *what* is important.

_____

_____

_____

_____

_____

_____

What will you do to enshrine them and make them visible?

_____

_____

_____

_____

NOTES AND REFLECTIONS:

THIS WEEK'S FOUNDATION THEME WAS
RESILIENCE AND CHANGE

What was this week like? Describe it here in three words:

_____ . _____ . _____

Topics we covered this week were:

- Day 29—The Iceberg: Introduction and Values

- Month One Check-In

- Day 30—Mentoring

- Day 31—Obstacles and Challenges

- Day 32—Troubleshooting and Decision Making

- Day 33—Getting Unstuck

- Day 34—Coaching

- Day 35—Teams in Focus: Team Identity and Culture

Wrap up theme of the week:

_____

_____

_____

_____

What are you looking forward to?

_____

_____

_____

_____

What questions do you have?

_____

_____

_____

_____

_____

_____

What To-Dos have surfaced? (List your top 3–5)

1.

2.

3.

4.

5.

Update your tracking sheet!

WEEK 6 · LONELINESS

"Loneliness is not lack of company; loneliness is lack of purpose."
—Guillermo Maldonado

FOCUS QUESTION:
What does loneliness mean to you?

This week's focus is going to be on Loneliness. This week we are going to be exploring topics including the Dip, and Change, Boundaries and Routines, along with Problem Solving.

Our roadmap for this week is:

- Day 36—Iceberg: Beliefs, Habits
- Day 37—Boundaries
- Day 38—Getting Organized
- Day 39—Change and the Dip
- Day 40—Routines
- Day 41—Problem Solving
- Day 42—Team Effectiveness: Performance Measures and Roles

This week's theme is loneliness, as it's likely that the "honeymoon stage" of remote work has worn off for you. You may even have hit several dips along the way. This week will support you in being where you are, looking at your internal landscape, setting boundaries, and getting organized.

A reminder that other daily topics covered Networking and Team Culture, both of which are an antidote to loneliness. Most likely you are part of a larger team, even if your team is miles away. Be sure to continue to lean into, and reach out to, your colleagues, peers, and boss.

Loneliness, along with lack of boundaries, are two areas which many remote professionals highlight as challenges. What are you doing to build your networks and proactively reach out to others?

Ways to build connection might include:

- Follow a passion project and join a community of others with the same interest. For example, I am part of several online writers' communities, which are a great resource to tap into.
- Build in time to your plan for outreach and relationship building.
- Create a learning plan and expand your network that way.
- Engage a mentor.

WHAT ARE YOUR TOP 3 GOALS THIS WEEK?:

1. _____

2. _____

3. _____

By the end of the week I want to be sure that . . .

_____

Be sure to use the daily tracker to capture additional notes.

ICEBERG: BELIEFS, HABITS

"Your visions will become clear only when you can look into your own heart.
Who looks outside, dreams; who looks inside, awakes."
—C. G. Jung

FOCUS QUESTION:

What beliefs do you hold? What habits have you developed to support you in your work?

WHAT?

Self-awareness is critical as a remote worker. Without it, we may find we trip over ourselves at every step. The challenge is that others may not see us, and with that, we may become blind to what isn't working.

Last week, on Day 29, we started exploring the Iceberg. Today we go a bit deeper into the next few layers of the iceberg, including beliefs and habits.

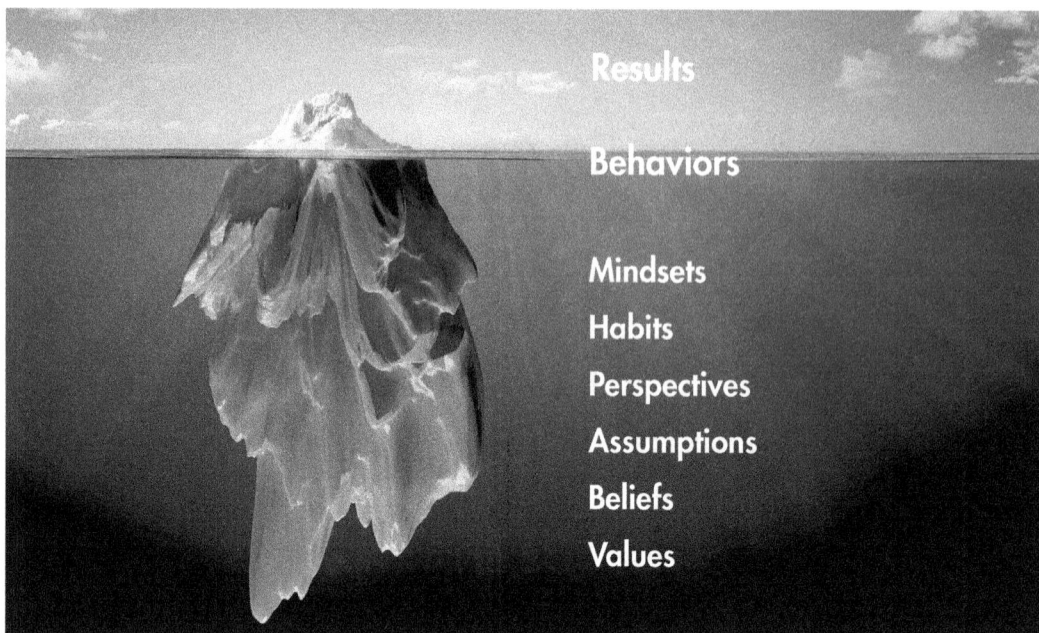

Results
Behaviors
Mindsets
Habits
Perspectives
Assumptions
Beliefs
Values

SO WHAT?

BELIEFS

Beliefs are the things we hold dear. They are the principles and philosophies we guide our work by. These are lines which we do not cross. Return to what you explored and noted on day 29 around your Values. What are the belief systems you hold dear with your work?

Here's a quick example:

I may have a belief that collaboration is valuable, and, hence, I may overextend and always focus on bringing others in the conversation.

Alternatively, I may also hold a belief that commuting is a waste of time, and, therefore, I don't make much effort to reach out to my peers, preferring to be a "lone wolf."

Beliefs are the principles and philosophies which guide you. These are often invisible lines you do not cross.

Beliefs can be enabling or derailing. They can help or hinder you. Limiting beliefs might include themes such as "You can't have it all" or "I can't do that in the virtual space" or "It won't work here." Note the beliefs you are holding. They may sound like a small "voice in your head" or on your shoulder.

Note the beliefs which you hold around your work and/or business.

HABITS

Habits are things we do repeatedly. They are things that we may do consciously, and often unconsciously.

Habits might include:

- Reviewing documents twice before sending.
- Checking for any assumptions that need to be named.
- Ensuring that enough background information and/or resources is included.

As an individual, what habits are getting results?

_____

_____

_____

_____

As a team, what habits need to be practiced consistently?

_____

_____

_____

_____

Did You Know

Here are some of the many great books around habits:

BJ Fogg's *Tiny Habits*

James Clear's *Atomic Habits*

Charles Duhigg's *The Power of Habits*

Stephen Covey's *7 Habits for Highly Effective People*

FIELD WORK—NOW WHAT?

1. Note the beliefs you hold around your business.

2. Using the Habits table, work through identifying the behaviors and results which flow from these habits.

HABITS	WHAT BEHAVIORS DOES IT LEAD TO?	WHAT RESULTS DOES IT LEAD TO?
Getting into the office at 6:00 am	One hour of focused project work, uninterrupted	Better design, more detail, more creative projects Getting things done more quickly

NOTES AND REFLECTIONS:

DAY 37

BOUNDARIES

"It is necessary, and even vital, to set standards for your
life and the people you allow in it."
—Mandy Hale

FOCUS QUESTION:
What boundaries have you created in your work to help you thrive?

WHAT?

Boundaries are a significant issue when working remotely. Boundaries may be around your:

- Working hours—when you are "on" and when you are "off"; when you are available
- Roles
- What teams you are part of
- What you are focusing on
- Work-life issues

Let's look at a couple of these more in-depth.

Boundaries and availability. Discernment around availability can help you protect the necessary time for strategic thinking and action needed in your business, networking, and keeping yourself at peak performance.

Questions to consider:

- What times of day are you "at your best" for doing different types of work? Consider different activities—coaching calls, setting up new business, marketing, relationship building, etc.

- What items are not getting done? What time do they need for completion? Ideally, when could they be completed?

- What are you doing to renew and/or keep at your prime? This might involve building in time for physical activity, renewal, etc.

- What are you doing to not only "do the work" with your business, but move the business forward? This is one of the greatest challenges for business owners at all stages of their business. Business inflection points occur regularly throughout the entire lifecycle of a business.

- What space are you leaving for other important parts of your life, i.e., family, relationships, etc.?

Did You Know?

Boundaries—What are the boundaries you are putting around your work?

Put a time around it—Parkinson's Rule asserts that our tasks expand to the time we give them. How much time do you want to earmark for a task?

Things like design of new programs or presentations can often take as long as we give them. To speed up the process, create an outline, draft it out, and keep it moving!

SO WHAT?

On another level, boundaries can become blurred in our home/work life, especially if we are working from home and have not set up a dedicated area for work. Be sure to check out the following Teams365 post about "setting yourself up for success in the remote space" and making sure you have what you need - https://www.potentialsrealized.com/teams-365-blog/teams365-2067-remote-work-setting-yourself-up-for-success

Consider the different boundaries that are important in your work. These might include boundaries:

- Between different tasks and projects you are working on
- Between the different teams you are part of
- Between your working hours and non-working hours
- Between when you are *on* and *off*
- Between priorities
- Between your work and home space

What do you notice as you explore these boundaries? What conversations do you want to have?

Visit www.potentialsrealized.com/teams-365-blog/teams365-2087-remote-working-myth-boundaries-arent-important

While saying "yes" can be important, so can saying "no." How to do it: "If you need me to do X, what would you suggest I defer or stop working on?"

What are the boundaries you want to create to enhance your focus, traction, and results?

_____

_____

_____

_____

Visit www.coachingbusinessbuilder.com/blog/solopreneur-myth-boundaries-and-availability

Creating a boundary between your work and your office. Having a boundary between your work and office space can be important in terms of longer-term productivity. Is it useful to get into the habit of putting things away at the end of the day? Yes!—for security issues especially, if there are others living in the space.

Can you close a door or put it away?

What flow of work will help you throughout the day?

PERSPECTIVES ON BOUNDARIES FROM THE DIGITAL DOZEN

Sujit—it doesn't need any more attention than getting clear on scope, budget, and time.

Serge—boundaries can be flexed. I work on my own terms. There are seasons when I am busy, and seasons when I am not.

Jane, virtual facilitator—we want to be conscious of what boundaries are needed.

Jo—what else is important for us to explore as a team? What do we need to keep in mind as we move through this discussion? What point of view is not yet being represented?

Mo, the creative solopreneur—I want to look at having flexibility in my schedule. I don't want to just have a 9–5 job. I want to work when I want to.

Alex—we'll work around the stakeholders' needs.

Malcolm—when I was your age, I was pleased to have a role.

What else do you think you want to keep an eye on around boundaries in your work?

_____

FIELD WORK—NOW WHAT?

Consider where you are with boundaries around your working hours, roles, projects, and other areas.

What's important to communicate and protect?

_____
_____
_____
_____
_____
_____

Note your boundaries around:

Working hours:

_____
_____

Roles:

_____
_____

Projects:

_____
_____

Other:

_____
_____

GETTING ORGANIZED

"For every minute spent in organizing, an hour is earned."
—Benjamin Franklin

FOCUS QUESTION:
What does getting organized mean to you? What does it look like?

WHAT?

We explored getting organized back in Day 5, Setting Up Your Office, of this *90-Day Guide*, and it's a topic we are returning to as we move along the pathway of working productively in the remote space.

Today's topic is about getting organized in the remote space. Core to efficiency in the remote space is getting organized. Without the visible systems of an organization, getting organized in the workspace will involve:

- Systems—see more on that in Day 15, Systems for Working Remote.

- Paper-based organization

- Furniture organization

- File organization

- Organizing how you operate and work every day

What are the core areas for you to explore?

Working remote may mean a smaller office footprint than you might have been used to, or a more open workspace which is shared with friends and loved ones.

Keeping focused, keeping things secure, and keeping things organized are key for success.

Today I wanted to cover five areas you might want to consider as they relate to getting and keeping organized:

1. **File management**—from our paper-based files to electronic ways we file and access information, keeping files in check is critical.

2. **Version control**—when working with other team members in collaborative documents, being able to access and work on the most up-to-date documents is key.

3. **Building in time for planning**—planning often falls to the bottom of the list for remote work. When boundaries are fluid as we work odd hours with our stakeholders across the world, the ability to build in time for planning sometimes "goes by the wayside." When are you building in formal moments to plan—virtually and otherwise?

4. **Batching considerations**—remote workers are often pulled from task to task, especially if we become reactive around key tasks coming in via email. A challenge for the remote team today is to ensure that we do make headway on all the different tasks involved, including the more focused, deeper work required for tasks.

5. **Keeping on top of rote tasks**—reporting, finances, filing, etc. Regularly dedicating 15 minutes to more rote tasks can help to keep the clutter (physical and mental) at bay. Physically also filing things in an orderly fashion—e.g., a box for receipts—can also help to diminish the mental clutter created by the open loop of invoices which have not been entered.

One final thing to keep in mind in terms of getting more organized is systems. In *PlanDoTrack*, I point to the importance of five main areas of systems for entrepreneurs and other remote workers. Consider these areas:

1. **Financial systems**—invoicing, accounts payable, cash flow, accounts receivable, etc.

2. **Client and stakeholder systems**—connecting with and sharing information with others—this might include such things as email templates, contact lists, meeting notes, or past reports on collaboration.

3. **Marketing**—websites, social media feeds, frequently asked questions.

4. **Content**—do you know what you have created? Do you have an accessible listing of what there is?

5. **Project management**—from Waterfall to Agile project management, it's key to have a strong series of systems to keep your projects moving and communication happening around them.

What systems are going to help you streamline and keep on top of your work?

Did You Know?

Small areas you may want to check out as they can disrupt your organizing process:

- What is lighting like? If a window is behind you, you will be in the shadow. Can you reorient your work space so you are facing the window? That will change the lighting.

- Sitting is the new smoking. What can you do to get up on a regular basis and do work?

- Getting office supplies—who provides this? How do you invoice it?

- Being sure to back-up

- Consider what you need to have on hand and create easy access for things you need.

SO WHAT?

One area which can quickly become overwhelming is paper. In addition to having a file, it will be important for remote workers to have a strategy to corral the paper and know where to place it. Whether you organize by project (New newsletter) *or* task (Readings), take 5 minutes today and think about the files which you are likely to need to use or access.

Paper can pile up, and getting into the habit of keeping notes in one booklet or dedicating a notebook for major projects can keep things corralled.

Write it down! It's more likely that you will retain it. Multiple studies point to the value of writing things down, in terms of retention and also thought process. For more on this topic, take a look at this *Educational Leadership* article, "Research Matters: The Magic of Writing Stuff Down: http://www.ascd.org/publications/educational-leadership/apr18/vol75/num07/The-Magic-of-Writing-Stuff-Down.aspx

Helen Buttigieg shared a wonderful organizing tip with me several years ago. It's called RAFT, and it helps us to sort through and *action* piles of paper. What do you want to:

> R—READ
>
> A—ACTION
>
> F—FILE
>
> T—TOSS

Given that paper and digital clutter is a pain point for many remote professionals, earmark time on a regular basis (i.e., weekly) to sort through your paperwork.

For more on this, refer to Helen Buttigieg's *Organizing Outside the Box: Conquer Clutter Using Your Natural Learning Style.*

FIELD WORK—NOW WHAT?

What actions are going to move you forward?

_____

_____

_____

_____

_____

_____

Take 5 minutes today and think about the papers which you are likely to need to file. RAFT them.

NOTES AND REFLECTIONS:

DAY 39
CHANGE AND THE DIP

"Intelligence is the ability to adapt to change."
—Stephen Hawking

FOCUS QUESTION:
What do you notice about the change cycle you are in right now?

WHAT?

In the process of change there are many different ups and downs.

In my work as a coach, we often explore something that is called the Dip. It might look, and sound, like this:

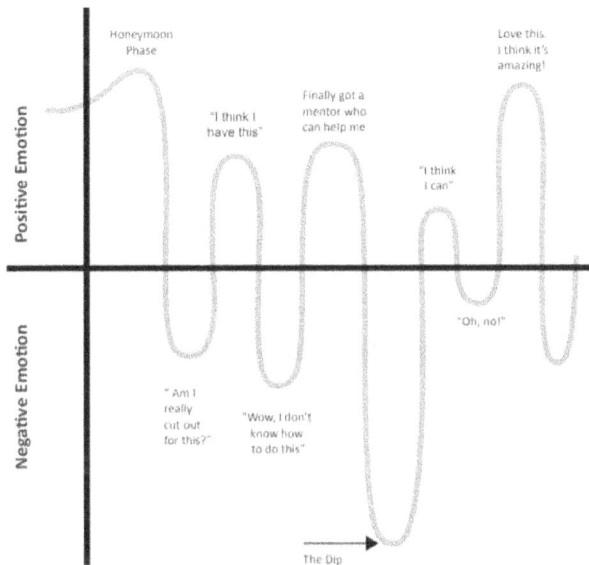

Positive Emotion

Negative Emotion

Honeymoon Phase

"I think I have this"

Finally got a mentor who can help me

Love this. I think it's amazing!

"I think I can"

"Oh, no!"

" Am I really cut out for this?"

"Wow, I don't know how to do this"

The Dip

The dip refers to the low point where we really hit "rock bottom." When we get there, we can either stay there and cocoon (pretending that nothing is different), or we can push off the bottom and move back up the change curve.

Anecdotally, I have seen the Dip occur in different contexts throughout my career. In international postings, we knew that it would likely occur two-thirds into the first half of the posting. So, if a posting were per year—at that phase it was as if you realized that there was "no going back." It was important to either adapt *or* evolve.

The Dip can happen on longer-term projects.

A number of factors can get in the way of and impede remote work:

- Lack of trust
- Misunderstanding on the part of management
- Poor infrastructure to support remote work
- Lack of clarity around tasks, responsibilities, and/or quality of work
- Lack of systems to support work (See the 10 systems focusing on remote work)
- Not having your office space set up (check out Day 5 Setting Up Your Office and Day 38 Getting Organized)
- Not having the right technical systems which will allow you to get the work done
- Loneliness
- Lack of motivation (check out the post on motivation)
- Lack of tools to do work
- Poor systems for communication
- Lack of clarity of role
- Not understanding how your work relies on or dovetails into the work of others
- Lack of information to do work

When this happens, it is important to:

- Notice that you are in a dip—this is not going to be forever
- Explore options to help you return to homeostasis and/or get you out of the dip
- Reach out to others—this is where your boss, a mentor, and peers can be a great support
- Move into problem solving and consider what you are going to do

Here's a brief excerpt from Blog post #756 of my *Teams365* blog:

> What we often don't talk about in leadership is the "DIP." Just as in any change process, such as cross-cultural integration when you move locations for work, or change through a coaching process, it's typical to start off with great gusto in what's commonly known as the

"honeymoon" phase. At this point, mentor and protege are raring to go—they can't wait to get started and into dialogue with each other. Goals are clear as is usually the way forward.

As the meetings progress, some partnerships find an ever-evolving spiral of conversation and goal touchpoints, whereas others drop down into the Dip. The Dip is a place which sometimes feels like you are spinning your wheels, or not getting traction. Proteges and mentors may feel like mentoring is a waste of time.

In fact, the Dip is natural! It's part of the change process; what you can see in the illustration of the cycle of adaptation. It's actually from a recent conversation I had with a leader who was going to work globally and wanted to think about what to expect. I've seen the Dip throughout my own international assignments, and I've seen it mirrored not in the hundreds, but, over more than two decades of work in the intercultural sector, in the thousands.

The Dip can and does happen in any change process. What to do if you see it? Here are a few things to consider:

- Revisit your goals
- What have you accomplished?
- What do you want to aim for next?
- Where might you need recharging?
- What will "shake" things up a bit?

  You might have noticed there were several other places where we can see the Dip—in coaching, global assignments, and any change process. Where have you experienced the Dip? What did you do?[69]

Change is an inevitable part of any business context, but it may be even more augmented for you. As a remote professional, you will want to think about how you naturally react to change.

According to Michael D. Watkins, in *The First 90 Days*, there may be four stages, or waves of change. These include:

- Stage 1—Transition
- Stage 2—Immersion
- Stage 3—Reshaping
- Stage 4—Consolidation[70]

Think about the process you have gone through in recent weeks. Where are you in terms of shifting into your new role (Transition), getting immersed in what you need to do, including where to go (Immersion), reshaping the way you do things (Reshaping), and then consolidating what you need to do (Consolidation)?

Another useful change model is that of RW Rogers. His change model first published in 1983 identified five different ways people may approach the change process.

You may have members on your team who are **innovators** (those who are eager to create change), **early adopters** (those who embrace the change early on), **early majority** (those who get on the bus relatively early), **late majority** (those who slowly adapt/get on the bus with change), and **laggards** (those who resist change).

Being aware of who will be advocates for change on the team is just as important as recognizing those who might need more support or conversation/attention throughout any change process.

What do you recognize in yourself about how you respond to, and initiate, change?

We all react to change in different ways. For those who find it challenging, it may be useful to:

- Write it out
- Speak it out— Reach out to an Employee Assistance Program (EAP), mentor, coach, with a peer partner, with your leader
- Get outside of your comfort zone

Becoming comfortable to operate in a context where we are outside our norm is an important part of developing resilience and focus.

WORDS TO LIVE BY

"If you really want to do something, you'll find a way; if you don't, you'll find an excuse."
—Jim Rohn

_____

"The road to success is always under construction."
—Lily Tomlin

SO WHAT?

What things are going to help you get outside your comfort zone?

What new experiences are you excited to explore?

Getting outside the comfort zone can build new experience and practice in certain areas. We may be able to focus more on getting things done and evaluate how that can help us in the future.

STAGES OF CHANGE AND THE DIP

Change is an inevitable part of the world of the remote worker. Every day we may be experiencing new change processes—new project starting, getting a chance to work with others, and then focusing on what others may need to do. What elements are going to help you as a remote worker through the ups and downs of change? This might include such things as:

- The honeymoon stage
- The Dip
- Hitting rock bottom
- When you get paralyzed

Paralysis can be part of the remote worker experience. Whether we don't know where to go next, or we sense we are over our head, or we are waiting on someone else for information or direction, being okay with paralysis is a part of the remote worker experience.

- **Being able to articulate/speak what is going on and reach out to others for support is key.** This is where having a mentor can be invaluable. It may also be useful to have a regular series of one-on-ones earmarked with your boss so you can raise issues as they come, and frequently enough so they can be resolved or moved before things mushroom.

- **Know your triggers**. What really gets you stuck? What do you need to self-manage around this?

- **Know who can help you**. Who are the people who can help you as a remote worker?

- **Talk it out**. Given that we are solitary for a lot of the day, many remote workers can benefit from having a space and place for talking it out. Who and where do you want to go to talk it out?

- **Know where to go for inspiration**. Is there a location where you can go to think deeply, focus, or get grounded?

- **Know where to go to for a change**. Even changing scenery or location can help in terms of creating a new perspective around issues.

What are your practices for when you get paralyzed?

FIELD WORK—NOW WHAT?

Think about what your change curve looks like. Use this space to sketch it out:

What is important to note?

_____

_____

_____

_____

What tips will you activate around change and the Dip?

_____

_____

_____

_____

What is your natural reaction to change?

_____

_____

_____

_____

NOTES AND REFLECTIONS:

DAY 40

ROUTINES

"The big things that come our way are . . .
the fruit of seeds planted in the daily routine of our work."
—William Feather

WHAT?

Routines are an important part of maintaining consistency. Be intentional with the routines you want to set. These might include getting to work at a certain time of day, being sure to switch off by a certain time of day, leaving your desk for lunch to participate in a workout, scheduling in two out-of-office networking events each month, and/or earmarking time each season to participate in a learning event (internal to your business, industry wide, or MOOC—massive open online course).

What routines are important for you to establish early on?

_____

_____

_____

Stability and flow can be created for many in the hybrid and remote space via:

- Practices
- Habits
- Routines

Where to Go

Here are more resources regarding practices, habits, and routines.

- **Practices:** Check out KPMG's online article, "Leading Practices for Remote Working: How to Navigate the Current Environment," at bitly.com/remoteworkkpmg

- **Habits:** Check out Charles Duhigg's the *Power of Habits*, James Clear's *Atomic Habits*, and BJ Fogg's *Tiny Habits*.

- **Routines:** Check out Amanda Cross's blog post, "21 Ways to Switch Up Your Remote Work Routine," at https://blog.bonus.ly/remote-work-routine.

SO WHAT?

Practices

Practices provide anchors for us in terms of getting things out and into the space of conversation. A practice may be a meeting, a focus, or a connection with people you enjoy. What is the purpose of your work right now?

To create something. Could you put on your calendar an event which you host every week or month? What would it take to create that item on a regular basis? What could you create over the course of a month or year?

To connect people. Host a meeting at a consistent time weekly or monthly. Put it out in the calendar before the end of the year to make sure that it works.

To equip people. What are the different strategies which will help people?

What practices do you want to create?

_____

_____

_____

Habits

As James Clear writes, "Habit formation is the process by which a behavior becomes progressively more automatic through repetition."[71] Habits are useful in that they may free up more thinking space for creative thought and problem solving. Think about the habit of driving. When you first started driving, likely all your thought needed to be dedicated to that. As it became more automatic and a habit, chances are that your brain now goes on autopilot while you drive and think. Have you ever found yourself at a location, not quite knowing how you got there?

Hebb's law asserts that "Neurons that fire together wire together;" in other words, things that we do consistently become a habit.

What habits are going to help you thrive?

_____

_____

_____

Routines

What are the routines? Routines are essential for remote workers. They help us stay grounded in a context that may be very fluid.

Write out the activities you undertake on a consistent basis. Maybe they include:

- Going into the office once a week—what's the learning here?
- Getting to the gym 4–5 days a week—what's the value?

Routines can create a workflow that keeps us at peak. It is important to consider elements like what creates *flow* for you, and how you are balancing time on and time off.

What routines are going to help you thrive?

_____

_____

_____

FIELD WORK—NOW WHAT?

Map out the practices, habits, and routines which will help you do your best work:

How are they helpful?

_____

_____

_____

_____

What doesn't help?

_____

_____

_____

_____

DAY 41
PROBLEM SOLVING

"A problem is a chance for you to do your best."
—Duke Ellington

FOCUS QUESTION:
What are the roadblocks the team is facing?

WHAT?

It's quite common for remote workers to feel adrift or lost in the woods, not quite sure where you need to go.

When this happens:

- Focus on what you need to do.
- Review the requirements again.
- When you think you can't go any more, then review, make a plan, and start afresh the next day.
- Take a break or a walk—reframe the situation. The movement may help you shift perspectives.

What are the elements of momentum?

As I write in *Coaching Business Builder* and *PlanDoTrack*, **Daily steps + Consistent Action = Momentum**

It's often the quick wins which make a difference. What are the small steps and short chunks (i.e., 15 minutes) you can take towards your goals today?

What you might be undecided for: Where to go? What to prioritize?

What is going to give you some momentum? Creating a structure. Putting boundaries around it. When things are too broad, we may not focus as much as we could. Putting some frame around it can help us focus on what's important.

What things will help you the most in your work?

What else can you do to get anchored?

When feedback is not positive, review the requirements again. Is there a sample you can learn from or use as a prompt? Is there some past work you have completed that could be used to inform or inspire this?

What can you repurpose here? It's not always about creating, but also repurposing; and that might involve exploring another way of presenting the information—getting it out to a new community, getting it in front of new eyes.

Did You Know?

Where it's easy to feel adrift as a remote professional:

- Where am I going?
- What impact is my work having?
- What quality is my work, and how does it compare to that of others?
- What will this lead to?
- How does this fit into the bigger picture?

SO WHAT?

Here are some more problem-solving suggestions:

- Ask for samples of work.
- Consider a best-practice example.
- Get some coaching around it.
- Focus on the high-level overview of what's important.
- Go to the opposite. What's not being said? What are we not exploring?
- Take a break. Sometimes it's as simple as taking a break.
- Put a time window around it—what do you need to know in order to do it?
- Do some research—what are others doing around it?
- Mix it up. Would it be useful to undertake another task in the process?

What about the negative; what's not being said here? What's the focus element for others? How much do you know about what's getting in focus from others? This topic connects into the Dip—also found earlier this week.

Bringing on other team members may be the thing you are needing. We can't always do it alone or by ourselves. We too need support.

What else is important to note about all of this?

Link then to what you want to do as a remote worker.

Think about the bigger picture.

Expose yourself to some new learning—what else do you need to explore? What else is important to focus on? What would your mentor say? Imagine yourself in five years and deconstruct it—what do you need to do now in order to get there?

What can you do as a professional, and what can you think of excising?

What does *the team* really need?

What do *you* really need?

FIELD WORK—NOW WHAT?

Identify a major challenge or obstacle you are facing.

_____

_____

_____

_____

What's really important about it?

_____

_____

_____

_____

6

TEAM EFFECTIVENESS: PERFORMANCE MEASURES AND ROLES

"Don't lower your expectations to meet your performance.
Raise your level of performance to meet your expectations."
—Ralph Marston

FOCUS QUESTION:

What does successful performance look like? What are the roles required on your team?

WHAT?

Performance Measures

In brief, performance measures examine "What will success look like?" Just as important as it is to be clear on our goals, we also need to be sure we are clear on how we are being measured.

In the remote space, consistency from one location to another is essential. Being specific and clear about what good and poor performance looks like is critical at the goal and team level.

While the SMART-E Goal framework helps us to focus on what's important and what the details are, shared performance measures spell out what success looks like.

Part of this may involve a deeper dive into the components of a task.

Let's use the example of Ned working on a project report. He is also collaborating with Sujit, the project manager, and Alex, an external stakeholder who works for an NGO, and they've brought in Mo, the creative solopreneur, to help out.

A component of remote success for this process may be to have Jo host a meeting for this micro-project team to go into details about what the end result is going to look like. They can tap into the use of the Is/Is Not tool, which helps to clarify what the task looks like. Jo gets the entire team to brainstorm and agree upon the details for success of each section. They come up with the following list:

THE REPORT IS	THE REPORT IS NOT
A deeper dive into specific examples from each area. Specifically, 3 case studies from each of the staff and their work.	Just photographs
Including 2 photographs per case study	A replacement for other types of reports
Including 3 testimonials across the 3 cases from external stakeholders	Focused on the wider context
Including a bulleted list of the benefits of the project (micro, macro, local, and regional)	A 56-page report

Just as the process is focused on specific tasks, shared performance measures help to clarify what's required, ensuring that everyone is working on the same page.

In this example, the report around team work in the remote space may also include things like hours of work, expectations around start and end time, use of company data or equipment, and/or personal research during company hours. Being explicit about these elements for everyone creates clarity. It's important to be upfront and explicit around expectations with new staff (and reinforce for all staff) to build trust.

Key Point: Trust is enhanced when standards are made explicit.

Did You Know?

What things are going to help you discern?

Questions to consider with discernment:

- What's a high yield?
- What's not important?
- What will help in the short term?
- What will help in the long term?
- As you consider your vision, where do you want to go?
- What else might be necessary?
- What is out of focus?

- What is a red herring (something that looks important but really isn't)?

- What else do you need to focus on?

Focus—When we are too focused, things may drop out of our radar which are important.

CASE STUDY—THE DIGITAL DOZEN

The Digital Dozen strive for high performance in their work. Let's take a look at what several of them focus on in their different roles.

Back to the example of the project report, Jo, the virtual team leader, asks the team to consider the strengths-based work they have done, to help the team be more successful with their project report. She and the team match the team members' strengths to different roles needed.

Sujit offers that he is really good around project scoping and resourcing. He's also offered to set up a timeline.

Ned sees himself as a workhorse and can sit down and power through. He offers to be the one to bring the pieces together.

Mo is great at working to create vision and is detail-oriented. She will do a round of edits before handing off to Jo, who will be orchestrating the whole project. Jo is committed to one-on-one check-ins as well as facilitating three team meetings throughout the one month this project will be worked on.

What are your preferences in terms of project roles?

SO WHAT?

ROLES

Another key driver for high performance is roles, and gaining clarity around the roles we play in a team. In any project or team we may play a variety of roles like "finisher," "visionary," "social coordinator." People might feel that their work does not connect with others, when in reality it does. A significant focus for a remote leader can be to ensure that people are clear with their roles and how they intersect. Helping people learn more about each other's roles serves to boost trust and, therefore, connection.

In addition to roles, alignment is also important.

ALIGNMENT

Where are your tasks aligned? What do you want to keep focusing on? What are the things where alignment may be shifting outwards?

Prioritizing Your Workflow

What key priorities do you have for undertaking your work? What are the priorities of the teams you belong to?

What are the tools you have to ensure that the time and resourcing you have is going to match what you want to create?

What is the alignment with the bigger-picture goal?

What alignment exists on the individual level? Collective team or organizational level?

Thinking about one of the projects you are assigned to, what are the roles involved; who is the initiator, the completer, the workhorse, the detailed one? Thinking about the different roles needed in a project, along with *who* is best placed to complete them, can provide a boost to project completion.

ACTIVITY

Use the following chart to consider the different roles needed in a project you are working on. Consider what each person's focus or tasks are, along with who would be good at that.

ROLE	FOCUS/TASKS	WHO IS GOOD AT THIS?
Visionary		
Starter		
Finisher		
Cheerleader		
Strategist		
Analyst		
Problem solver		

Joker		
Granular thinker		
Detail-oriented person		
Hunter—finds resources		
Other		

FIELD WORK—NOW WHAT?

Consider applying the *Is/Is Not* tool to another project or task you have.

IS	IS NOT

What are your shared performance measures this quarter? (i.e., What will success look like around the top 3-5 activities?)

_____

_____

_____

_____

On a scale of 1-10, how clear are the shared performance measures?

_____

_____

_____

_____

Note "what success looks like" with all key projects, and, as a team, discuss what it means.

Consider the roles different group members can inhabit.

_____

_____

_____

_____

_____

_____

_____

_____

NOTES AND REFLECTIONS:

THIS WEEK'S FOUNDATION THEME WAS
LONELINESS

Congratulations—you are now through the first six weeks of your role. What was it like? Describe it here in three words:

_____ . _____ . _____

Topics we covered this week were:

- Day 36—Iceberg: Beliefs, Habits
- Day 37—Boundaries
- Day 38—Getting Organized
- Day 39—Change and the Dip
- Day 40—Routines
- Day 41—Problem Solving
- Day 42—Teams in Focus: Performance Measures and Roles

Wrap up theme for the last week:

_____

_____

_____

_____

What are you looking forward to?

_____

_____

_____

_____

What questions do you have?

_____

_____

_____

_____

_____

_____

What To-Dos have surfaced? (List your top 3–5)

1.

2.

3.

4.

5.

Update your tracking sheet!

WEEK 7 · LEADERSHIP AND PLANNING

"The quality of a leader is reflected in the standards they set for themselves."
—Ray Kroc

Welcome to Week 7! This week's theme is Leadership and Planning. Regardless of your role, *everyone* needs to be a leader in the remote space. It's likely that you will be utilizing and leaning into many of the core skills traditional leaders have focused on—delegation, influence, etc.

Our roadmap for this week is as follows:

- Day 43—Assumptions
- Day 44—Perception Does Not Equal Reality
- Day 45—The Messy Middle and Mid-Point Check-In
- Day 46—Influence
- Day 47—Empathy
- Day 48—Presentations 101
- Day 49—Teams in Focus: Team Practices and Commitment

For more on this topic, listen to *Remote Pathways* podcast episode 17. You can listen in on any of the podcast players or at www.remotepathways.com/podcast.html. Check out that episode download as a bonus!

It's hoped that this guide not only will equip you for your current role but may be one that you return to next time you step into a new role.

1. _____

2. _____

3. _____

By the end of the week I want to be sure that . . .

_____

Week 7 Theme—Leadership and Planning

What leadership skills do you need in today's context?

On page 128 of *The Infinite Game*, Simon Sinek writes:

> Qualities like honesty, integrity, courage, resiliency, perseverance, judgment and decisiveness . . . are more likely to engender the kind of trust and cooperation that, over, the course of time, increase the likelihood that a team will succeed more often than it fails. A bias for will before resources, trust before performance, increases the probability a team will perform at higher levels over time.

Key issues for remote workers also include such topics as support, boundaries between their work and role, support, and flexibility. Key to successful work and leadership is also the 7 Remote Enablers—communication, clarity, connection, culture, consistency, community, and collaboration—as well as trust and reducing the us/them divide.

As you step into this week, what's important for you to note? What is really important for you to put attention around?

DAY 43
ASSUMPTIONS

"Begin challenging your assumptions. Your assumptions are the windows on the world. Scrub them off every once in a while, or the light won't come in."
—Alan Alda

FOCUS QUESTION:
What assumptions are you making?

WHAT?

Assumptions frame our focus. They frame our actions, which then frame our results. It's like a lens that we wear. Assumptions shape our decisions, which then shape our actions and, therefore, our results.

What are the holes in your assumptions?

Making assumptions explicit is critical in the remote and hybrid space. Assumptions are often implicit or *unspoken* in the virtual and remote space. There can be assumptions around resourcing, budgeting, information, priorities.

For example, I may be thinking things but need to spell out the rationale, provide context, and talk about how this connects to others on the team. I may also need to "spell out," with much greater detail, the thinking that has gone into my decision. Lack of clarity and misunderstanding happen when we do not provide enough detail. Unnamed assumptions can lead to a lack of alignment around work, goals, and priorities. It also can lead to conflict, or things' being completely missed.

Assumptions can also be made when we are moving too quickly. They occur when we don't stop to pause and read things through or think things through.

What are the different perspectives around things? What key elements are going to help?

Judith Glaser often wrote that coaching is about making the implicit, explicit.

What can we do to make sure that we are naming and owning the assumptions we make?

When assumptions reside underwater, they usually do find a way of showing up. If you are seeing a disconnect in your work, or a lack of alignment across the team, it may be a signal that it's time to explore the assumptions being made.

6 Questions—Assumptions

1. What's another way of looking at this topic?
2. What assumptions are you holding?
3. What assumptions do you need to make more explicit in your work?
4. What assumptions do you need to check out with others?
5. What blind spots are these assumptions creating?
6. What's important to note?

SO WHAT?

Here are some ways to unearth assumptions.

Ask:

- What assumptions are we making? Go around the room to find out the different assumptions that people are making.
- What are you thinking about as you have made this decision? Can you walk us through it?

Go through process mapping and actually break down a complete task or activity from start to finish. Each activity may get its own Post-it note, and from there you can assign who is responsible for the task and how it connects with another task or person. It's enlightening to make this pathway clear for the sake of the team.

FIELD WORK—NOW WHAT?

Note the assumptions you are making.

_____

_____

_____

_____

How are they helping?

_____

_____

_____

_____

How are they hindering?

_____

_____

_____

_____

What assumptions need to be made explicit?

_____

_____

_____

_____

NOTES AND REFLECTIONS:

PERCEPTION DOES NOT EQUAL REALITY

"Life is all about perception. Positive versus negative. Whichever you choose will affect and more than likely reflect your outcomes."
—Sonya Teclai

FOCUS QUESTION:

What perspective are you holding around your most important priority? Is that grounded in reality?

WHAT?

With communication touchpoints being elongated so people see us for only brief windows of time, not only are things magnified (so if we are having a bad moment people might think we are having a bad day), but they are also taken out of context.

With this in mind, perception does not always equal reality. One of the tenets of this work is "Check your assumptions." What you see may not be what you get.

Is what you are seeing really "True?" Is it the complete picture?

Perception can be defined as a way of understanding or interpreting things.

Reality can be defined as the state of things as they actually exist, rather than as they may be perceived or imagined.

Think back to the image I shared earlier. Did you see the rabbit or the duck?

Examine the assumptions you may be making around projects, priorities, and/or key relationships. What is important in the work that you are doing?

At the same time, when communicating issues, it's important to communicate as much as you can about context and be explicit about assumptions you are making.

Did You Know?

Reflect back on the perceptual illusion shared earlier. What do you notice about what needs to shift as you look at it?

SO WHAT?

When we name assumptions, they are "there," and we can speak to them and debate with them. The ability to have constructive dialogue and debate is key in the remote world, given how infrequently we may meet, and how each person may hold different pieces of the puzzle.

FIELD WORK—NOW WHAT?

What things are you holding as "true"?

_____

_____

_____

_____

_____

_____

What may need more exploration or reframing?

_____

_____

_____

_____

_____

_____

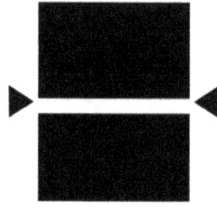

THE MESSY MIDDLE AND MID-POINT CHECK-IN

"If you find yourself stuck in the middle there is only one way to go, forward."
—Richard Branson

FOCUS QUESTION:
What do you notice at the Messy Middle?

WHAT?

Today is the mid-point of the 90-day process. The mid-point of many projects is often characterized by complexity and confusion, plus a lot of murkiness. It is often called the *Messy Middle*. It can be a place of losing momentum. It also can be a place of doubt. The Messy Middle may also feel like the Dip, so you may want to go back and refer to that at this time.

At the mid-point things can feel anchored or they can feel unclear. At the mid-point you may feel empowered or you may be facing doubt.

FACING DOUBT

What do you do when you don't know where to go?

- Listen to your intuition and be focused on the bigger picture.
- Focus on what your goals are. Imagine them and visualize success.
- Surround yourself with a focus on what you need.
- Ask for help.

- Return to explore what is core to you.

- Focus on providing value to others, and they will reach out to you. You can also make requests in terms of what updates you need and how you need to be supported. What can you do in order to have a supportive work space?

- What outer accountability do you need? What will be magnetic?

Practically, moving through the messy middle:

- Know your anchors

- Revisit your vision

- Consider what strengths, or superpowers, you can lean into

- Focus on what's important in the big picture, to isolate milestones and anchors

Messy Middle

In any process, the middle becomes messy. We can get stuck and mired down.

At this point it can be useful to ask:
- What are the enablers?
- What are the factors which will help things move forward?
- What else can you focus on as it relates to equipment and ideas that you have?

SO WHAT?

You can do anything you need and focus on what's important to you. What is the legacy you want to leave? Your digital footprint will remain and can be magnified beyond where you are. What do you notice about the star you have in sight, and what the shooting star of your imprint might look like?

What's the melody you want to lean into? What additional melodies can you incorporate? What can you make together as a team?

That's what 1 + 1 equals.

Always give 10% more.

Mindset shift: There is nothing that cannot happen today.

How can you move a mountain? How can you create some new melody? How much is in the shooting star of the world?

FIELD WORK—NOW WHAT?

Consider what is happening to you at this space:

What do you notice about what's very important for you?

_____

_____

_____

_____

What does the Messy Middle mean?

_____

_____

_____

_____

MIDPOINT REVIEW QUESTIONS

Key accomplishments in the last 45 days:

_____

_____

_____

_____

Things which have helped my progress:

_____

_____

_____

_____

Obstacles I've faced:

_____

_____

_____

_____

How I've moved through them:

_____

_____

_____

_____

Strengths I've leveraged:

_____

_____

_____

_____

Key goals for the next 45 days:

_____   _____

_____   _____

_____   _____

_____   _____

_____   _____

DAY 46
INFLUENCE

"True leadership cannot be awarded, appointed, or assigned. It comes only from influence, and that cannot be mandated. It must be earned."
—John C. Maxwell

FOCUS QUESTION:
What does influence mean for you?

WHAT?

Influence is an especially important skill in the remote and hybrid space as we have to work THROUGH people. It's not possible to micro-manage, we can only micro-monitor.

Relationship Management is also about the skill of Influence. This includes our abilities in:

- Being a great listener and knowing what is important to others (team members, stakeholders, your boss, etc.).

- Knowing our people and their preferences.

- Being sensitive to others' "What's In It For Me" (WIIFM).

- Skills in tactful communication—being able to diplomatically and sensitively communicate alternative points of view.

- Building trust and rapport quickly. Without this foundation of trust, the skill of influence is moot.

- Understanding political currents and the nuances of groups/teams/organizations.

Did You Know?

Influence occurs on multiple levels, including:

- Our processes
- Our systems
- The way we do things
- Our level of commitments
- How we treat each other
- How we share information

What is infectious in the virtual space?

SO WHAT?

As a remote worker, the skill of influence becomes even more important. We don't get to see people on a regular basis, so a "direct control" model is not possible. Given our distance, it's key that we need to work through others to get things done.

What helps you be influential in your work:

- Podcasts
- Learning opportunities
- Secondment opportunities
- Reaching out and picking up a new hobby or skill

When connections are there between remote team members, it can be much easier to influence and have things go viral. A strong team culture will help people share and connect with what's important to them.

Robert Cialdini asserts that there are seven principles around influence[72] including:

- **reciprocity**,
- commitment and **consistency**,
- **social proof**,
- authority,
- liking,
- **scarcity**
- unity

Each one of these is a lever which can be used.

As I wrote in *Reconnecting Workspaces* (pages 1566-157):

> **Reciprocity:** Humans are guided by give and take. We give back the behavior we have received. If you help me, I will help you. If you have been given a favor, you will return it. As a consumer or in a relationship, we are more likely to say yes to those that we owe. Be sure to be the first to give and that what you give is something that is unexpected.
>
> **Scarcity:** This principle notes that we want more of what we can't get. When something is scarce, we tend to want it more.
>
> **Authority:** People follow those who are credible and have expertise. Signal to others what makes you a credible expert. What have others said about your work? What track record do you bring to make you an authority?
>
> **Consistency:** Be consistent with the things your customers and teams are looking for. Ask for small commitments that can be made regularly.
>
> **Liking:** People will say yes to those they like. We like people who are similar to us, who pay us compliments, and who cooperate towards mutual goals. To employ these factors in online negotiations, share a snippet of personal information with each other before you begin negotiating. In one study, 90% were able to come to agreement.
>
> **Consensus:** When we feel uncertain, we look to the actions and behaviors of others.
>
> **Unity:** This was the final area added, which involves our yearning to be part of something.

As you think about your team experience, what things do you need to influence? Which of these seven principles could be a lever or something you could cultivate so that you can work more effectively through others? If you don't know, consider starting with Reciprocity, by reaching out first to a colleague to share information, or explore the Liking principle by finding some common ground with another team member.

FIELD WORK—NOW WHAT?

Think about what areas you need to influence. Where does your work become an influence through others?

_____

_____

_____

_____

DAY 47
EMPATHY

"When people talk, listen completely. Most people never listen."
—Ernest Hemingway

FOCUS QUESTION:
Where do you need to develop more empathy?

WHAT?

Empathy is a skill set critical for teamwork and leadership. In fact, I probably could do a whole series of blog posts on this topic. Let's zoom into this question: "What are some practical ways to build more empathy across virtual teams, while also boosting connection"?

Skill in focus—communication or relationships—empathy or collaboration

One important skill to develop in the virtual world today is empathy. One of the challenges is that we don't get to see beyond the screen. What are some ways we can be building more empathy and understanding with other virtual team members?

What comes to mind in terms of ways you can boost more connection and understanding among team members?

Learn More

There have been some great writings by others on the topic of empathy. Consider these articles:

- "Empathy in Leadership—10 Reasons Why It Matters," by Tanveer Naseer
- "Empathy in Leadership: Coaching Leaders to Manage Their Stories," by Matthew Taylor

- "The Importance of Empathy in the Workplace," from the Center for Creative Leadership. [73]

SO WHAT?

Here are five ways we as virtual teams can build our skills in empathy while building connection:

1. **Provide opportunities for team members to get to know each other—online and offline.** While some virtual teams will never meet, building in time for "getting to know" each other is critical. This could entail dedicating some time to sharing two of my favorite warmups: "What's outside your window?" or "What's on your desk?" [74]

2. **Create formal learning partnerships with others on the team.** Many virtual teams benefit from having peer partners to meet with on a regular basis. This helps us to learn more about each other and what projects we are working on. As we listen and learn, more trust, connection, and understanding are created.

3. **Be present and listen.** We continue to see how important the ability to focus on virtual conversations is. Nothing will destroy trust and connection faster than hearing the other person on the end of the phone or streaming typing away doing an email while you are speaking together. What will it take to be present, focus, and deeply listen in your virtual conversations?

4. **Listen for the deeper layers.** Typically, in listening, we may be staying at the surface, hearing with one ear and thinking about what we are going to say back to the other person. In the deeper listening needed by virtual teams today, listen to what the person is saying. Notice the pace, pitch of the conversation. Notice the emotion behind the words. What is being said?

5. **Take time to share more about your world, your work, your priorities.** An important part of empathy is understanding. It's a two-way street—being open to share and being receptive to listening. how much are you sharing about your world, your work, and your priorities?

There are multiple ways we can be focusing on the skills of empathy as we build connection on teams. What are some approaches you as a team want to focus on?[75]

Empathy has been a key skill during the pandemic. As Kendra Cherry writes, "In addition to helping you connect with others, being empathetic also helps you regulate your emotions in times of stress."[76]

As the old adage says, we may forget what people say, but we don't forget how they made us feel.

FIELD WORK—NOW WHAT?

What can you do to be more empathetic? What is important to explore about this topic?

DAY 48
PRESENTATIONS 101

"Designing a presentation without an audience in mind is like writing a love letter and addressing it 'to whom it may concern.'"
—Ken Haemer

FOCUS QUESTION:

What presentations are you going to be leading? What's going to make it a WOW?

WHAT?

Communication is at the heart of great remote work. Presentations are one of the most important vehicles for change in the workspace.

Not only do great presentations have a storyline, but they also have a great structure. Start with the end in mind. What do you want people to leave the conversation having explored? Learned? Gained insights into?

Presentations at their simplest forms have three main components:

Open—It's key to capture people's attention in this first phase. What are you going to talk about? What's the story you want to open with? The question? or Other?

Body—What are the three to five main bullet points of your presentations? Is there an example to illustrate each one?

Close—In the close, you want to summarize your main points. It should last about 5% of the total presentation time.

What are the elements you want to include?

_____

_____

_____

What is the Open of your presentation?

_____

_____

_____

What is the Body of your presentation?

_____

_____

_____

What is the Close of your presentation?

_____

_____

_____

Elements which can make a presentation stand out in the virtual space include:

- Visuals
- Media use
- Interactivity
- Case studies and examples

I explore many of these topics in the Stand Out Virtually Challenge and One-Day Studio Masterclass, as well as in my ICF-CCE approved *Virtual Facilitation Essentials* program. Learn more about these programs at StandOutVirtually.com.

SO WHAT?

Another important part of the presentation is the slide deck.

For each of us, our market may be different, and what is visually appealing to one group may not be attractive to another.

With this in mind, here are some questions to consider as you go about designing your slides for your next presentation:

- What is the message you want to communicate through your images?

- What are the main colors which represent your brand (or your messaging)?

- What are your clients inspired, touched, or moved by?

- What is the emotional message you want to communicate?

- What images would communicate these messages?

- What icons describe the story you want to communicate?

- What else is important to check out around color?

Did You Know?

For more on color use, check out:

- Canva's Color Wheel: www.canva.com/colors/color-wheel

- Color Theory for Designers, from *Smashing Magazine*—https://www.smashingmagazine.com/2010/01/color-theory-for-designers-part-1-the-meaning-of-color/

FIELD WORK—NOW WHAT?

Think of an upcoming presentation. What elements do you want to include in your *Open*, *Body*, and *Close*? (Write these separately.)

What does the audience want? What are they listening for?

_____

_____

_____

_____

_____

_____

What are your three main points? How are you reinforcing these as you go through?

_____

_____

_____

_____

_____

_____

_____

_____

_____

_____

List out five ways you may want to create more memorability in your presentations:

1.

2.

3.

4.

5.

DAY 49
TEAM IN FOCUS—PRACTICES AND COMMITMENT

"Until one is committed,
there is hesitancy, the chance to draw back. Concerning all acts of initiative (and creation),
there is one elementary truth, the ignorance of which kills countless ideas and splendid
plans: that the moment one definitely commits oneself, then Providence moves too.
All sorts of things occur to help one that would never otherwise have occurred.
A whole stream of events issues from the decision, raising in one's favor all
manner of unforeseen incidents and meetings and material assistance,
which no man could have dreamed would have come his way.
Whatever you can do, or dream you can do, begin it.
Boldness has genius, power, and magic in it.
Begin it now."

—William H. Murray

FOCUS QUESTION:

What are the consistent activities your team is undertaking to build your
relationships and focus your results? What are you committed to, no matter what?

WHAT?

Two additional components of the Six Factors of High Performing Teams are *practices* and *commitments*.

Practices are consistent activities the team undertakes focused on building team relationships and clarifying team results. Practices create safety and build a solid process. What activities do you undertake regularly to build relationships and focus on results?

Practices can include team meetings, a social evening out or online, quarterly team development sprints, a 2 p.m. huddle. What things are going to support you as a team?

Some examples of virtual team practices are:

- **Weekly coffee breaks** which the entire team attends. You could incorporate one of the weekly Thursday Team Building Tip Questions I share to spark dialogue across the team. View them at www.potentialsrealized.com/teams-365-blog/category/team-building-tip.

- **Virtual Get Things Done afternoons**—every quarter I host a Virtual Get Things Done afternoon. People are invited to bring their list of things to do and join us for a 4-hour co-working block. We meet at the top of every hour to check in. Benefiting from peer accountability and a focused support, hourly check-ins also serve to keep the focus and push people through work, which might not be as focused.

- **Virtual co-working sprints**—Throughout 2021, I have hosted a series of 21-minute virtual co-working sprints geared to get people into action around their work, called the 21 for 21 Virtual Co-working Sprints. I hope you will join us for the next one!

- **Structured team meetings** to build connection and focus on work.

What other types of virtual team practices will support the team in maintaining and building relationships, keeping the team moving, and getting things done?

Did You Know?

Rotational leadership of meetings will support team members in owning the process. It will also create more "novelty," likely leading to a boost in engagement.

What can you do to jazz up your team meetings?

Explore Day 53 Meetings 101 for more on meetings.

SO WHAT?

Commitment is an essential part of teamwork. It signals how I have your back and what we are going to do, no matter what.

Practices are the things we do to ensure we stay connected.

What is important for you to note in this area?

FIELD WORK—NOW WHAT?

Practices:

As a team, discuss what team practices you have scheduled to focus on *relationship development* and your *results*. Consider team meetings, peer support meetings, virtual co-working sessions, etc.

Commitments:

As a team, discuss what you are committed to *doing? Being?* Taking a stand *for?*

_____

_____

_____

_____

_____

_____

_____

_____

As it relates to the *doing*, what are you going to do, *no matter what*:

This month?

_____

_____

_____

_____

_____

_____

This quarter?

_____

_____

_____

_____

_____

_____

WEEK 7 REVIEW
THIS WEEK'S FOUNDATION THEME WAS
LEADERSHIP AND PLANNING

Congratulations! You are now through the first seven weeks of your role. What was it like? Describe it here in three words:

_____ . _____ . _____

Topics we covered this week were:

- Day 43—Assumption
- Day 44—Perception Does Not Equal Reality
- Day 45—The Messy Middle and Mid-Point Check-In
- Day 46—Influence
- Day 47—Empathy
- Day 48—Presentations 101
- Day 49—Teams in Focus: Team Practices and Commitment

Wrap up theme for the week:

_____

_____

_____

_____

What are you looking forward to?

_____

_____

_____

_____

What questions do you have?

_____

_____

_____

_____

_____

_____

_____

_____

What To-Dos have surfaced? (List your top 3–5)

1.

2.

3.

4.

5.

Update your tracking sheet!

WEEK 8 · FOCUSING AND GETTING THINGS DONE

"Always remember, your focus determines your reality."
—George Lucas

Welcome to Week 8! Part of the mantra of my *PlanDoTrack* and *Coaching Business Builder* workbook and planners are **Daily Steps + Consistent Action = Momentum**.

Key to making things happen in the remote space is *focusing* and *Getting Things Done!*

This week's theme is the neuroscience of remote work, as well as what's going to help you get things done. Daily focus includes such key topics as collaboration, meetings, and networking.

Here's our roadmap for the week:

- Day 50—Mindset
- Day 51—Ongoing Learning
- Day 52—High-Leverage Activities
- Day 53—Meetings 101
- Day 54—Get It Done: Consistent Action
- Day 55—Collaboration
- Day 56—Teams in Focus: Tools in Your Toolbox

WHAT ARE YOUR TOP 3 GOALS THIS WEEK?:

1. _____

2. _____

3. _____

By the end of the week I want to be sure that . . .

_____

THE NEUROSCIENCE OF REMOTE WORK

When I wrote *Effective Virtual Conversations* back in 2017, I felt that it was very important to include items around the neuroscience of design. Here are several things to keep in mind:

NEUROSCIENCE AND THE BRAIN

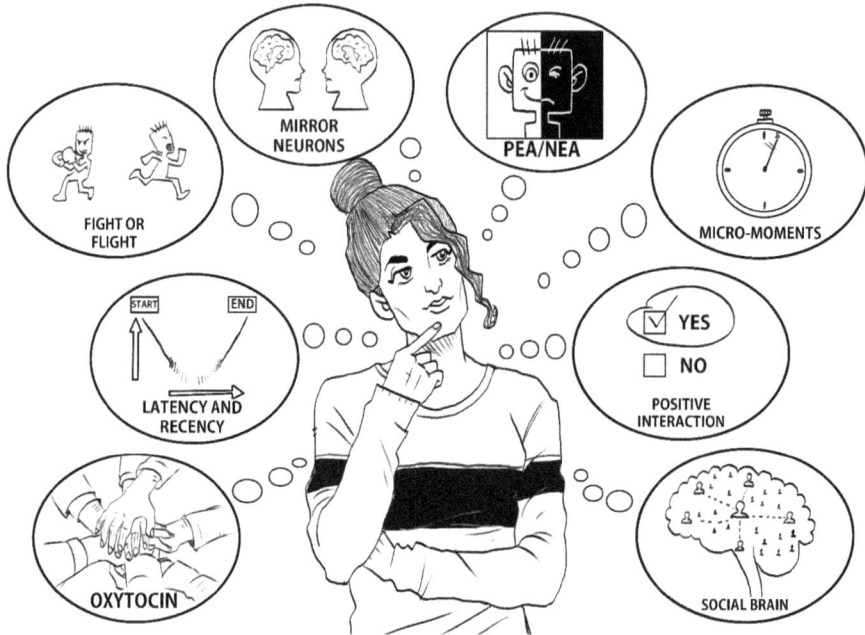

Effective Virtual Conversations, (C) Britton, 2017

Let's zoom into several of these.

PRINCIPLE	DESCRIPTION	TO CONSIDER
THE SOCIAL BRAIN	We learn best when we are learning with others. Learning something, and then having to discuss something and or even teach it to others, can work well.	What can you do to build in more areas of connection, and conversation with others?
PEA/NEA	Questions influence whether our brain opens up or shuts down. This is significant, given the importance of communication in the remote space.	To keep the brain open, use questions like: What's possible? If you were to win $50M, what would you do? To learn more, read about the work of Boyatzis, Smith, and Van Oosten in "Coaching for Change."

POSITIVE INTERACTION	Teams that provide more positive emotional bids to each other may be more open. John Gottman's research has found a 5:1 ratio of positive feedback to negative feedback. A few year's later, Barbara Frederickson found a 3:1 ratio, commonly known as the Losada principle. While this has been disputed due to statistical error, anecdotally, what do you notice about conversation patterns?	What can you do to help teams notice more positivity on their team, and provide not only constructive feedback but also positive feedback?
LATENCY AND RECENCY	We remember the start and end of things. Those things that happen in the middle are often forgotten. Think about the "messy middle" of processes and conversations you have been part of.	Stress key messages at the start and end of a conversation. Be intentional in how you remember things in the middle.
MICRO-MOMENTS	Micro-moments was a term coined by Google back in 2015: "Micro-moments occur when people reflexively turn to a device—increasingly a smartphone—to act on a need to learn something, do something, discover something, watch something, or buy something."[77] In my work as a virtual facilitator, it's also an indication of what's going to shift things. It is often the small things that make the greatest shift.	What do you notice about the small things that could make a big difference for the groups you work with?
MIRROR NEURONS	A growing body of research points to how our brain pattern can resemble others' that we are in touchpoints with. For example, if you are connected with people who are negative, your brain patterns may also reflect that.	What are you mirroring, or picking up, in your conversations?
SOCIAL LEARNING	Social learning asserts that we learn best with others.	Consider the social elements of learning: Peer partners/learning Partners Breakouts Teach-backs Application assignments

What are some other ways you can get your brain working in tandem with you?

DAY 50

MINDSET

"Thoughts are behaviors we haven't learned to observe yet."
—B. F. Skinner

FOCUS QUESTION:
What is your mindset?

WHAT?

Over the last few weeks, we have explored the various layers of the iceberg. One which has been touched upon in different contexts is that of mindset.

Carol Dweck defines *mindset* as "a self-perception or 'self-theory' that people hold about themselves." The Oxford Library defines mindset as "the established set of attitudes held by someone."

Mindset has been said to have an impact on both motivation and what you get done.

Of interest may be Agile Mindsets, Digital Mindsets, and Growth Mindsets.

As you scroll through the workbook, you'll notice we have touched on related topics, such as in Day 9, the focus on 15 Skills, Mindsets and Practices, and experimental mindset in Day 82 Experimentation.

In today's post we are going to take a look at what Learners' Mindset and Experimental Mindset mean in the virtual space.

IN FOCUS: LEARNER'S MINDSET AND EXPERIMENTAL MINDSET

Ongoing learning is a critical mindset for remote workers. It's likely that the context will continue to change, just as the remote world is changing rapidly every day. A learners' mindset embraces ongoing learning, which is often referred to as continuous development or always be learning.

Related to this is experimentation. *Experimentation* means that you are trying things out. Starting with an initial hypothesis, experimentation may mean that we are seeing how things work.

An experimental mindset means that we are:

- Open to outcome

- Curious about what makes it happen

- Unattached to the end result

- Aware that we don't know everything and are open to learning and seeing what happens

- Focused on data; taking time to note what happens, the process we follow and the outcome which is possible

Mindset

Mindset is an important topic to explore with your team, given the ongoing changes in the remote and hybrid workspace. Given this, it is likely that you as a team will need to keep on learning new skills and adjusting practices.

SO WHAT?

More has been written on this topic from Carol Dweck in her growth mindset material.

Knowing when "good is enough" can also save heartache. If you are trying to do too much, it can be a challenge. *Good enough* gets us out of the trap of needing things to be perfect. Having a conversation with your colleagues around what *good enough* means is important so you know when to move on. One of the challenges is that work can be interrelated, even if we don't recognize it. So if I am late in providing information, how will that impact others?

FIELD WORK—NOW WHAT?

Consider what is important to you to note around mindset:

_____

_____

_____

When have you adopted a growth mindset?

_____

_____

Experimental mindset?

_____

_____

Learners' mindset?

_____

_____

What experiments do you want to try?

_____

_____

_____

_____

NOTES AND REFLECTIONS:

ONGOING LEARNING

"Wisdom is not a product of schooling but of the lifelong attempt to acquire it."
—Albert Einstein

FOCUS QUESTION:
What learning do you want to undertake?

WHAT?

Learning can take many forms. As a remote professional, it can be very important to build in time for ongoing learning.

- What are the things you are wanting to learn?
- What are the best modalities to learn these?
- Where else might you explore these learnings?
- What does the team really need? What do you really need?
- What just needs to get done? When can you say enough is enough?

Expose yourself to some new learning:

- What else do you need to explore?
- What else is important to focus on?
- What would your mentor say?

Imagine yourself in five years and deconstruct it:

- What do you need to do or not do in order to get there?

- What can you do as a professional, and what can you think of excising?

- Where are you learning too much?

- Where do you need to put it into practice?

Taking time to build your confidence in these areas can be critical for success. We need to ensure that we get off our books and put it into the world. It's unlikely that it's going to work the way we want it to . . . .

Learning Opportunities

Here are more learning opportunities to consider:

- Books; "we read to know we are not alone." —spoken by C. S. Lewis in William Nicholson's play, *Shadowlands*

- Podcasts

- Membership in a book club or virtual community, e.g., *Reconnecting Workspaces Book Club*

- An online course in your area of focus

It may be useful to identify in your annual plan the skills you want to develop. This can also be part of formal performance review discussions with your boss and/or mentoring with your mentor.

SO WHAT?

What can you do in the next while to get into action so you can get some data to close off on some of the options?

THE ECOSYSTEM OF REMOTE LEARNING[78]

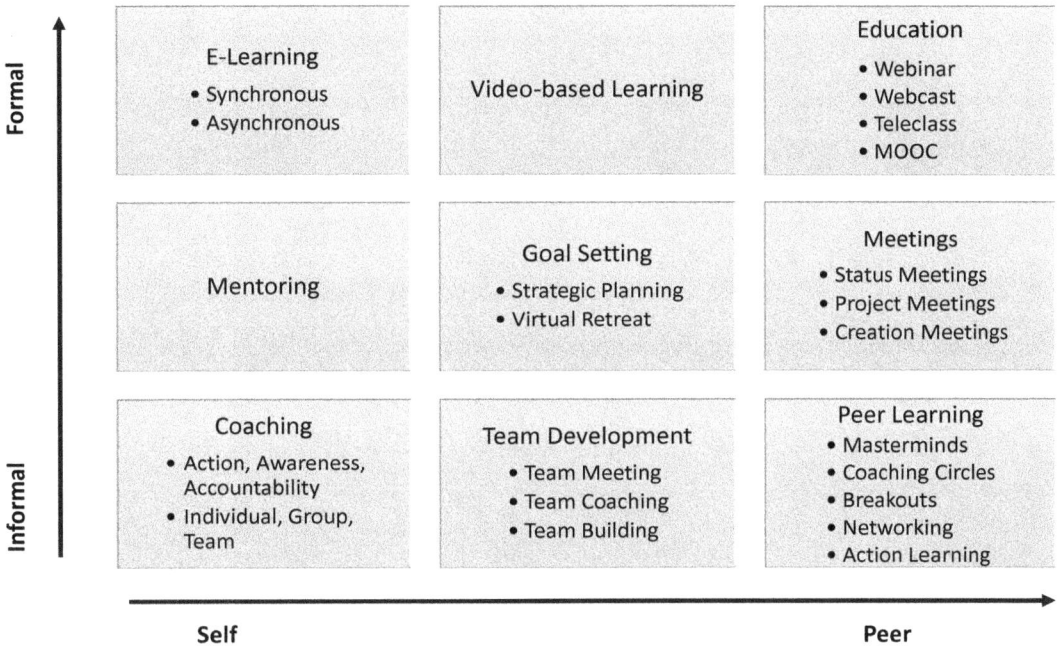

	Self		Peer
Formal	**E-Learning** • Synchronous • Asynchronous	**Video-based Learning**	**Education** • Webinar • Webcast • Teleclass • MOOC
	Mentoring	**Goal Setting** • Strategic Planning • Virtual Retreat	**Meetings** • Status Meetings • Project Meetings • Creation Meetings
Informal	**Coaching** • Action, Awareness, Accountability • Individual, Group, Team	**Team Development** • Team Meeting • Team Coaching • Team Building	**Peer Learning** • Masterminds • Coaching Circles • Breakouts • Networking • Action Learning

In my 2017 book, *Effective Virtual Conversations*, I explore the concept of the Ecosystem of Virtual Learning. Across both the formal and informal landscape, we can learn in a variety of ways—in a self-guided way, as well as with peers.

Some of the learning approaches you may want to consider are the following:

- E-learning—*synchronous*, happening live, where you might be learning with a live instructor, or *asynchronous*, where you may be connecting in with others

- Formal education—webinars, webcasts, teleclasses, MOOCs (Massive Open Online Courses)

- Video-based learning

- Mentoring

- Goal setting—planning sessions, strategic planning, short-term planning, Get-It-Done-Days, virtual retreats

- Meetings—team meetings, status meetings, creation meetings, co-working sessions, project meetings

- Coaching—with a focus on goals, action, awareness, and accountability

- Team development—team meetings, team coaching, team building

- Peer learning—masterminds, coaching circles, breakouts, networking, action learning

- Virtual, local, and in-person learning opportunities—local Meetups, workshops, retreats, and conferences

Need to Know

In the first 90 days it is likely that there are core areas for you to focus on:

- What to do
- How to do it
- Where to go
- Who to know

Ask your leader and peers what is most important to learn about and/or take action on. Ask them to help you understand the learning arc at your organization or for your role. What are the things you need to learn in:

- The 1st month?
- The 1st quarter (3 months)?
- The 1st year?

EXPAND YOUR HORIZON

As we have explored so far in Day 51, ongoing learning is important for remote and hybrid professionals at all stages of their careers.

Ongoing learning is deemed to be part of today's landscape. While Elaine Beich indicated in 2007 that knowledge was doubling every two years, today's workplace may be more about synthesis and curation of information than retention. Such learning tools as Alexa and Google have changed the way we access and even retain information.

With this in mind, developing new skills in search, research, and retrieval can be important.

What things do you want to do in order to expand your horizon?

Think about:

- Taking a MOOC—EdX.
- Attending a conference—yes, in person. We still can't replace the in-person context.
- Team focus on development—in person or virtual/remote. What's important to you?

What are you going to focus on?

TYPES OF LEARNING

Regardless of the type of learning you are undertaking, it can be useful to explore a mix of formal and informal learning, as well as social learning and on-the-job learning.

Informal learning includes such activities as reading, observation, attending lunch-and-learns, and mentoring. It may be valuable to explore informal learning opportunities, including peer pairs/accountability partners, and/or mentoring. Is there someone who is ahead of you in terms of their level of experience, from whom you'd like to learn? Check out Day 30 - Mentoring. In a mentoring relationship, you are paired with another professional who can share their working experiences with you, and potentially connect into important information, networks and resources related to your role or industry.

Social learning occurs when we learn with others. This might include a group coaching process, a formal workshop, a retreat, job shadowing, or a team meeting. Social learning and seeing how others do things can be an important indicator of remote work success. What do you need with social learning?

On-the-job learning includes many opportunities for remote workers, from participating in special projects to job shadowing, where you can follow someone around. What are your on-the-job opportunities?

Other questions to consider:

What core skills will support your work?

_____

_____

_____

What is important to learn?

_____

_____

_____

How long does it take to get confident to know a new job?

_____

_____

_____

What is important to be exposed to?

_____

_____

_____

IN THE SPOTLIGHT—DIGITAL DOZEN:
A CONVERSATION WITH JANE, THE VIRTUAL FACILITATOR

As a learning professional, Jane, the Virtual Facilitator, has worked with thousands of professionals around the world in online training. Here are some questions she would be able to answer.

- What training is available?
- What skills would you recommend that I develop as a remote worker?
- What feedback should I be asking for?
- Where else can I go to learn more?
- How much time should I earmark for training?
- I'd like to access online learning for a fee. How would that work?
- I'd like to do a job rotation or undertake a secondment. How might that work?
- What external organizations or associations would you recommend I connect into?

- I'd like to learn more in ___ skill area—what would you recommend?

- What would you recommend about keeping my skills sharp?

- What internal and external relationships do you think are important for me to invest in?

- What do you think the biggest challenges are for my position right now?

- Who would you recommend I connect with?

- What skills do the most highly performing staff exhibit?

- What other pieces of advice do you have for me?

FIELD WORK—NOW WHAT?

From informal learning to formal learning to on-the-job learning, there are many ways we can engage with and absorb information. Take time this week to identify the key skills you want to learn, and in what way. Explore the learning opportunities which exist. Ask your mentor what they have learned which has served them best.

Get clear input from your leader and peers around *what to do*, *where to go*, and *who to know*.

Identify the skills needed to thrive in your work. Determine core skills for Month One, Quarter One, and Year One.

_____

_____

_____

_____

Add a learning component to your work—write it down as part of your One-Page Plan, or develop a One-Page Plan for learning for the year.

Make a list of the different learning events you are currently tapping into.

_____

_____

_____

_____

What other learning options do you want to explore?

_____

_____

_____

_____

What new learning will help you get ahead?

_____

_____

_____

_____

New skills might include knowledge in related fields, skills in emotional intelligence, and skills identified throughout the book. *Activity:* Make a list of the skills-based learning you want to undertake this year. What do you notice?

On-the-go learning might also include job shadowing (which can be done virtually), mentoring, and e-learning courses, as well as industry learning events. What types of courses are going to help you keep learning?

A wide variety of different courses can help you get ahead. Consider what is available to you as part of your organization, and also what can be considered towards any professional development for credentials you hold. Is there an intersect with these and with what jobs are available in your organization? Take a look at any job postings available online, and consider what new skills you want to have.

As another activity, do a skills audit for what you currently have and what you want to have in the future:

SKILLS I CURRENTLY USE EVERY DAY IN MY WORK	SKILLS I WANT TO CULTIVATE

Choose from the following, plus any other skills you consider relevant:

- Generic skills
- Communication
- Conflict management
- Relationships building
- Emotional intelligence
- Influence
- Collaboration
- Project management
- Intercultural effectiveness
- Technology
- Program design
- Organizing
- Service delivery
- Marketing
- Financial

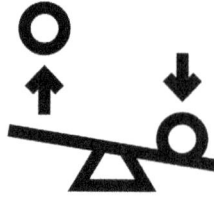

DAY 52

HIGH-LEVERAGE ACTIVITIES

"Productivity is never an accident. It is always the result of a commitment to excellence, intelligent planning, and focused effort."
—Paul J. Meyer

FOCUS QUESTION:

What are the high-leverage activities you engage in?

WHAT?

In any given day, the remote professional will have a wide variety of tasks which need to get done.

Getting in the practice of identifying high-leverage activities can ensure that the most important things get done first. Stephen Covey referred to this as the Big Rocks. You might have 3–5 big rocks that need to get done first, so that you can then focus on the smaller things.

What you need to know:

- What are your boss's priorities?
- What are the priorities of the team right now?
- What are you good at?
- Where do you need to put more attention?

Identify the top 3–5 list each week. Keep this visible and in front of you.

High-Leverage Activities

Consider the high-leverage activities for yourself, which might include:

- Mentoring
- Coaching
- Meeting with your boss
- Planning
- Networking
- Presenting to a professional association
- Time with peers
- Networking
- Reviewing things online
- Turning off notifications including Slack

Focus on *need to know, nice to know*, and *where to go*.

Originally from Master Trainer Bob Pike (www.BobPikeGroup.com), this is a useful framework which can help us cut through huge volumes of information. Originating in the training and performance improvement sphere, it helps us focus on what's important.

SO WHAT?

As I wrote in *PlanDoTrack*:

1. **Focus when you can, even if it is for a short while.** Productivity is not always about the long haul; it can also be about the short burst of focused effort. This is especially true in my world, where I am regularly juggling roles, hats, responsibilities, and clients. As much as I would love to have huge swaths of time to undertake my work, it's unlikely. Therefore, focused bursts of work, coupled with #2 below, help me (and the business) keep moving!

2. **Be clear on the top 3–5 goals for the day, week, and month**. My world was the world of contingency planning on steroids, so being clear on what top 3 or 4 to-dos were for the day, or the week, or the month, created a powerful anchor to planning, and also allowed me to feel satisfied when not *everything* on the list got done (which was almost every day).

WHERE TO GO?

- For more on this topic, refer to the Time Management Tips listed in Day 18 Time Management and Staying at Peak.

- Refer to *PlanDoTrack*.

FIELD WORK—NOW WHAT?

Take time, today and every day, to identify the top 3–5 activities which need to get done:

1.

2.

3.

4.

5.

Have your top 3–5 goals visible on a daily, weekly and/or monthly basis. If you have a copy of *PlanDoTrack*, be sure to complete the top 5 boxes of the different planning tools.

NOTES AND REFLECTIONS:

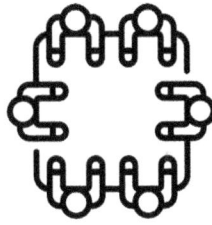

DAY 53

MEETINGS 101

"The meetings can be a lot of fun or they can be frustrating."
—Bob Weir

FOCUS QUESTION:
How much time did you spend in your meetings?
What's going to make them most effective?

WHAT?

Research completed in 2016 found that professionals can spend upwards of 40% of their time in meetings. This ballooned during the pandemic! In 2021, a Microsoft survey, found:

- An increase in time of 148% in meetings (according to time spent in Microsoft Teams)
- 40.6 billion increase in emails delivered between February 2021 versus February 2020
- 45% increase in weekly Teams Chats per person
- 66% increase in people working on Office documents[79]

Think about your last week; how much time did you spend in meetings, either in person or virtually? Getting better at the strategic use of time is critical

Tips for Meetings:

- Ask yourself the eight meeting questions found in today's text box.

- Have a focus

- Log in early

- Keep to time, or even end a few minutes early so people have breathing space

- Identify the important components of the meeting.

As I went to write *Effective Virtual Conversations* back in 2016–2017, I was curious about how much time people were spending in meetings. If anything, the quantity and duration of meetings has increased rather than decreased in recent years. From face-to-face meetings to ones where some are in a room and others are virtual, meetings can take up the majority of people's time if we let them. What are you doing to ensure you are maximizing your meeting time?

8 Essential Meeting Questions

Before any meeting (internal or external), be sure to ask the following questions:

1. What's the purpose?

2. What takeaways do we want?

3. Who needs to be on the call?

4. What preparation is needed for us to be most effective in the meeting?

5. What pace to do we want in order to keep it engaging?

6. What will help keep the focus?

7. What's absolutely essential, versus what will be nice to cover, or where people can go for more information around topics?

8. What follow up might be required?

(Excerpt from Britton, *Effective Virtual Conversations*, 2017, p. 304)

SO WHAT?

As you set out to strengthen your meeting processes, ask yourself:

1. **Is it a meeting that's really necessary?** We often think we need to meet for meeting's sake. Is a meeting really necessary, or can it be covered in another way?

2. **What is the purpose of the meeting?** Is it to provide information? Invite discussion? Make a decision? Brainstorm? Coordinate across the team? Support learning? These are all very different reasons to hold meetings. Consider *what* is the purpose of the meeting, and then *what* the best platform is, and *who* should be at the table. Does it even need to be a face-to-face meeting, or can it be completed some other way? For example, a learning event may be offsite or on WebEx/Zoom or other.

3. **What outcome are we looking for?** Without a clear direction, meetings can derail quickly. Has the outcome been circulated beforehand, so people can prepare with whatever is needed? As well, are they able to build in time based on the outcome?

4. **What involvement are we asking for?** Helping frame expectations is another key part of the process.

5. **What can and should be done, prior to the call?** Is there any preparatory work attendees need to do, or information they need to bring? Provide sufficient time and warning before the meeting for them to complete this. Then remind them of it before the call.

6. **Create regular feedback loops and agreements to make sure that the meeting is covering what you want it to cover.** Taking time to create agreements on how the meeting will run is important. While some organizations scoff at having ground rules for meetings, creating shared agreements with those you are meeting with regularly creates a culture where people own the meeting and are active participants. (Source: *PlanDoTrack* blog)

7. **Stream where possible to help everyone keep a focus.** Multitasking is the bane of any virtual meeting. Seeing each other eyeball to eyeball helps to maximize focus and minimize the urge to engage in multiple other tasks while you are meeting.

8. **Use platforms which facilitate dialogue and engagement.** Choose platforms that let you screen share, so you can each input and share pertinent information from your devices. Many platforms allow you to move into breakouts for smaller group discussion, and several offer the use of whiteboards or annotation to capture information and decisions made. Many platforms also provide a recording function that can also help to streamline record keeping. Virtual meetings don't have to be a bore.

9. **What follow-up is needed?** One reason many meetings get poor reviews is because no follow-up or concrete action flows out of the meeting. Spend a few minutes highlighting the key takeaways, actions, and timelines, along with who is responsible for taking action. In many platforms, chat logs are recorded. A quick way to remind people of the meeting outcomes and responsibilities is to have someone type these items into chat while the meeting is taking place. Everyone attending can validate these agreements, reducing the need for a lengthy back-and-forth on what's been decided and who is going to do what. Depending on the formality and requirements of your organization, the chat log can serve as some, or all, of the meeting notes.

10. **Finally, is a meeting really what is needed?** We host virtual meetings for a variety of reasons—to share information, provide updates, brainstorm new ideas, problem solve, or plan. Let people know what type of meeting they are coming to attend, rather than assuming that they know.

Setting everyone up for success is a key principle for virtual work. What's going to help maximize the impact and effectiveness of your next meeting?

FIELD WORK—NOW WHAT?

Consider the one or two things you can be doing to make your meetings more productive and efficient:

_____

_____

_____

_____

Quick hacks to make your meetings more productive

TYPE OF MEETING	PURPOSE	HACKS/KEEP IN MIND
Project meetings	Status updates and making sure everyone on the team is on the same page	Status updates Red, Yellow, Green
Three-way meetings	Feedback loops between multiple teams	Three-way meetings are often over-looked in matrix management but are an important part of keeping things flowing.
Feedback	Feedback	Feedback conversations need to be specific and regular. Feedback is only useful if it is close to the event. (More on feedback coming in Day 58.)
Status meetings	Updates on how projects are going	Status conversations need to be specific and regular. Status information is only useful if it is close to the event

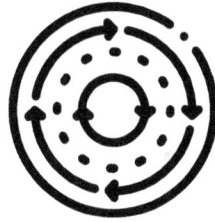

GET IT DONE: CONSISTENT ACTION

"Small disciplines repeated with consistency every day lead to great achievements gained slowly over time."
—John C. Maxwell

FOCUS QUESTION:
What actions help with consistency?

WHAT?

Consistency in business is important. Consistency in the remote space is essential, and even more so in an era of disruption. As things ebb and flow, consistent action can level out.

In today's noisy social space, it may take longer for things to be heard or seen. Part of consistency may not be doing more; it may be repurposing things. So, if you have developed something of value, for example, an article, could it be repurposed into something else? A great example of this is an article I wrote for the Coaching Tools Company. Over the span of six or seven years, I wrote thirty articles for them. Many of these were repurposed from blog posts, videos, and other media.

Consistency also builds trust. It signals, "I can be relied upon. I am here for you in the long run."

What things do you want to do on a consistent basis?

- Reaching out to your boss and other peers you need to relate to
- Scheduling meetings with stakeholders
- Reviewing your metrics
- Getting out of the office for energizing or working out
- Focusing on both *results* and *relationships*

90-DAY GUIDE FOR SUCCESS | DAY 54 | 323

- Following through
- Creating content
- Sharing something in the social space—do a series rather than a one-off

What activities can you focus on in terms of creating more consistency?

Get it Done!

One of the most important tasks you have as a remote worker is to *get things done*. Set your timer and see what you can do in 15 minutes or less.

- Clean up your office
- File your materials
- Back up your drive
- Draft the email you've been putting off
- Do some research
- Focus on your accounting/receipts
- Place an order

Sprint or Marathon?

What type of flow is best – sprint or marathon? Consider these items:

Marathons—Everyone moves at their own pace. What can you do to build up your capacity to focus and work? The energy of a marathon is different than what's required for a sprint. Where are you building muscle mass? Where are you training to go for the long haul?

Areas we may need to go into the long haul as a remote worker:
- Longer term projects
- Creating our body of work

Sprints are useful:
- With projects
- With tackling big pieces of work in intensive components

SO WHAT?

IN FOCUS—21-FOR-21 VIRTUAL CO-WORKING SPRINTS

One of the series I undertook this year was the *21-for-21 Virtual Co-Working Sprints*. This series provided 21 minutes of focused co-working each day, geared to get people moving and into action in very focused bursts. One of the greatest benefits raised by others from this was the momentum that people created while undertaking the sprints, leading to getting more done with a boost of motivation. What is important for you to do on a consistent basis?

FIELD WORK—NOW WHAT?

What consistent action do you want to be undertaking?

_____

_____

_____

_____

What projects do you want to get done?

_____

_____

_____

_____

NOTES AND REFLECTIONS:

DAY 55

COLLABORATION

"Alone we can do so little; together we can do so much."
—Helen Keller

FOCUS QUESTION:

Where can partnering or collaboration support you in creating
a better product or delivering a better service?

WHAT?

As a solopreneur, we may hold a myth that "I need to do it all alone." While you may be choosing to run a solopreneur company, it may not mean that you have to do everything alone. Maybe you are building a team of part-time or full-time workers or are looking to bring different people onboard as subcontractors for specific projects. Regardless, being able to build your team is critical.

The benefit of collaboration is that 1 + 1 = 3. Translation: we are able to create more by working together than by working alone.

At the heart of collaboration are the following behaviors:

- Trust
- Candor
- Connection
- Flexibility
- Self-awareness
- Working across differences
- Relationship development

As you grow your team, key themes to explore include:

- What do you want to delegate, and to whom? Check out posts on the *Teams365* blog on delegation for additional inspiration and information on this topic.

- What does "grow your team" mean? Is it a full-time, part-time, or subcontractor role?

- What type of support do you need? Spend time today making a list of everything you need.

SO WHAT?

Just like many other activities in the remote space, it can be important to plan for your collaboration. You will want to set intentional meetings before, during, and afterwards to discuss some of the questions you'll find in the text box.

As a team we also need to collaborate—with each other and across our team, as well as with others outside of the team.

Consider these questions:[80]

- What do we need in order to excel?

- What will help us be at our best?

- What is going to be the major challenge for the year ahead? The major opportunity?

- What development opportunities do we want to build in (retreats, team coaching, mentoring etc.)?

- What requests do I need to make of you right now?

- How will we measure our success?

And, as a bonus:

1. What will help to expedite or magnify what's working?

PARTNERSHIP AND COLLABORATION QUESTIONS TO CONSIDER

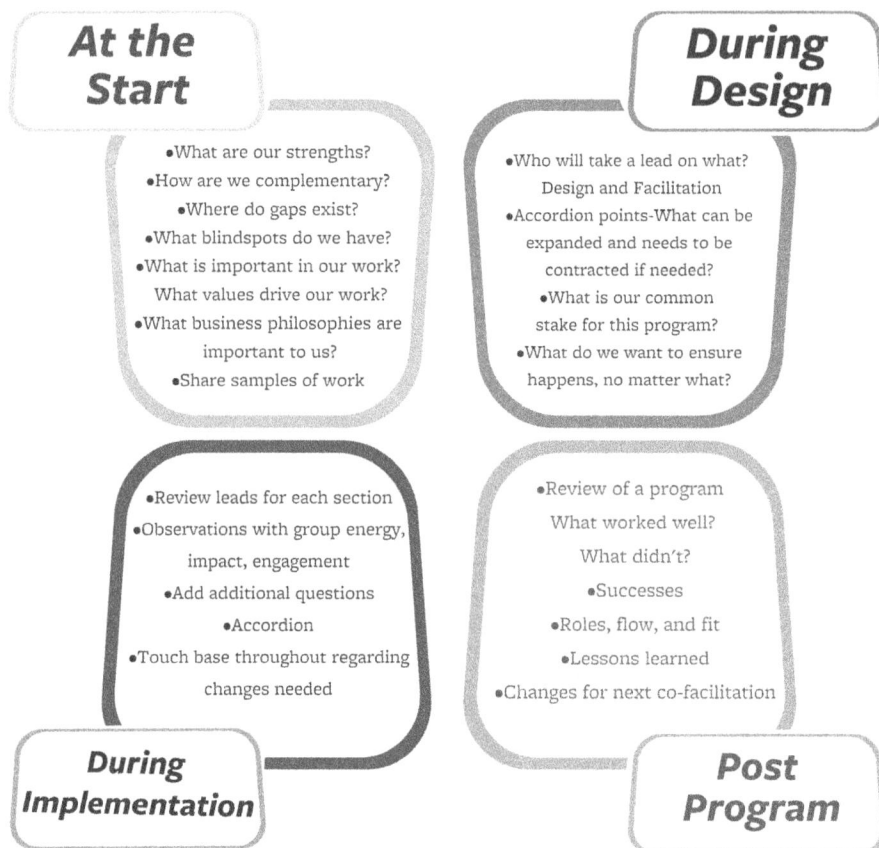

At the Start

- What are our strengths?
- How are we complementary?
- Where do gaps exist?
- What blindspots do we have?
- What is important in our work? What values drive our work?
- What business philosophies are important to us?
- Share samples of work

During Design

- Who will take a lead on what? Design and Facilitation
- Accordion points-What can be expanded and needs to be contracted if needed?
- What is our common stake for this program?
- What do we want to ensure happens, no matter what?

During Implementation

- Review leads for each section
- Observations with group energy, impact, engagement
- Add additional questions
- Accordion
- Touch base throughout regarding changes needed

Post Program

- Review of a program What worked well? What didn't?
- Successes
- Roles, flow, and fit
- Lessons learned
- Changes for next co-facilitation

Partnership Questions

- What do I bring to this partnership?
- What strengths and talents do they bring?
- Together, what is possible?
- What's important to both of us in terms of getting things done?

FIELD WORK—NOW WHAT?

What does self-awareness mean? It means knowing our strengths and areas for improvement, as well as what the triggers are for us—these get magnified.

This may mean exploring different skills in the areas of personal development and relationship management.

What things do you want to put more attention around?

_____

_____

_____

_____

_____

_____

_____

_____

What are the questions to ask at each stage of your partnership process?

_____

_____

_____

_____

NOTES AND REFLECTIONS:

TEAM IN FOCUS: TOOLS IN YOUR TOOLBOX

"Talent wins games, but teamwork and intelligence win championships."
—Michael Jordan

FOCUS QUESTION:
What's going to help you thrive as a team?

WHAT?

Throughout the Guide there have been many questions, tools, and processes which you may consider.

Teams, and members of teams, can thrive when they have the right tools in their toolbox. In our remote professional toolkit, we will want to have resources which include:

- Tools such as the prioritization matrix
- Planning tools for individual planning
- Project management planning
- Team planning tools
- Communication tools
- Presentation tools
- Productivity tools
- Communication tools
- Strengths-based resources
- Measurement tools or metrics

Where to Go

For inspiration around team development, check out websites including:

- MindTools.com

- BetterTeam.com/team-building-activities

Mantras to operate by

TRUST + CONNECTION = Great Teams

FOCUS + PASSION = Great Virtual Professional, Business Leader, or Owner

SO WHAT?

Teams move through phases, and they can move up and down the staircase of phases in terms of focus and needs. When needs are not met, teams are likely to cycle back down to a lower level. What do you know about your team's needs right now? What do you need in the Forming, Storming, Norming, Performing, and Adjourning phases of team development? Refer to Chapters 3 and 4 in *Reconnecting Workspaces* for more on this topic, or search to learn more about Tuckman's Model of Group Development.

In addition to this, there are five other areas you will want to build tools in.

Area A: Activities/resources to help the team to get to know each other

- *What's outside your window?* As I wrote in Effective Virtual Conversations, we often only see people in their screen but aren't able to see what's beyond the screen. Have people share what's outside their window or call in from a different location so you can learn more about their context.

- *A fun opener/icebreaker (3–5 minutes).* Spend this time in your next team meeting so people can get to know each other better.

Area B: Tools to help with focus and prioritization

One challenge of being part of a matrix is the fact that you are often part of many different teams, with competing priorities.

Two useful prioritization tools are the Urgent/Important Matrix (Eisenhower principle) and the Action Priority Matrix. These are covered in *Reconnecting Workspaces* Chapter 18 on Personal Productivity and Time Management.

Minimizing the impact of digital distraction is a key issue for teams today. See what I had to say about reducing digital distractions at my *Teams365* blog post #2340 at https://www.potentialsrealized.com/teams-365-blog/teams365-2340-remote-productivity-tip-reducing-distractions-in-the-remote-space.

Several different tools which help team members focus in the virtual space include:

- The Urgent/Important Matrix (Also known as the Covey Eisenhower principle)
- Strategic Issues Mapping
- SWOT, the trusty strategic planning tool

Area C: Helping teams connect

Helping teams connect with who is who and who is working on what is of critical importance to a remote team. It's an area we often don't think about on the surface, sometimes given the diversity of roles and locations. It can be very useful in the medium and long term to facilitate regular conversations with the team around who is doing what, and to also earmark time for the team to regularly connect and get to know each other. Discussion in this area might include[81]:

- Undertaking inventory of projects people are working on, so that lessons learned can be shared.
- Identifying key strengths and experience bases which exist in the team—there may even be a "go to" team resource person around different areas—i.e., technology questions, or around different themes/focus areas team members work on, etc.
- Short team openers and closers such as Bingo, with team members asked to find someone who [insert different categories, such as has visited 3 different continents, speaks multiple languages, is a twin, etc.)

Area D: Planning tools

A fourth area to consider is that of planning tools. On a personal planning level, you will want to consider what the best level of planning is. For some it's annual, monthly, quarterly, or weekly. Do you have a quarterly One-Page Plan where you can keep your high-level goals over the period of a week?

Planning within your top 3–5goals can be important for you in terms of identifying core elements to keep an eye on. Whether these items get attention first or you schedule out blocks for them, you will want to experiment with them.

On a team planning level, bringing people together regularly—i.e., biweekly or weekly, along with a focus on this quarterly and annually—will help keep your teams aligned. You will also want to make sure you are updating systems regularly, and always consider what needs to get updated and shared across the team.

Area E: Communication and planning

Communication tools can vary dramatically. Look at the communication area. In brief, team members will want to make sure they are focused on items including email, instant messaging, text, etc. What are the preferences, and what are the *boundaries*?

Areas for presentations include Zoom, Skype, and engagement tools such as polling (Poll Everywhere, Miro, Mural).

FIELD WORK—NOW WHAT?

Identify what you want to focus on and add to your toolbox so you thrive in the remote and hybrid space.

_____

_____

_____

_____

_____

_____

_____

_____

_____

NOTES AND REFLECTIONS:

THIS WEEK'S FOUNDATION THEME WAS
FOCUSING AND GETTING THINGS DONE

Congratulations! You are now through the first eight weeks of your role. What was it like? Describe it here in three words:

_____ . _____ . _____

Topics we covered this week were:

- Day 50—Mindset
- Day 51—Ongoing Learning
- Day 52—High Leverage Activities
- Day 53—Meetings 101
- Day 54—Get it Done: Consistent Action
- Day 55—Collaboration
- Day 56—Teams in Focus: Tools in Your Toolbox

Wrap up theme:

_____

_____

_____

_____

What are you looking forward to?

_____

_____

_____

_____

What questions do you have?

_____

_____

_____

_____

What To-Dos have surfaced? (List your top 3–5)

1.

2.

3.

4.

5.

Update your tracking sheet!

WEEK 9 · ADDITIONAL CONVERSATIONS TO HAVE

"One good conversation can shift the direction of change forever."
—Linda Lambert

Business happens through relationships and conversations. Conversations take a variety of forms in the remote and hybrid space, ranging from verbal dialogue to meetings to chats and instant messaging.

You will have ongoing conversations with your boss, peers, and stakeholders, as well as mentoring and coaching conversations. This week we explore additional conversations every remote and hybrid team member needs to have:

- Day 57—Virtual Conversation Skills
- Day 58—Feedback
- Day 59—Difficult Conversations
- Day 60—Troubleshooting and Month Two Check-In
- Day 61—Pitfalls
- Day 62—Negotiation
- Day 63—When Are You at Your Best? Circadian Rhythm

Relationships are critical in the remote space. What is going to help you as a remote worker? What things are going to get in the way of your productivity?

Conversations are going to help you with clarity, insights, and actions in a variety of settings, including:

- Matrix relationships (*See Day 28*)
- Role clarity—what your job is and isn't
- Task clarity—what you need to do, and *not* Do

As we get moving into Week 9, write down your top 3 goals for the week, and be sure to use the daily tracker to capture additional notes:

WHAT ARE YOUR TOP 3 GOALS THIS WEEK?:

1. _____

2. _____

3. _____

By the end of the week I want to be sure that . . .

_____

NOTES AND REFLECTIONS:

VIRTUAL CONVERSATION SKILLS

"To effectively communicate, we must realize that we are all different in the way we perceive the world and use this understanding as a guide to our communication with others."
—Tony Robbins

FOCUS QUESTION:

What type of virtual conversations do you want to have?

WHAT?

> The oxygen of the remote workspace
> is a great virtual conversation. —Jennifer Britton

In my book, *Effective Virtual Conversations*, I explored the nine most common types of virtual conversations, varying across formality and whether it's an individual focus or peer focus.

In conversation, it is important to create a two-way conversation. It should be a dialogue, which means two. The varied tools available in the virtual conversation space can support a conversation. Today we will be looking at elements which can be incorporated, regardless of the type of conversation you want to have.

5 Engagement Levers™

Effective Virtual Conversations
©Jennifer Britton. All Rights Reserved. 2020

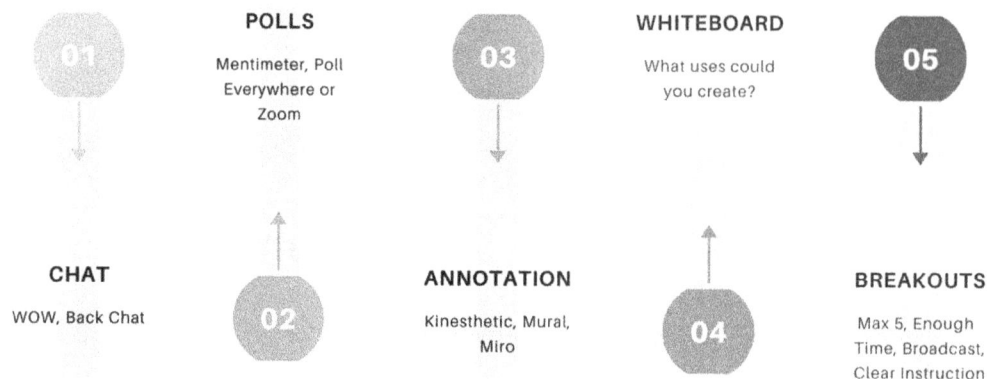

01

POLLS

Mentimeter, Poll Everywhere or Zoom

03

WHITEBOARD

What uses could you create?

05

CHAT

WOW, Back Chat

02

ANNOTATION

Kinesthetic, Mural, Miro

04

BREAKOUTS

Max 5, Enough Time, Broadcast, Clear Instruction

The Five Engagement Levers™ available to you are:

- Polling
- Chat
- Breakouts
- Whiteboards
- Annotation

How are you using each one of these to make your call more engaging?

Check out *Reconnecting Workspaces* for more on this topic.

Polling Resources

Polls are a great way to find out what people are thinking, especially in large groups. Check out these resources to boost your interactivity in virtual conversations:

- Mentimeter
- Poll Anywhere
- AsktheAudience
- Kahoot
- Internal Polling functions in Zoom

Check out the *Effective Virtual Conversations* tips around polling which have been shared over at the *Teams365* blog at Potentials Realized.com. Check them out.

SO WHAT?

One of the areas I know is super-challenging to get used to is virtual calls. For teams who were used to being together, here are a few things you may want to keep in mind:

1. **Make everyone virtual.** Rather than trying to jam people into one space, invite everyone to dial in from their own device. That way you all have an equal voice, and no one is left out because they can't hear or see the person presenting.

2. **Give people permission to move around.** I've had a large number of people new to streaming say that they felt uncomfortable. While it may take time to get used to seeing yourself on the screen, give people permission to move around during the call. It's only human. We don't want to make the saying that "sitting is the new smoking" come true.

3. **Experiment with what is possible.** Each week or month, try to do something different. Be sure to leverage the Five Engagement Levers™, to ensure that all voices are in the room.

4. **Use breakouts and other engagement techniques.** As a group, you don't all need to be together for an entire call. There may be opportunities for you to be in different types of conversations along the way. What breakouts and focus areas can you create?

5. **Use polls on phones and the platform to take a pulse check of where the group is.**

FIELD WORK—NOW WHAT?

Consider what's going to boost your virtual conversations. Explore these resources and add at least one component to the conversation.

NOTES AND REFLECTIONS:

FEEDBACK

"There is no failure. Only feedback"
—Robert Allan

FOCUS QUESTION:

What feedback do you want to receive? How? How do your colleagues want to receive feedback?

WHAT?

Feedback conversations in the remote space may feel different, given that we don't see people in action. Great feedback is linked to trust and connection and is grounded around what success could look like. Virtual feedback can feel trickier, especially if you don't know your colleagues well.

Good books on the topic of feedback include the following:

- *Thanks for the Feedback* by Douglas Stone and Sheila Heen
- *Difficult Conversations* by Bruce Patton, Douglas Stone, and Sheila Heen
- *Radical Candor* by Kim Scott
- *Fierce Conversations* by Susan Scott

SO WHAT?

Keep in mind that, in general, feedback is useful when it is:

- Specific,

- Focused on observable behaviors, and

- Provided as close to the event as possible.

For the past several years, I have been sharing what I call the REVET model to feedback. It helps to shape both preparation for and implementation of feedback conversations.

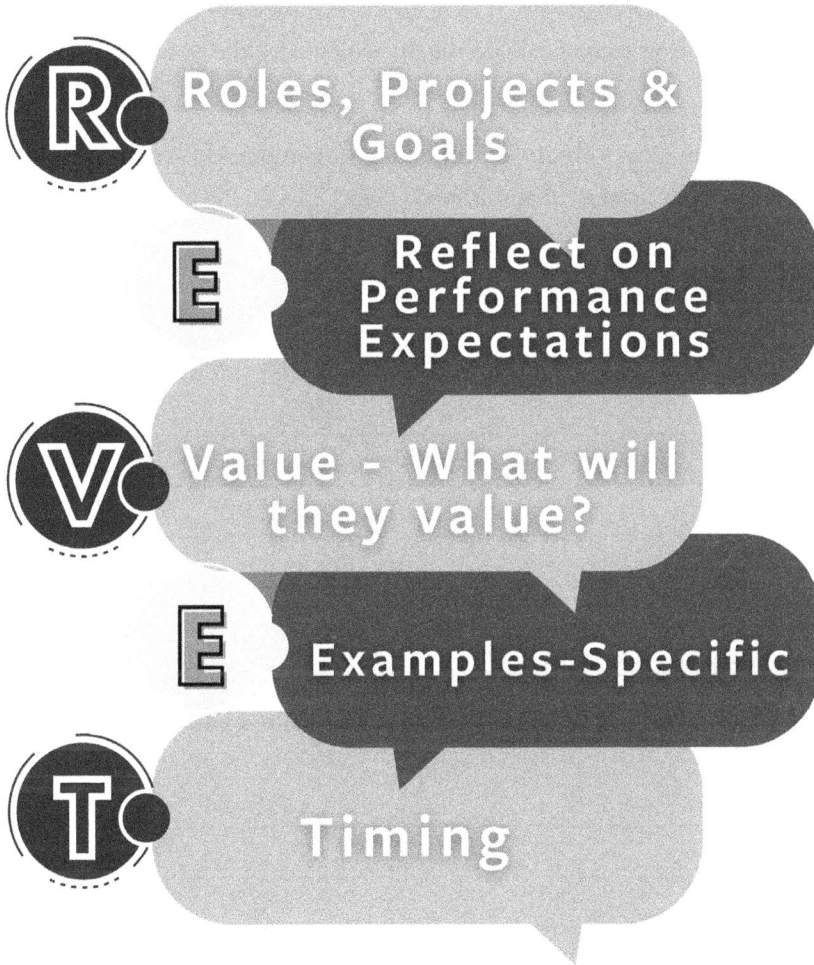

In preparing for feedback, consider:

R—Roles, projects, and goals. What are the roles the person inhabits, and what projects are they involved with? What are their goals? Considering these questions helps us to make sure that feedback is relevant to them.

E—Reflect on performance expectations. What expectations are set about performance? What does success look like? What key issues are they focused on, and most likely value feedback around?

V—Value. What do they value? Think about the style of the person you are speaking to. Some people value feedback delivered frequently and "off the cuff." Other team members may prefer feedback offered in a structured fashion, or in writing, with a time lapse between receiving the feedback and then having the performance conversation. If you have not yet thought about feedback, now is the time.

E—Examples. When have you seen this occur? What examples do you have? Providing specific examples is absolutely essential for an effective performance conversation. These need to be specific examples you have personally witnessed. If they aren't, you may not be the right person to provide feedback in that manner. You could facilitate the discussion with the person and those who see them every day, one on one.

T—Timing. What is the most appropriate time for the conversation—mid-morning? Lunchtime? Evening? What distractions need to be minimized?

FIELD WORK—NOW WHAT?

What type of feedback is important for you in your work?

_____

_____

_____

_____

Who do you need to design feedback with?

_____

_____

_____

_____

Work through the REVET model as you prepare for a conversation with them.

After preparing for the conversation, you want to *have* the conversation.

A final consideration is follow-up. When will you follow up and check in to see what action has been taken, and what you can do to follow-up?

_____

_____

_____

_____

_____

_____

_____

_____

Tool: Use the REVET model below:

ROLES, Projects and Goals

_____

_____

Reflect on Performance **EXPECTATIONS**

_____

_____

What will they **VALUE**?

_____

_____

Provide **EXAMPLES** of when you saw this in action:

_____

_____

When is the best **TIME** to have this conversation?

_____

_____

NOTES AND REFLECTIONS:

DIFFICULT CONVERSATIONS

"All faults may be forgiven of him who has perfect candor."
—Walt Whitman

FOCUS QUESTION:
In order to do your best work, what issues need to be raised?

WHAT?

It is not uncommon for disagreements and conflict to get "swept under the rug" in the remote space. The danger is that these issues have a tendency to fester and grow and often become something much bigger than they originally were.

In today's focus, we are going to explore the topic of difficult conversations.

Kim Scott's book, *Radical Candor*, hit the bestseller list back in 2017. According to Scott, *Radical Candor* is all about being firm and kind in providing feedback.

Sharing Our Stories

Taking time to share our stories has one of the most significant influences. Our stories demonstrate our *Why*—the thing that drives us forward. Our stories also are a unique tapestry of *Who* we are, our DNA, our journey, our aspirations and hopes, our learning and moments of defeat.

Our stories help to translate/transmit who we are, and what we take a stand for. Our stories will signal where we put our foot down, where we say no.

Sharing our stories creates connection and creates a common ground.

Stories are part of a collective global process. What things do you want to communicate?

How can the team also share their stories? What might they do as a collective?

Create a collaborative story. What is possible when you co-create stories with others?

What does success mean for you?

SO WHAT?

Rather than leaving difficult conversations to resolve themselves, it can be useful to be proactive in addressing them. Here are three things you can do:

Script it out—rather than let things run through your head (which tend to loop back time and time again), spend a few minutes writing it out. Think about what you would say if you sat down with them virtually to have a conversation. Write out what you would say. What's at the core of this? What is it that you need to articulate?

Practice the 24-hour rule—don't respond right away. Sleep on it. Draft out a message and then review it with clear eyes in the morning. Does it capture what you want to say? Is there something that is going to come back and haunt you later in the process?

Find the release valve—what is going to get this off your chest? What will help you come to resolution or peace around this issue?

Always keep the end in mind—just like new drivers in snow are taught to "always keep an eye to your end result." What are you aiming for in terms of an outcome with this conversation? What's important?

FIELD WORK—NOW WHAT?

What elements are important to be more direct about? More candid?

_____

_____

_____

_____

_____

_____

You may find that these are a feedback conversation or a different conversation. Using the tools included throughout this guide, prepare for the conversation, keeping in mind the end results you want to achieve.

NOTES AND REFLECTIONS:

DAY 60

TROUBLESHOOTING

"A problem well put is half solved."
—John Dewey

WHAT?

Troubleshooting is a fundamental skillset for all remote team members. The role of the leader often becomes that of troubleshooter, helping team members identify and work through solutions to the issues facing them.

One useful tool can be the Problem Tree approach, using a series of questions to get to the core of an issue. Robert Mager is well known for this approach. Take a look in *Reconnecting Workspaces* at the Problem Tree shared around performance issues.

The Problem Tree: Each time you have a challenge, you'll be able to rely on problem solving. When facing a challenge there are different approaches you can use. Consider these:

- Do nothing—ignore and hope it goes away

- Hit it head on—the relationship or result is important

- Stand your ground—the outcome/result is important

- Let them move ahead—your relationship is important

- Take on a perspective of race cars—another way to approach conflict and crisis

What else is important to note about the approaches you want to undertake?

What to, do when?
The Performance Analysis Flow Diagram

What's the Problem? — Can we Apply Fast Fixes? — Other Factors — Do they Already Know How? — Are there more clues? — Select and Implement Solutions

Does the performance concern you? — Expectations Clear? — Is the environment supportive? — Genuine Skill Deficiency? — Can task be Made Easier? — Select Best Solution (s)

Yes — Describe Discrepancy

NO — Clarify Expectations
Yes — Resources Adequate?

NO — What gets rewarded?
Yes — Address Situational Issues

Yes Not Sure — Did it in the past?

NO — Any Other Obstacles?
Yes — Simplify Task

Draft Action Plan

Is it Worth Solving?

NO — Provide Resources
Yes — Performance Quality Visible

NO — What other issues are impacting
Yes — Identify Behavior

Yes — Used Often
NO

NO — Person has Potential to Change
Yes — Remove Obstacles

Implement and Monitor

Worth Pursuing? (What's the cost?)

NO — Provide Feedback?
Yes — Problem Sufficiently Solved?

NO — Identify

Yes — Provide Feedback
NO — Provide Practice

NO — Replace Person

Yes — Train

Done

NO

Done

Yes — Problem Sufficiently Solved?

Yes — Done

NO

Yes

Adapted from The Center for Effective Performance © 1997

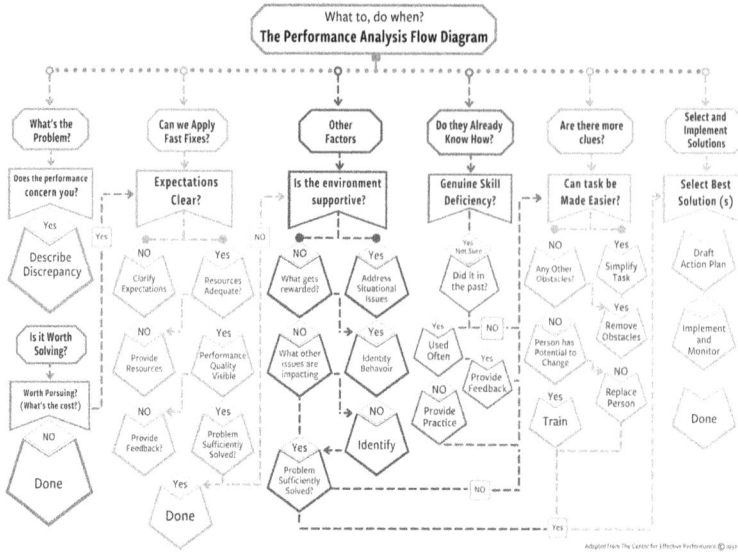

Perhaps at this point, two-thirds into the 90-day process, you thought that things would flow. You thought you had hit the Dip already, but here is another one! Whether it's a relationship that has broken down, technology and work approaches that aren't working, or a boss from hell, there are likely to be ongoing things that put you down the rabbit hole.

Motivational Dips

One of the pitfalls you can face is around motivation. Motivational dips are an area not everyone knows how to address. Some strategies for this include the following:

- Note where you are. Know that it's a place that needs attention, but don't over-dwell. Don't let it tap out all of your energy or focus. Be sure to move things forward.

- Do some shadowing with a team member and see what they are doing.

- Have a change of scenery—sometimes we get in our own rut.

- Leave it and let it simmer—Einstein always said that brilliance happens when we least expect it.

- Do a checkpoint—see what you've accomplished, and note where you need to go.

- Take a break!

SO WHAT?

Just like Dewey's quote inspires, now is the time to pull together all your resources to figure out what you can do to get out of the hole.

- Is there a conversation you want to have with your mentor?

- Who else can you call on for advice?

- What are the difficult conversations you need to have?

- What can you lean into and rely on?

- What else is important to note about this issue?

- What past experience can you rely on?

- What resources can you tap into?

- What's the horn or signal you want to make when you need assistance?

FIELD WORK—NOW WHAT?

Take a current problem you are facing and work through the problem tree.

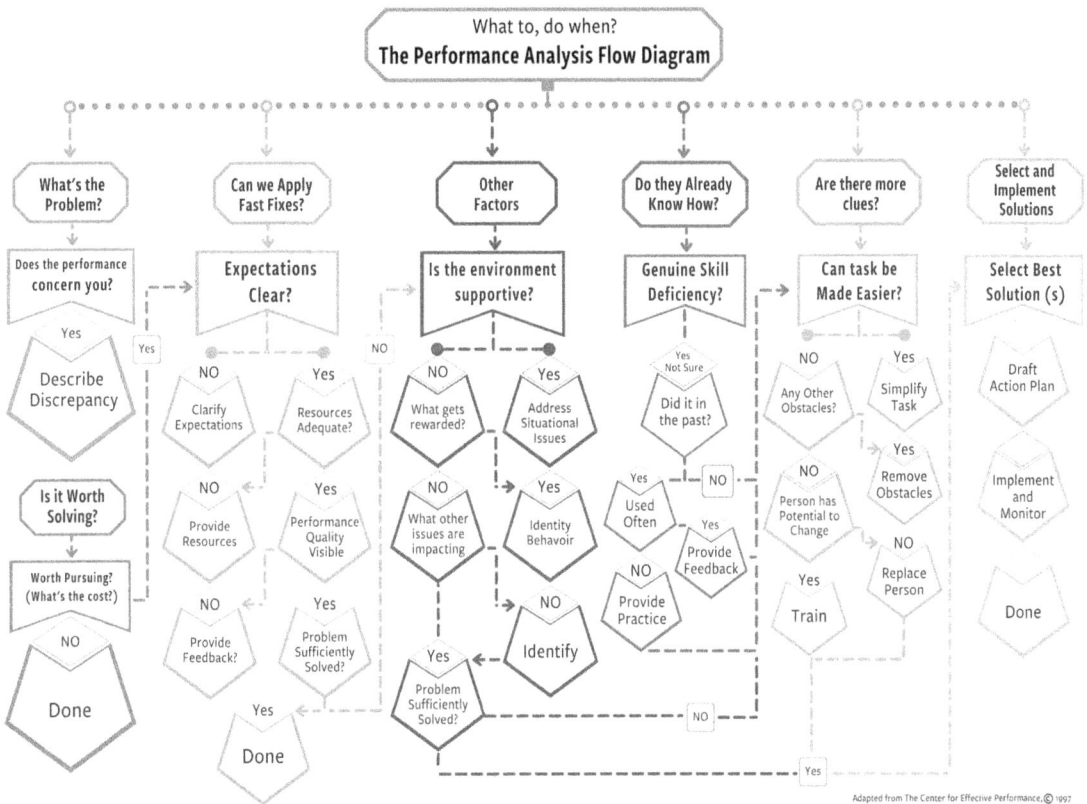

What to, do when?
The Performance Analysis Flow Diagram

Adapted from The Center for Effective Performance,© 1997

NOTES AND REFLECTIONS:

MONTH TWO CHECK-IN

We started this process two months ago. Use this worksheet as a quick pulse check to see how things are going.

What have been your key achievements this past month?

_____

_____

_____

_____

_____

What are the projects, tasks and activities you have:

Started

_____

_____

_____

_____

Completed

_____

_____

_____

_____

In process

_____

_____

_____

_____

What relationships have been critical to your success?

_____

_____

_____

_____

_____

_____

_____

_____

Which ones need attention?

_____

_____

_____

What has been your biggest learning?

_____

_____

_____

_____

_____

_____

_____

Mantras in the Remote Space—
Sound Bites to Be Reinforced

Some of the key mantras we may engage with are the following:

- Remote does not mean disconnected.

- Less is more!

- No person is an island.

- A few minutes of planning saves us an hour of unfocused effort.

- Avoid death by conference call.

- Go the extra mile.

Check out my YouTube Video on these at the Effective Virtual Conversations or Reconnecting Workspaces playlist. You will find my channel at www.youtube.com/EffectiveGroupCoach.

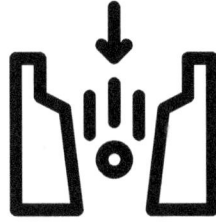

DAY 61
PITFALLS

"Life's journey is not traveled on a freeway devoid of obstacles, pitfalls, and snares. Rather, it is a pathway marked by forks and turnings. Decisions are constantly before us."
—Thomas S. Monson

FOCUS QUESTION:
What are the solutions to the pitfalls you might face?

WHAT?

Pitfalls happen every day. It is important to address these issues quickly.

- **Going rogue—doing your own thing.** Be sure to schedule regular one-on-ones to make sure you are up to the standard required. When it comes to getting things done, consider the milestones and checkpoints. It's often easier to meet more frequently at the start of a project or task to make sure you are on target.

- **Losing connection with the team.** Revisit the Six Layers of Connection and consider how you want to boost your connection across these layers.

- **Neglecting to continue to learn.** Things change quickly in the remote and hybrid world so be sure to keep on learning. As a team ask yourselves regularly about the best practices you are evolving and can share with others.

- **Losing motivation.** It can be inevitable that we lose motivation. This may happen at the Dip (see Day 39), or it may happen in the "messy middle" of a project (see Day 45). As shared in the text box in Day 60, consider what is going to get you out of a motivational dip.

- **Not getting feedback.** Have discussion with others about the type of feedback they are looking for. Be sure to do a debrief, post-mortem, or retrospective of important projects, as these can help you stay on track and focus on ongoing learning. This could be a great team conversation—what I need from you. What I would like from you.

- **Being culturally inappropriate.** This is a big pitfall in the virtual space, and sometimes we do things we don't even know are taboo. Have agreements for team members to share things (big and small) that are either taboo or welcomed in their culture. This could include things such as gift giving, meal etiquette, communication patterns, how to start meetings, the role of hierarchy, or how group or individually focused the culture is. Explore your biases and learn to note what you are needing further education or coaching around.

- **Not being sure of priorities.** Given that you may report into many different teams, losing sight of priorities can be a real concern for remote and hybrid teams. Is it time to call a three-way meeting? Is it time to use one of the prioritization tools? This could include one that ranks the impact and importance with feedback from leaders and members of both teams.

Getting Feedback

Feedback is a critical part of avoiding pitfalls. Ongoing feedback creates an environment of dialogue.

In my work, I use a three-step framework for feedback with peers to build an ongoing climate of dialogue and feedback. The three questions people comment on are:

1. What I appreciated . . . .

2. What I see as one of your strengths is . . . .

3. Next time, I'd suggest . . . .

Try this out as you provide feedback. Use this at the end of major projects. Cultivate an environment of appreciation and openness around what's working and what's not.

SO WHAT?

Questions to consider: What one thing will have the most impact if you don't do it right? What one might have the greatest ripple effect? Who else can advise you on this?

FIELD WORK—NOW WHAT?

Identify some of the key pitfalls you are facing.

_____

_____

_____

_____

_____

_____

_____

What's going to help?

_____

_____

_____

_____

_____

_____

_____

What are the conversations you need to have?

_____

_____

_____

_____

_____

_____

_____

DAY 62
NEGOTIATION

"Let us never negotiate out of fear. But let us never fear to negotiate."
—John Fitzgerald Kennedy

FOCUS QUESTION:
What things might you need to negotiate this week?

WHAT?

Negotiation is a core skill set for all employees in the remote space. Whether or not we are trying to get to a core understanding and focus, we want to be creating *win-win* solutions.

Negotiation takes place all the time, from asking for a raise to pushing back on tasks that we get asked to do.

At the heart of negotiation are several key premises, as outlined in the seminal book, *Getting to Yes*—

1.   What are your goals?

Focusing on underlying needs. What are your needs and goals in this conversation? This is often known as your position. What are the other parties' needs and goals in this conversation?

2.   What is your BATNA—Best Alternative to a Negotiated Agreement? What is the end result that you can live with?

What is the line in the sand you don't want to cross?

3.   What are the different perspectives? Think about the other person. What's important to them? What's important to you?

Tips for Successful Negotiations

Consider these tips when stepping into your next negotiation:

- Know who you are negotiating with. What is their position? What's important to them? What do they want to achieve?

- Ask open ended questions. These are likely to start with *What? Why?* or *How?*

- Listen for what is being said. Consider what their position is.

- Look to create a win-win, so both parties get what they want.

- Be clear with your outcomes.

- Don't rush—take your time!

SO WHAT?

Heidi Grant[82] notes that a focus on Promoting is important in negotiation. She cites the work of Galinsky, who asked negotiators the following before every conversation:

> Please take a couple of minutes to think about the aspirations you have in a negotiation. What are the negotiation behaviors and outcomes you hope to achieve during a negotiation? How could you promote these behaviors and outcomes?

What are the different perspectives?

What's your strategy?

Finally focus on the issue, not the personality. It can be all too easy to always think about the person, not the topic at hand.

FIELD WORK—NOW WHAT?

Think about an upcoming negotiation. What's important to note?

_____

_____

_____

_____

_____

What do you need to take into account?

NOTES AND REFLECTIONS:

DAY 63

WHEN ARE YOU AT YOUR BEST?
CIRCADIAN RHYTHM

*"You can create something that is pure genius,
but you have to get your timing right."*
—Lang Leav

FOCUS QUESTION:

When are you at your best?

WHAT?

Our circadian rhythm plays out in the backdrop of work and may become more pronounced in a remote or hybrid workspace. Today's focus is on your circadian rhythm, which is grounded in the study of chronobiology.

What time of day you are at your best? We all have different rhythms. For decades the phrases "night owl" and "early bird" have been in the lexicon of workers. When are you at your best? The science of chronobiology explores what helps people perform at different times of the day.

To Consider . . .

Questions to consider:

- What times of day are you "at your best" for doing different types of work—coaching calls, setting up new business, marketing, relationship building, etc.?

- What items are not getting done? What time do they need for completion? Ideally, when could they be completed?

- What are you doing to renew and/or keep at your prime? This might involve building in time for physical activity, renewal etc.

- What are you doing to not only "do the work" with your business but move the business forward? This is one of the greatest challenges for business owners at all stages of their business. Business inflection points occur regularly throughout the entire lifecycle of a business.

- What space are you leaving for other important parts of your life, i.e., family, relationships, etc.?

SO WHAT?

Our own internal motivation and drivers have a tremendous influence on *how* and *when* we get things done.

Spending time working through the questions included in the text box can create more awareness around your own internal rhythms. Often these can act as levers for impact, helping you get more work done, in quicker amounts of time.

For more on this topic, check out Daniel Pink's *When: The Scientific Secrets of Perfect Timing*. He writes,

> Our moods and performance oscillate during the day. For most of us, our mood follows a common pattern: a peak, a trough, and rebound. That helps shape a dual pattern of performance. In the mornings, during the peak . . . most of us excel at . . . analytic work that requires sharpness, vigilance, and focus. Later in the day, during the recovery, most of us do better on . . . insight work that requires less inhibition and resolve.[83]

FIELD WORK—NOW WHAT?

Work through the questions included in the "To Consider" text box. What do you notice?

_____

_____

_____

_____

Spend time making a list of the tasks you have to get done in a day or week. List them in the left column. Now in the right column, with your circadian rhythm in mind, when would they best be completed?

_____

_____

_____

_____

_____

_____

_____

_____

_____

_____

_____

_____

Consider blocking off times in your calendar to schedule in these activities.

NOTES AND REFLECTIONS:

WEEK 9 REVIEW
THIS WEEK'S FOUNDATION THEME WAS
ADDITIONAL CONVERSATIONS TO HAVE

It's the end of another week. What was it like? Describe it here in three words:

_____ . _____ . _____

This week we explored the following topics:

- Day 57—Virtual Conversation Skills
- Day 58—Feedback
- Day 59—Difficult Conversations
- Day 60—Troubleshooting and Month Two Check-In
- Day 61—Pitfalls
- Day 62—Negotiation
- Day 63—When Are You at Your Best? Circadian Rhythm

Wrap up theme for the week:

_____
_____
_____
_____
_____

What are you looking forward to?

_____
_____
_____
_____
_____

What questions do you have?

_____

_____

_____

_____

_____ _____

_____

_____

What To-Dos have surfaced? (List your top 3–5)

1.

2.

3.

4.

5.

Update your tracking sheet!

WEEK 10 · TECHNOLOGY

"There was a time when nails were high-tech. There was a time when people had to be told how to use a telephone. Technology is just a tool. People use tools to improve their lives."
—Tom Clancy

Welcome to Week 10. What's important for you to note in your world right now?

This week's theme is one that you are likely *very* aware of—technology. There's a part two to this as well—relationships.

- Day 64—Reliability
- Day 65—Alchemy, Blends, and Follow-Up
- Day 66—Visibility
- Day 67—Productive or Busy?
- Day 68—Conflict
- Day 69—To Do/Not to Do
- Day 70—Chunk It Down

WHAT ARE YOUR TOP 3 GOALS THIS WEEK?:

1. _____

2. _____

3. _____

By the end of the week I want to be sure that . . .

_____

TECHNOLOGY SKILLS

Tech skills and comfort in working within the unknown can be a "make it or break it" in our work in the remote and hybrid world. Technology can either create a lot of stress, or become just part of how we work.

Here's what I wrote about technology skills in *PlanDoTrack*:

> From navigating the different virtual platforms from communication to meetings, from chats to learning management systems to instruments. These platforms can change on a regular basis—be sure to check with your peers, boss, and mentors about the most up-to-date platforms you are using, and the tips and tricks they are leveraging to make them work.

Technology can be an enabler and a derailer. It can build trust or erode trust. That's why part two of this week's theme is relationships.

Technology is the vehicle for relationships in the virtual space. What's possible when you leverage the best of technology?

RELATIONSHIPS

The larger the group or team you have, the more connections are possible. As Keith Ferrazzi noted in his 2014 HBR article, the larger the team, the larger the number of touchpoints. He references Richard Hackman's research, which found that it required "10 conversations for every person on a team of five to touch base with everyone else, but that number rises to 78 for a team of 13."[84]

What's important for you to take a look at in your connections? What are you doing to be proactive about building connections? What is still not clear to you?

Activity: Make a map of the core relationships you have with others. Who do you need to interface with on a regular basis? (If you don't know yet, ask your peers, boss, and mentors.) What is the level of frequency of touchpoints? What is important to note about these relationships? How are these facilitated by technology? What changes might you need to make?

When building your partnerships, consider how you can build on strengths. You might consider undertaking the StrengthsFinder assessment together *or* have them complete the Positive Psychology Strengths VIA Survey. Earmark a conversation for dialogue and sharing about who they are, what their top five strengths are, and how they can bring them to current projects.

DAY 64

RELIABILITY

Reliability is the precondition for trust.
— Wolfgang Schauble

FOCUS QUESTION:

What signals reliability in the remote space?

WHAT?

In *The Culture Map*, Erin Meyer writes, "When you meet your workmates by the water cooler or photocopier every day, you know instinctively who you can and cannot trust. In a geographically distributed team, trust is measured almost exclusively in terms of reliability."

Reliability is a critical component for remote work success. How are you showing up? Things get magnified in the remote space, as we do not see each other regularly. So if you are always rushing onto calls, or showing up late or flustered, what does it signal?

Keep in Mind

Reliability is often related to consistency. Consider these elements in showing up consistently with your peers and other stakeholders:

- Be proactive! Proactivity is key in the world of the remote worker. Being able to get ahead of whatever curve is critical.

- Prioritize what's important in your space.

- Keep it simple.

- Track.

SO WHAT?

Here are some things you can do to signal reliability and follow through:

- Let people know about the process and/or timeframes they can expect.

- Be clear with agreements and expectations.

- Focus in on end results and success factors.

- Add value—clarify what people value.

- Walk your talk—If you say you are going to do it, you do it. You model it in your own work and process.

- Let people know what they can expect from you—detailed deliverables, and timelines.

Another important component of this is that things get magnified easily in the remote space. What elements are important to focus on?

FIELD WORK—NOW WHAT?

Consider *what* you are doing to signal reliability:

What is being communicated?

_____

_____

_____

_____

What is being *magnified*?

_____

_____

_____

_____

DAY 65

ALCHEMY, BLENDS, AND FOLLOW-UP

"The most successful people I know are also the most reliable."
—Unknown

FOCUS QUESTION:

What's the blend you want to create? Alchemy is all about the blend of things.

WHAT?

Combinations | Blends | Openness | Solutions

Today's solutions often require a combination of different elements. As remote workers, we may find that we get stuck and need to be able to jettison ourselves out of this mire. Being open to solutions and being able to blend things together can be the ultimate solution. Alchemy is the art and science of blending things together.

Did You Know?

Alchemy is seen as transformation, creation, and combination.
Alchemy was practiced across Europe, the Middle East and Asia.

SO WHAT?

Alchemy requires a freedom and openness to experimentation. If we feel constrained, we may adopt a mindset of fear or doubt and/or failure. This can serve to stymie or minimize the innovation and change needed to succeed in the virtual space.

Here are some techniques we may use to practice alchemy in the remote and hybrid space:

- **Reframe** the situation and look at things from different perspectives.

- **Cross-pollinate**—adopt a stance where you can combine elements from different areas. There may be a problem or project you are working on in one area which could be a useful solution in another. Multidisciplinary approaches are useful in solving complex issues, and learning from others can help spark new solutions.

- **Blend techniques and tools**—To perform at our best, we can pull from a wide range of tools and techniques, from experiential education to design thinking; from coaching to mentoring. All of these approaches help us to become clearer, and more capable of moving our ideas forward. Without the experimentation and the permission to blend, we may get stuck in ruts. (Refer to days 31 to 34 around getting unstuck, obstacles and challenges.)

- **Learn from and participate in other industry learning**. Part of innovation means being able to blend different ideas together. How are you learning about different areas and different topics?

What journeys or pathways may provide a new insight or set of ideas for you? Whose journey do you want to become more familiar with? What are the key elements, and what decision points do you need to make? How do you connect these into the *impact*, *results*, and *relationships* you want?

What elements do you want freedom from? What blend will help you do your best work; will soothe you when you make a mistake; or will call you forward when you get stuck?

FIELD WORK—NOW WHAT?

What are the different elements you can weave together to create new ideas? Innovation? Change?

_____

_____

_____

_____

_____

_____

_____

_____

_____

_____

_____

_____

DAY 66
VISIBILITY

"Cultivate visibility because attention is currency."
—Chris Brogan

FOCUS QUESTION:
What does being more visible mean to you? What's important about being more visible?

WHAT?

Another mantra of remote work I share in *Effective Virtual Conversations* is this: "Out of sight does not equal out of mind." What are you doing to keep in touch with your leader, peers, stakeholders, and customers? Visibility can take many forms, from emails to streaming virtual meetings to video messages.

What do you want visibility to look like?

Pre-pandemic employees noted that the ability to work remotely offers a wide range of advantages. Among employees who were given this benefit, the overwhelming majority (80%) believed that it had provided a better work-life balance at their current company; 65% thought it had reduced stress; 60% stated that remote work led to their taking fewer sick days; 56% said that it had improved morale at their current company; and 52% believed it had reduced absences.

In 2016, "Dell reported saving about $12 million US per year in real estate costs by encouraging employees to work from home."[85]

In 2021 it was estimated in the City of Toronto that the available office space in 2021 rose to 12.4%, a significant change from 2019's 2.2% availability rate, or 2020's 7.8%.[86]

According to an Indeed survey in 2018[87], 62% of Canadian employers offered their employees the option to work remotely. Almost half (47%) of respondents who work for companies without a remote-work policy feel frustrated and wish their company offered this benefit—so much so, that 33% have considered looking for a job at a company that offers remote work, and 14% are actively looking. Strikingly, over a third (36%) of employees would consider taking a pay cut to have the option to work remotely, with 7% saying that they definitely would.

The downside of remote work:

Pre-pandemic Canadian employees are also aware of the potential downside of remote work[88]. More than a quarter (28%) of respondents thought that it contributes to less visibility and access to leadership at their current company, and 25% think that it leads to less collaboration. Almost one in ten (9%) believed working remotely stunted career growth at their current company.

Visibility Tips

Visibility could include:

- Proactively reaching out on a regular basis to your boss and your peers
- Offering to undertake a special project aligned with your strengths and passions, to contribute to your organization or your field
- Writing a blog post or article for your organization or industry
- Attending virtual networking events

SO WHAT?

As a remote worker, you are more likely to need to take charge of your career. Being proactively visible can be of benefit for career growth, and also hearing about what opportunities are available.

Whether you are attending in-company events, industry events or other, networking is a key activity for all remote workers.

CASE STUDY—BOOSTING YOUR VISIBILITY VIA NETWORKING

As I share in *Teams365* Blog #764 (originally published February 3, 2016):

1. **Connect with the other person.** In any networking function, we may meet a range of people. When you are talking to one person, really connect with them. Don't think of who else you might want to meet in the room. Be present in your conversation and listen. Watch for the sticky factor, and continue to move on when the time is appropriate.

2. **Be genuinely interested—be curious.** Ask them questions. Listen—remember, people like to talk about themselves, so develop a short list of questions.

3. **Be clear on what you want to get out of the networking experience.** Why are you going? Is this the right group? What is going to be worth your investment? Whether business owners are building their business or people are looking for a new role, it can be very easy to quickly fill up your schedule with lots of things to do and meetings to attend. The more you explore, the clearer you may become with where your time is best spent.

4. **Follow up.** Quickly follow up with those you connected with, the next 48 hours of meeting. Exchange email, business cards (v cards) and/or social media accounts.

5. **Spend a few minutes after each networking event** reflecting on:

    •   What worked well?

    •   Who did you meet and connect with?

    •   What value was there in attending?

    •   What would you do differently next time?

FIELD WORK—NOW WHAT?

Think about visibility and the different strategies you can use to be more visible in your team, with your boss, with your peers. Don't just think about it; what's also in your calendar?

_____
_____
_____
_____
_____
_____

What time have you earmarked for this to happen?

_____
_____
_____
_____
_____
_____

PRODUCTIVE OR BUSY?

*"It is not enough to be busy, so are the ants.
The question is: What are we busy about?"*
—Henry David Thoreau

FOCUS QUESTION:

Productive or busy? What can I do to figure out how much time I am working?

WHAT?

Are you productive or busy? Are you working *in* the business or *on* the business?

Working *in* the business involves doing work to keep the business moving—administrative tasks and the like.

Working *on* the business can include planning, relationship building, and service delivery.

In today's world, there can be a perception that we are busy and doing a lot of work.

What is the work that will give you impact?

What are the things that will help to generate business?

In today's prompt, make a list of all the things you have done this week. What is important in terms of getting things done? What is "busy" work—i.e., work that is not really having an impact? An example of this in my business could be over-creating content.

Consider This . . .

Take a look at your list of tasks this week and consider which are:

- Busy tasks—not adding value
- Tasks which are important for the short term
- Tasks which are important for the medium term
- Tasks which are important for your overall career

What shifts might you make?

SO WHAT?

Rather than spending time sharing content (i.e., making sure that posts are found on the different social platforms I know people will be at, I focus on creating new content. This may be wasted effort.

In fitting items in to the time we have available, we want to make sure that we are focusing on the work that is going to get us moving ahead in the long term, and in the big picture.

PRODUCTIVE OR BUSY?

What are you doing in your business right now? Are you productive, or are you busy? This question can take us into the landscape of high leverage work. (Refer to our earlier focus on High Leverage Activities on Day 52.) What pieces of work will move you ahead; deliver, or over-deliver, to your customers; create a foundation for the remainder of your business; create a platform for you to grow upon; add to your body of work?

Activity: Take some time today to make a list of all of the activities you have been involved with this year/month so far. What activities are keeping you busy?

KEEPING THINGS MOVING

It's easy to get stuck, feeling like we are in concrete in the remote space. This may happen when we are:

- Overanalyzing on a project and don't take action.
- Second-guessing ourselves.
- Over-thinking something.
- In an eddy, continuously swirling around an issue.

In most of these instances, action is needed. In my speaking around *PlanDoTrack* and *Coaching Business Builder*, the tagline of **Consistent Action + Daily Steps = Momentum** has emerged. In the remote space, keeping things moving can be as important as getting it right. This is true because we are often working without full context, details, or pieces. Our component may connect in with other work that's happening in a far-off distance. Our context may be stable, while someone else's may be very challenging.

Here are some ideas to keep things moving, especially when you get stuck:

- Step away from it for a while.
- Take it out of the office—move to a new place and tackle it there.
- Get grounded—take 2 minutes to brain dump everything by talking it out; or, if you know it's valuable (and it usually is), undertake a mind map for 2–3 minutes, getting everything that is in your head on paper

What things do you want to do if you get stuck?

FIELD WORK—NOW WHAT?

Consider whether you are productive or busy. Are you working *in* the business or *on* the business?

_____

_____

_____

_____

In today's prompt, make a list of all the things you have done this week. What is important in terms of getting things done? What is "busy" work—i.e., work that is not really having an impact?

_____

_____

_____

_____

_____

_____

_____

_____

_____

_____

_____

_____

DAY 68
CONFLICT

"Peace is not absence of conflict; it is the ability
to handle conflict by peaceful means."
—Ronald Reagan

FOCUS QUESTION:
I'm having conflict with a colleague. What might be at the core?

WHAT?

Conflict can be due to a number of factors, from different styles and approaches to working, through to different resources available or information. What do you need to clarify first? What is at the heart of the conflict? If it is a style difference, what adjustment do you need to make to your style?

Address or even prevent conflict early on. What things might get magnified? What misunderstandings might occur? How might my message be perceived? Is what I have written, what I hope to have understood?

What else do you think you should focus on?

The way forward may not be an easy pathway. What will help things go more smoothly?

What are you proud of? How are you celebrating? What are you doing to acknowledge and note your learning?

The ability to work through differences and conflict is a key skill for leaders and team members. What we know from research is that complementary skill sets often make a team strong. We may have different styles, which means that what we value and how we interrelate with the world is different.

Several factors can lead to conflict, including different styles (refer to Day 3); different approaches with conflict; and competing resourcing, information, and tasks.

Sometimes our roles are in conflict with each other.

Conflict may also be created by unequal resourcing. Leaders should be aware of inequitable resource issues. If you perceive one, build a business case around what is required with your skills.

Another consideration is how you approach conflict. What is your natural style in navigating conflict? There are many different approaches.

Different conflict models may have different names, but we may demonstrate one of many styles including:

- **Accommodate**—often when the relationship is important but the results are not, we will accommodate to enable the other party to have their preferred outcome. In accommodation, the other party wins, at our loss.

- **Compromise**—compromise may be important when the outcome is important for both of us, as is the relationship. In compromise, I win some and you win some, but neither party really wins completely.

- **Avoid**—there are instances where it makes sense to avoid conflict and sweep things under the rug. The challenge and danger with this, over time, is that the issue can fester, and the small minuscule issue can grow into an elephant. Where it may be appropriate to avoid conflict is when the issue is not important, and the relationship is not important. In avoiding, I lose and you lose.

- **Collaborate**—collaboration takes time and may be the preferred solution when relationships and results are both important. Not every situation warrants collaboration, and as Morten Hansen writes in his books, "Don't collaborate just for collaboration's sake. While collaboration often takes more time, it can be the best outcome. In collaboration I win, and you win."

- **Compete**—We may choose to compete to achieve an important outcome when the results are key, and the relationship is not as important. When competing, we need to be aware of when it becomes too aggressive. In competition I win, and you lose.

As you consider these five different styles, what are examples of each one, and how would you and others benefit from adopting that approach in each example? When might the approach be beneficial?

Did You Know?

What's at the heart of your conflict?

Conflict in teams can emerge for many reasons[89], including:

- Competing demands
- Unclear roles
- Lack of clarity around where we are going—our vision, our goals

SO WHAT?

Regardless of the source of conflict, becoming more proficient and confident in navigating conflict is very important.

In navigating conflict, you will want to consider these questions:

- **What is more important here—the end result or the relationship?** This will influence everything from our stance and approach to conflict. For example, if the end result is really, really important in the short term, I may adopt a stance of competition where I do everything I can to "win" at the other's expense. If the relationship is more important because I need to work with this person, or team, on a regular basis, then I may choose to collaborate. In collaborating, I may let the other party win or spend more time.

- **What do I know about how I approach conflict?** We each have our own unique approach to conflict, which also shapes how we view conflict. Many team members may have been socialized that conflict is not a bad thing. In fact, part of the team development process is the storming stage, where a team needs to figure out who they are, what is important, and how they want to operate. That stage is naturally conflict ridden.

  It can be important during the storming stage for team members to be aware of their natural approach. Are they more conflict avoidant—i.e., preferring to sweep it under the rug? Or are they more head on with conflict—i.e., raising issues and placing them on the table for immediate exploration?

- **What is the common ground we share?** This is a third essential area to consider when thinking about conflict in teams. Helping people find that expanse where they do align is critical for conflict resolution. It may be only a small sliver, but helping people see the area in which they align is core.

In supporting teams through conflict, there are some specific things we can do as we wade through the choppy waters of conflict. Consider these the next time you are working with a team:

- **Normalize it.** A natural part of the formation of groups and teams is conflict and the recognition of differences. Helping teams understand that they are not alone can be useful in taking off some of the pressure of the thinking that "they are all alone."

- **Give time for the team to work through it.** It takes time and space to have these conversations. Prioritize this as something which does need time.

- **Consider the resources which will support you as a team around this.** Having a common framework and skills you can all use in navigating conflict supports the process of resolution. If people don't know how to have the conversation around conflict, it can be challenging. Consider investing resources in some skill development for the team, and/or bringing someone in who can help you with this.

- **Focus on supporting enhanced self-awareness in the team.** In today's teaming environment, we all benefit from enhanced self-awareness—awareness around how we naturally approach work, our styles, as well as our approach to conflict. Many times, teams may be experiencing conflict due to differences in work styles. If some team members are driving for results and working to get things done quickly, whereas others want to make sure things are done correctly, conflict is likely. Helping team members understand their natural style can be of great benefit and may reframe differences to being *simply* differences, rather than something which is wrong or a problem.

- **Consider the end result.** Sometimes it is very easy to get mired in our own perspectives, and in what we believe needs to happen. Helping team members reconnect with the end result is critical for success. Connecting with the bigger picture also helps team members find those slivers, or 2%, where they do align.

What is important for your team to notice about conflict? What's the issue they need to work through?

FIELD WORK—NOW WHAT?

Explore the conflict styles of you and your colleagues. What is important to note?

_____

_____

_____

_____

_____

_____

_____

_____

_____

For more on this topic, explore *Remote Pathways* podcast episode 12.

TO DO/NOT TO DO

"The only man who never makes mistakes is the man who never does anything."
—Theodore Roosevelt

FOCUS QUESTION:

I need to get clearer on my tasks. The last few projects have not been as clear.
What can I do?

WHAT?

In any given day it is likely that we will have more to do than time available. Having a Not-to-Do list can be as important in the remote and hybrid world.

So What Do I Do?

Now what about the things that are on our *Not-to-Do* list?

Make a list of all the things you need to do. Separate them according to what you can . . .

- *Delegate*—pass on to others to complete
- *Defer*—do at another time
- *Dump*—really say *no* to.

SO WHAT?

Getting clear on what we need to focus on and what can be let go of, is key to success for ourselves and the people we work with.

What are the things *you* want to do?

Consider your work that is to be done and map it to the amount of energy it's likely going to need. I know that my most important work, and the work that takes the most brain power, is proposals and writing. Without getting this out of the way early in the morning, it's often a big challenge to get these pieces complete in an efficient timeframe, later in the day.

When working on projects, it can be useful to move through the *To Do* and *Not to Do* exercises to clarify what projects and tasks look like.

PRIORITIZING YOUR WORKFLOW

What is going to have *impact*—high, medium, low? What is the effort?

When looking at impact, you may view it as both numbers (hard cost) and qualitative (soft cost).

FIELD WORK—NOW WHAT?

Impact/Likelihood Matrix

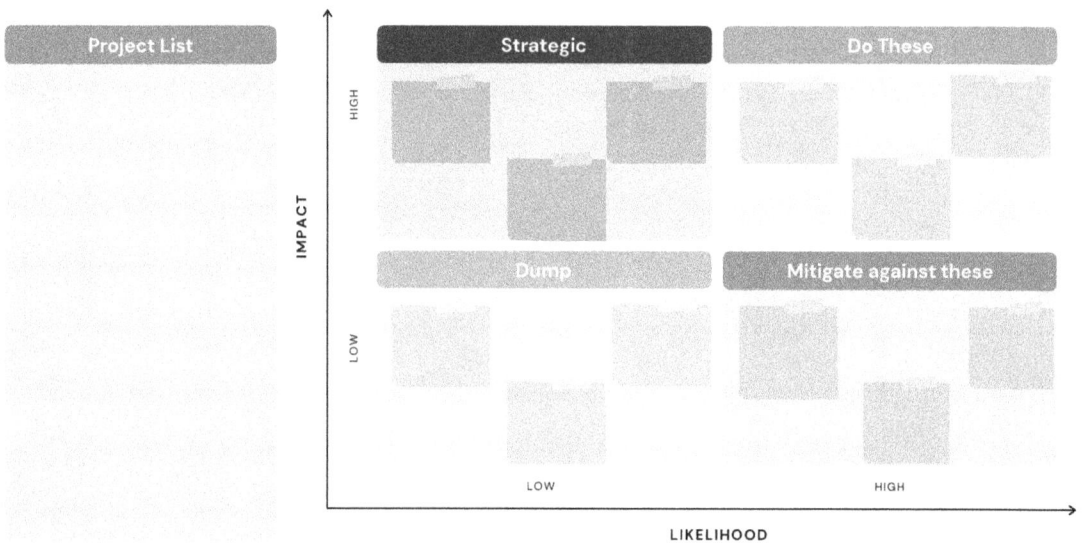

Make a separate list of all the things you need to get done this week. Then sketch out a list including the Impact and Likelihood listing (as you see here). Plot each activity in terms of what *Impact* it will have (Low to High) and the *Likelihood* that it will happen (Low to High).

As you look at your list, you'll see that they break out into four main areas:

- Items with low impact and low likelihood that it will move the needle—*dump* them or place them on your *Do Not Do* list.

- Items that have a High Impact and High Likelihood that they will happen—*lean into these*

- Items with Low Likelihood but High Impact—be strategic about these.

- Items with Low Impact and High Likelihood—Minimize and mitigate against these.

What's on your list?

While it can be useful to have tenacity, there are some things you may want to outsource:

- Bookkeeping
- Manual tasks
- Social media

Just as we know in strengths, it's harder to develop skills in areas where we are not so good. What things do you want to delegate?

NOTES AND REFLECTIONS:

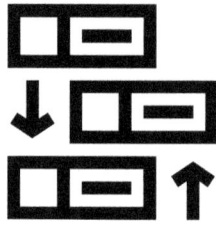

DAY 70

CHUNK IT DOWN

"Chunking makes our brains more efficient. The more you can chunk something, the faster and easier you can process it. Wayne Gretzky had chunked hockey like no one before or since. Talented people have supremely chunked whatever they become talented at doing."
— Kevin Maney

FOCUS QUESTION:

What needs to be broken down into smaller bites? Or in other words, how do you eat an elephant? One bite at a time.

WHAT?

The remote world can be a micro-world. From attention spans to what remains static, things are always changing. In order to get traction on big projects, when things do change, consider chunking things down.

Chunking things down may mean breaking things into discrete packets so you can complete things in one sitting. Related to project management, and time management, this tip gets you thinking about what you can do to break down the bigger pieces. It's hard to look at bigger issues at times.

Chunk it—consider what big tasks can be broken down into pieces, or what elements of similar buckets of work can be done in bigger blocks. For example, I have learned to schedule most of my coaching-call days in blocks, where I meet with people first thing in the morning for a few hours, step away and do my workout and several hours of writing, and then return to my desk. Other days may be earmarked for writing and speaking and learning, and still other days where it's all about time with teams.

Other Ways to Think about It

- Bundle like tasks.

- Break it down by making it visible. (Trello or Asana software can help)

- Block off time in your calendar for specific projects or tasks.

- Distill it down to the core.

- Delegate it to another.

- Just say no—delete or dump the task!

SO WHAT?

Consider the projects you have on the go. What discrete tasks and activities can flow out of this? You might choose to capture these subsets in project management software such as Trello or Asana. As you look at the discrete steps, add some more detail: What will success look like? Who is responsible? What resources are needed? How much time will it take?

Breaking projects down into more discrete packets can help us with the regular steps that are required.

In exploring other scheduling issues, another common pitfall is that tasks are scattered across a day, week, or month. When we have tasks that require "heavy lifting" and more brain power, it may require some time to get into the flow of the activity (i.e., 5–10 minutes). With this in mind, it can be useful to group things together that are a common type of activity.

Different activities may also lean into different parts of the brain. For example, if you need to update invoices, what accounting tasks can be grouped together? What tasks relate to other activities, such as conversations or planning or writing?

Pulling like activities together can help with minimizing cognitive load or the energy associated with switching between tasks.

Consider one of your current tasks. What could you do to chunk it down? What are the mini-pieces to that task?

FIELD WORK—NOW WHAT?

Review your To-Do and Not-to-Do lists.

Consider these questions:

- What things can be grouped together?

- What tasks make sense to bundle together?

- What else can get chunked down?

- Instead of adding on something new, it may be about simplifying or reviewing what is there already. What things do you want to simplify in your work right now?

NOTES AND REFLECTIONS:

THIS WEEK'S FOUNDATION THEME WAS
TECHNOLOGY

It's the end of another week. What was it like? Describe it here in three words:

_____ . _____ . _____

This week we explored the following topics:

- Day 64—Reliability
- Day 65—Alchemy, Blends, and Follow-Up
- Day 66—Visibility
- Day 67—Productive or Busy?
- Day 68—Conflict
- Day 69—To Do/Not to Do
- Day 70—Chunk It Down

Wrap up theme for the week:

_____

_____

_____

_____

What are you looking forward to?

_____

_____

_____

_____

What questions do you have?

_____

_____

_____

_____

_____

_____

_____

_____

What To-Dos have surfaced? (List your top 3–5)

1.

2.

3.

4.

5.

Update your tracking sheet!

WEEK 11 · TRICKY ISSUES

Welcome to Week 11. This week's meta-theme is Tricky Issues.

> "The greatest mistake you can make
> in life is to continually fear that you will make one."
> —Elbert Hubbard

My guess is by now, you may have encountered several tricky issues along the way. These might have included:

- Technology issues
- Interpersonal issues
- Team issues
- Technical issues
- Work-life issues
- Project issues
- And the list could go on and on . . .

Tricky issues often emerge or else get magnified when people don't feel safe, listened to, or heard.

Tricky issues also emerge when things are unclear. What can you do to clarify processes and practices?

Here are the areas we will cover this week:

- Day 71—Memorability
- Day 72—Micro-Monitor: Challenges and Opportunities
- Day 73—Intercultural Mindset
- Day 74—Delegation
- Day 75—Working across Time Zones
- Day 76—Simplify and Keep It Simple
- Day 77—Co-Working

WHAT ARE YOUR TOP 3 GOALS THIS WEEK?:

1. _____

2. _____

3. _____

By the end of the week I want to be sure that . . .

_____

Let's return back to the 7 Remote Enablers™ covered earlier in the book, about building skills and capacity in any and all of these areas:

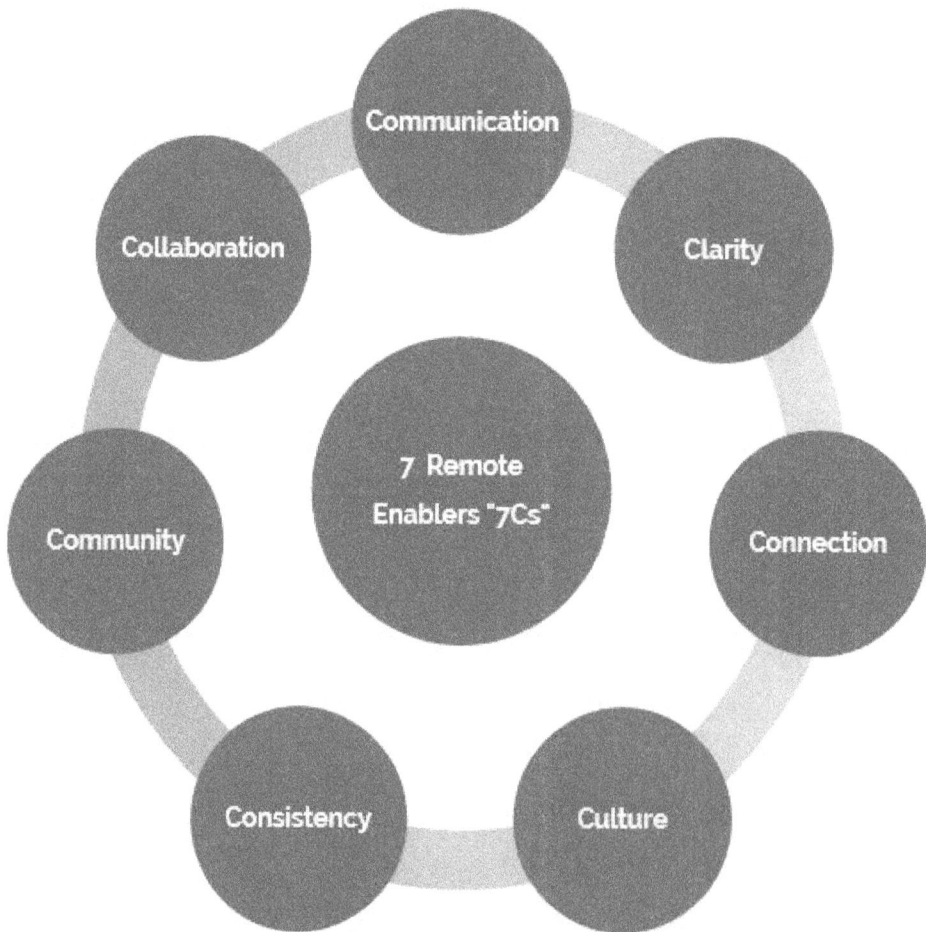

Earlier in the *Guide*, we discussed how Communication, Clarity, and Consistency were three areas to focus on for boosting trust. These elements are also important for mitigating against tricky issues.

Also critical to mitigating again tricky issues are the following:

- Connection
- Culture
- Community
- Collaboration

When people feel connected and part of a vibrant culture in an organization, issues which might be labeled as "tricky issues" may actually be seen as part of the constructive discourse and debate that happen at an organization.

On an individual level, many of our personality quirks can get magnified, especially when trust levels are low and people are feeling uncertain.

Someone who is naturally outgoing may be perceived as more dominant, while those who like to contribute may be seen as seeking the center of attention. What do you notice about the culture of the organization you have created?

When faced with a tricky issue:

- Consider what you've done in the past that might have been a similar situation. What did you do? How did you resolve it?
- Reach out to your network to find out what your peers or mentor have done.
- Bring it to a coaching conversation, and explore the different angles around the topic.
- Get to root cause—what's at the core of this?
- Consider different perspectives around the issue.

DAY 71
MEMORABILITY

"In this digital age, don't forget to use your digits!"
—Lynda Barry

FOCUS QUESTION:
What's going to help you stand out virtually?

WHAT?

Memorability in the virtual and remote space is important for many reasons. First, it is important in terms of *retention*—What you remember. Next, memorability is important in terms of your *impact*. Finally, memorability is also important in terms of your *visibility*. How do you stand out?

Memorability also helps with retention. If things are not memorable, it is unlikely that we will remember them. Some research has shown that digital retention is different than analog retention. It's currently thought that we retain more when we write things down than when we type it in. With this in mind, what do you want to digitize later?

Did You Know?

"Levers" we have available to create more memorability include the following:

- Visuals
- Metaphors
- Connection—this includes connection with others and connection to the context, the technology, and what we are presenting

- Interaction
- Action
- Awareness

SO WHAT?

Herman Ebbinghaus did initial research on what we retain and what we remember. He created what is now known as the *forgetting curve*. The forgetting curve asserts that we remember even less as days progress.[90]

And so how can we boost that? If we're not using something, not retaining something, within six days it's gone.

Ebbinghaus found several things that really made a difference—the meaningfulness of the information, the way it's represented, as well as some physiological factors, such as stress or sleep.

More recently, Todd Maddox, PhD, did research on the same topic of learning, memory, and performance. He writes, "The brain is hardwired to forget. Retention is the true goal of training."[91]

We really want to boost retention in a virtual event. Think about how many Zoom meetings don't stand out from another?

For years we've been saying the written word is retained much better. So where does that come from?

And that really came from a study by Mueller and Oppenheimer in 2014 called "The pen is mightier than the keyboard." They studied differences in university students with the difference between taking notes by hand or doing it by computer.

Some had to listen to TED talks and take notes. They found that those who wrote by hand did better. One of their outcomes was that "it is suggestive evidence that longhand notes may have superior external storage as well as superior encoding functions." So basically, you can remember handwritten materials because it is stored differently and it is encoded differently.

The researchers had two hypotheses about why note-taking is beneficial. The first idea is known as the *encoding hypothesis*, which says that when a person is taking notes, involves the processing that occurs when a person is taking notes. Encoding helps to enhance learning and retention.

Second, there's the *external capture*. When you take notes by hand, you can look back at your notes and think about them. It's a physical something that we can look back to in notebooks. I can pick up my notebook, look at it, and do a flip-through. This is a very different experience than if I'm going into my notebook on the computer; will I see things like this that actually jogged my memory?

So, in terms of that 2014 study, here is what they really found: in listening, we tend to capture notes verbatim, word by word, rather than reframing it in our own language. In other words, when we hear things, we tend to type it verbatim if we're using a keyboard, whereas, if we're writing it, we're also encoding it and making it our own. We're putting it in our own language.

FIELD WORK—NOW WHAT?

Consider what you can do to be more memorable and Stand Out Virtually.

_____

_____

_____

_____

_____

_____

_____

_____

_____

_____

NOTES AND REFLECTIONS:

DAY 72

MICRO-MONITOR: CHALLENGES AND OPPORTUNITIES

"Difficulties strengthen the mind, as labor does the body."
—Lucius Annaeus Seneca

FOCUS QUESTION:

What barriers are showing up in your work? Challenges. What might help you hurdle, or get around them? Opportunities.

WHAT?

Greatest challenges. Remote workers can experience a number of challenges:

- Not being in control of the workflow

- Working across time zones—I'm wrapping up at 4 pm my time, but a colleague is just stepping into work for the afternoon

- Working across cultures

- Not being self-aware

- Being aware of and managing our own biases

- Overutilizing strengths—our strengths become magnified in times of stress or complexity.

Things to do to learn more about yourself and boost self-awareness:

1. Learn more by doing. Focus on your strengths. Consider what others have provided in terms of feedback.

2. Understand your triggers—What gets you upset? What puts you at ease?

3. Consider what grounds you

4. Explore what you naturally gravitate to

5. Be aware of what you tend to do first

Two things to be cautious of:

- Navel gazing—spending so long trying to figure things out that the world around you changes.

- Projection—are you translating your issues onto someone else?

Did You Know?

When facing a challenge, consider:

- What is happening?
- What needs to be clarified?
- What is my read on the situation? What's another perspective?
- Who else can help me with this?
- What haven't I considered?
- What resource do I need?
- What am I not using?

SO WHAT?

Remote and hybrid work takes time and energy. It is not the same as working 1-1. What are you doing to ensure that you are setting yourself up for success?

We are all a work in progress. We can easily become overwhelmed or self-absorbed, when the focus usually needs to go elsewhere.

Opportunities. What opportunities are you facing in your work? These are things you will want to magnify, and possibly use as an antidote to some of the challenges you identified earlier.

Opportunities can take many forms, from special work assignments to learning programs to a day where you can job-shadow. In the workspace, it might also include finding windows coming up.

What are the current opportunities available for you to:

- Connect and network with others
- Showcase your skills
- Focus on your talents

- Explore what it means to have opportunities emerge and change

- Find where you want to contribute

- Determine what you want to learn

What lateral movements can I make in my career? Lateral movements can sometimes be as important as vertical movements. In today's VUCA context, having a generalist orientation can be of value.

- What's the level of opportunity?

- Who can connect you with opportunities that exist?

- What's the opportunity that you want to focus on first? What else might be of importance?

- Is it strategic? Tactical? Proactive? Short term or long term? What do you think and know about things?

Return back to vision. Where you want to go with your career? What is important to take note of and work around?

FIELD WORK—NOW WHAT?

Make a list of your current opportunities and challenges. Use the questions in the text box to come up with some new solutions for challenges, and some ways to magnify the opportunities.

CHALLENGE	REFRAME	OPPORTUNITIES	NEW POSSIBILITIES

INTERCULTURAL MINDSET

"Strength lies in differences, not in similarities."
—Stephen R. Covey

FOCUS QUESTION:
What is important to note about culture?

WHAT?

As I wrote in *PlanDoTrack,* "Remote and virtual teams may span across different countries, or different regions of the same country. Understanding our own cultural biases is one part of being an effective virtual and remote team member." Learning more about the cultural preferences of others is also important, while becoming aware of the assumptions we may hold. Intercultural skills are essential for virtual and remote professionals today. What is important for you to note or learn more about?

Keeping in mind the work of Geert Hofstede who has found through research that there are cultural variances across:

- Individualism-collectivism

- Uncertainty avoidance

- Power distance (strength of social hierarchy)

- Masculinity-femininity (task-orientation versus person-orientation)

- Long-term orientation

He also added a sixth item, *indulgence vs. restraint.* Find out more about his six areas at https:// hi.hofstede-insights.com/national-culture. Culture scales also often include direct and indirect communication—consider how direct your communication may be.[92]

Did You Know?

Another framework you may want to explore is that of Erin Meyer, author of *The Culture Map*. She distinguishes between eight different culture scales:

- Communicating: explicit vs. implicit
- Evaluating: direct negative feedback vs. indirect negative feedback
- Persuading: deductive vs. inductive
- Leading: egalitarian vs. hierarchical
- Deciding: consensual vs. top down
- Trusting: task vs. relationship
- Disagreeing: confrontational vs. avoid confrontation
- Scheduling: linear vs. flexible time[93]

SO WHAT?

As a team it can be very useful to have dialogue and even map yourself along these cultural continua, one at a time, having dialogue around where you naturally fall. This activity could take upwards of one entire team meeting of an hour.

As you look at each of the culture scales (Hofstede, Meyer, or other), have a discussion around these questions:

- What does activity under this culture scale look like?
- Where is your home-business context along this scale?
- Where are you as an individual professional along this scale? (Pause to have the team note what's similar/different/interesting along these continua.)
- Where are we as a team? (Pause to have the team come to consensus or agreement around where you are on this continuum and what that looks like behaviorally.)
- What is the culture of our team?
- What are the five or six adjectives we use to describe our team?

As a wrap up, ask the team to share what is important about each of those areas.

Helping the team understand who they are as a collective helps to create clarity around their own culture, "behavioral norms," and how things are done here. This provides consistency and greater alignment across the team.

What conversations are important to have in this area for you as a team?

What is important to note, and share, about your preferences, as they have been shaped by geographic factors and other preferences?

FIELD WORK—NOW WHAT?

Undertake discussion or exploration about the different cultures which you connect with every day. Even if you work in one country, there may be significant cultural differences between the way work is done on the East Coast versus West Coast.

What is important to learn more about?

_____

_____

_____

_____

What do you need to be more aware about in terms of your own cultural identity, assumptions, and biases?

_____

_____

_____

_____

NOTES AND REFLECTIONS:

DAY 74
DELEGATION

"Deciding what not to do is as important as deciding what to do."
—Jessica Jackley

FOCUS QUESTION:
What do you want to delegate?

WHAT?

Really, as a remote worker, can I delegate? Yes, you can!

This may involve the skill of influence. (Remember to look back at Day 46)

Can I outsource? Yes, you can.

Common things solopreneur remote workers may outsource include graphic design, social media, newsletter production, editing, and bookkeeping.

What would you want to outsource? What are the elements you want to retain for yourself? And how does your work intersect with the work of others?

What else is important to note about your focus?

We know of several things that remote and hybrid workers are not so good at, including:

- "The Pause" – slowing down to reflect, identify learning and then move forward
- Prioritizing
- Building in time to connect with others

Important qualities include resourcefulness, flexibility, resilience, contingency planning, learning on the fly, relationship building, and troubleshooting (MacGyvering)

What can you do to magnify these qualities?

Who can you collaborate with in order to mitigate against your weaknesses?

What do you notice about your blind spots—areas you have no knowledge about?

Self-awareness is key in the remote space. In this, you will want to focus on magnifying your knowledge. You may also find it useful to explore the Johari Window—things that we know, things that others know about us, things that are unknown. These become pronounced when we are under stress or pressure.

What things can you do to focus more on your work? To enhance your self-awareness? To help others expand their self-awareness?

5 *W*s and the H of Delegation

As you prepare to delegate a task, consider the following:

- What—what is going to be delegated?
- Why—what is important about this?
- Who—who is best placed to do this? Who would benefit and learn from the task?
- Where—where can they go for more information?
- When—what are the major milestones? When will you circle back and meet again?
- How—what steps need to be followed? What will success look like?

SO WHAT?

Delegation doesn't mean getting something off your plate. It should provide an opportunity for learning and growth for the person being delegated to.

Delegation is an art form and a necessity for getting more done in today's environment. We want to make sure that we are setting up for success those who are being delegated to.

FIELD WORK—NOW WHAT?

Identify the things you want to delegate. Consider the 5 *W*s as you plan to pass this on to others.

_____

_____

_____

_____

_____

_____

_____

_____

NOTES AND REFLECTIONS:

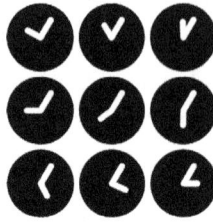

WORKING ACROSS TIME ZONES

"Time is precious."
—An old adage

FOCUS QUESTION:
What do you need to keep in mind around time?

WHAT?

The ability to work across time zones can be a key issue for remote workers. We may be focused on what is going to work best for us, without thinking about what is going to work best for our partners.

Note the times of day that you are at your peak. What time is that? Now note the times of day when your partners need to work.

Circadian rhythm. This hearkens back to Day 63 When Are You at Your Best? Circadian Rhythms. We all have some times of day which are better than others, in terms of our focus and ability to do deeper work.

When we are part of a global team, it will also be important to think about how your work feeds into that of others. If you have a deadline for a task to be completed by the end of the week, consider when your colleagues in other time zones may need to get the information from you.

Need to Know. What can get in the way? In spring and fall, not everyone switches their clocks at the same time. There may be several weeks when the time zone is off. Be sure to note this for future reference, and use a trusty time zone converter.

Did You Know?

Time zone conversions can be made easily at www.timeanddate.com.

Be aware that in October/November and March/April there are several weeks where North America and Europe are out of step, given that we change our clocks at different weeks of the year. Note when you and your colleagues go to Daylight Savings Time, etc.

Finally, there are states such as Arizona and provinces such as Saskatchewan that do not change time during the year.

SO WHAT?

A tip when learning more about your colleague: Find out exactly where they are based. Don't assume that there's only one time zone for that location. Many countries have multiple time zones. For example, in Canada there are six different time zones across the country. If you knew only that your colleague was in Canada, you might in fact be 3.5 hours off time for a meeting!

So ask the questions! Then Remember this great website to help you—www.timeanddate.com

FIELD WORK—NOW WHAT?

Where exactly are your colleagues based? What is important to note about where they are?

_____

_____

_____

_____

_____

_____

_____

_____

_____

_____

_____

DAY 76

SIMPLIFY AND KEEP IT SIMPLE

"Our life is frittered away by detail. Simplify, simplify."
—Henry David Thoreau

FOCUS QUESTION:

Less is more. What does it mean to simplify?

WHAT?

Keeping things simple is an important mantra for today's remote worker, given the various complexities that surround our work—from keeping your communications short and simple so they are understood to keeping your workflow simple and bundled.

What does *keeping it simple* mean for you?

Resources to Consider

Digital Minimalism: Choosing a Focused Life in a Noisy World by Cal Newport

Essentialism: The Disciplined Pursuit of Less by Greg McKeon

The Lean Startup: How Constant Innovation Creates Radically Successful Businesses by Eric Reis

SO WHAT?

Case study: Minimal Viable Product. Given rapid change, we may be working to a place where it is "just enough." This is often known as the Minimal Viable Product, or MVP. What absolutely needs to be done?

Many times, we go "above and beyond" what is required. When we think about the MVP, we are able to get things out, test them, get feedback, and then perfect them, rather than waiting to the time when they "might be perfect" but no longer relevant because it has taken us so long to get the product out into the market.

Today's quote also gets you thinking about what is absolutely necessary.

Consider these different areas where you may want to simplify and go back to the essentials:

1. Design

2. Communication

3. Writing (i.e., reporting)—what is the most important thing to know? What needs to be highlighted as well? What are the three bullet points?

FIELD WORK—NOW WHAT?

Instead of adding on something new, it may be about simplifying or reviewing what is there already. What things do you want to simplify in your work right now?

_____

_____

_____

_____

What can be "distilled down to its core," so that it's absolutely essential?

_____

_____

_____

_____

DAY 77
CO-WORKING

"Our belief is that mixing creative teams from different industries will spawn 'happy accidents' that inspire innovation, new products, and different ways of thinking."
—Steelcase executive

FOCUS QUESTION:
Where could you benefit from co-working?

WHAT?

As I indicated in *Teams365* blog post #1940[94], virtual co-working sessions can provide many benefits, including:

- A focused time to get things done—when was the last time you scheduled a block of time that was "meeting free" to get things done?

- Making a list of things that just need to get checked off

- Using the power of peer accountability in ensuring that you do what you say you are going to do in short bursts

- Connecting with others—the isolation effect of remote work can wear on many remote workers; this isolation may lead to a lack of focus, prioritizing "house" items over work items, etc.

SO WHAT?

Co-working in the remote space can help to boost creativity and connection. It can take many different forms in the virtual space, including:

- **Zoom calls**—Working real time for short blocks of time on Zoom.

- **Virtual retreats**—From virtual business planning sessions to team retreats, we can connect people through virtual retreat formats.

- **Lunch and learns**—Professional development opportunities abound for many professionals, and breakfasts, lunches, and dinners are very common. As I share in the call, it's not uncommon for me to speak to a group of 20 or even 200 virtually, over lunch. Contact me if you are looking for a speaker for your lunch and learn.

- **Social time**—"quarantinis" became a popular 5 p.m. activity in the early days of the pandemic. Today that's morphed into many different formats. What are you doing to create more social time with colleagues and friends and family, virtually?

- **Design (studio time)**—for many of the clients I work with, design or studio time is important. Getting together with others can create more focused work and impact. What are you wanting to design, and how might some virtual studio time support you? Again, contact me (info@potentialsrealized.com) for upcoming virtual studio days *and* sprints.

- **Conversations**—what conversations do you want to have this month? Who have you not reached out to recently?

- **Get It Done!**—getting things done is critical for success. One favorite activity with the annual lab programs I run is the Get It Done Days. What could 4 hours of focused work get off your list?

- **Games/challenges**—Challenges are one of my favorite marketing outreach activities. Throughout 2020 I hosted several Stand Out Virtually Challenges which supported others to learn more, and take action on, their virtual brands. Be sure to connect with us at Virtual and Remote Visionaries Hub for more on this topic at https://www.facebook.com/groups/314116869730339/

- **Team time**—Finally, what time have you earmarked for your team for team development?

What types of co-working experiences do you want to engage with?

For those who are remote workers, a virtual co-working session might connect people on Zoom or Skype for a one-hour or half-day session where team workers work live throughout the session, or else meet at the top of the hour, checking in on progress.

Lessons Learned from the 21-for-21 Virtual Co-working Sprints

For the first five months of 2021 I hosted the 21-for-21 Virtual Co-working Sprints. Daily, for a period of 21 days, I led a group of virtual co-working sprinters through 21 minutes of focused energy.

For many this provided an opportunity to tackle projects which weren't getting done. In fact, the *Reconnecting Workspaces* book was finally brought across the finish line in terms of updating and editing, based on the 21 minutes of deep focus created by taking pause midday.

Many lessons were learned by the dozens of professionals who joined me in these early 2021 sprints, including:

- There's power in the pause—even for 21 minutes.
- I can get a lot done in 21 minutes.
- When I am not interrupted for 21 minutes, I can achieve a lot.
- The *PlanDoTrack* Philosophy of "Daily Steps + Consistent Action = Momentum" really works! Daily steps really do add up to significant amounts.

I hope you will consider joining us for a future 21-for-21.

FIELD WORK—NOW WHAT?

Questions to consider:

What would be the benefit of scheduling a virtual co-working session?

_____

_____

_____

_____

When could you put a 1- to 4-hour block in the calendar with one or more colleagues?

_____

_____

_____

_____

What would you put on your "To Do" list?

_____

_____

_____

_____

Who would you like to develop some co-working relationships with?

_____

_____

_____

_____

NOTES AND REFLECTIONS:

THIS WEEK'S FOUNDATION THEME WAS
TRICKY ISSUES

It's the end of another week. What was it like? Describe it here in three words:

_____ . _____ . _____

This week we explored the following topics:

- Day 71—Memorability
- Day 72—Micro-Monitor: Challenges and Opportunities
- Day 73—Intercultural Mindset
- Day 74—Delegation
- Day 75—Working Across Time Zones
- Day 76—Simplify and Keep It Simple
- Day 77—Co-Working

Wrap up theme for the week:

_____

_____

_____

_____

What are you looking forward to?

_____

_____

_____

_____

What questions do you have?

_____

_____

_____

_____

What To-Dos have surfaced? (List your top 3–5)

1.

2.

3.

4.

5.

Update your tracking sheet!

WEEK 12 · EXPERIMENTATION

> "With experimentation comes surprise and discovery.
> —Kim Lee Kho

Welcome to Week 12! This week's theme is all about Experimentation.

Our roadmap for this week is:

- Day 78—Leveraging Your Support Network
- Day 79—Lightbulb Moments and Innovation
- Day 80—Flexibility
- Day 81—Renewal/Release Valve/Well-Being
- Day 82—Experimentation
- Day 83—What's Beyond the Screen?
- Day 84—What Doesn't Get Scheduled, Doesn't Get Done

This week's theme is ***Experimentation***. It's about innovation, support so you can do even better work, insight, renewal, and looking beyond the screen.

Living and leading in the remote world is all about experimentation. It's about focus and the ability to innovate and pivot.

WHAT ARE YOUR TOP 3 GOALS THIS WEEK?:

1. _____

2. _____

3. _____

By the end of the week I want to be sure that . . .

_____

DAY 78

LEVERAGING YOUR SUPPORT NETWORK

"One of the greatest values of mentors is the ability to see ahead what others cannot see and to help them navigate a course to their destination."
—John C. Maxwell

FOCUS QUESTION:

Who is in your network? How can others support you? How do you support them?

WHAT?

Back in Week 1 we started exploring different modalities for support. In one of the final weeks of your 90-day period, we're bringing it together again. As a remote worker, you are likely getting support from a variety of people, including a supervisor, coach, mentor, peers (internal and external), and others.

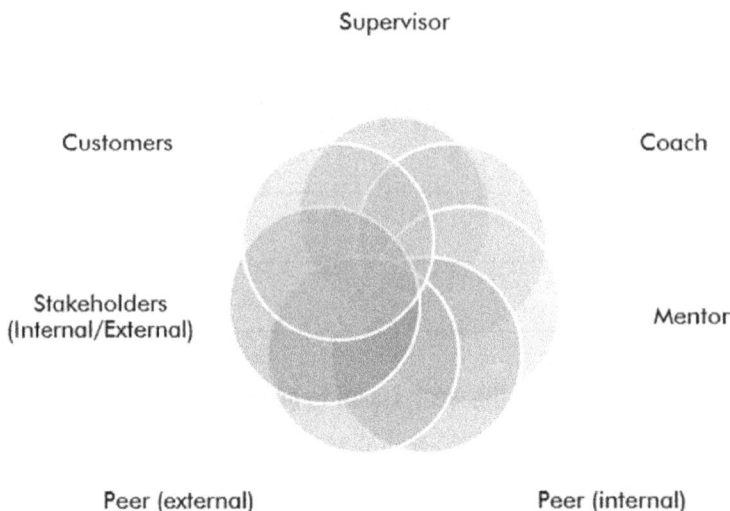

Supervisor

Customers

Coach

Stakeholders
(Internal/External)

Mentor

Peer (external)

Peer (internal)

The difference between mentoring and coaching is often seen as subtle, but there is a significant difference between the role of the coach and mentor. A coach is a thinking partner who helps you to tap into your own knowledge, may connect you with information you need, and will put a huge emphasis on accountability. They will hold your feet to the fire, help you hash out the things that didn't work, and also will take a neutral stance.

Your mentor can speak from their own experience; and while they may be happy to check in around what you are doing, they likely don't have as big a vested interest in this. Your mentor is a great resource to help you understand the hidden currents and dynamics of an organization or industry. Word of caution: They speak from their experience, which sometimes can be dated. Be sure to use your own intuition and good sense to figure out the best answer for yourself.

Tips for Leveraging Your Mentor

Topics you might want to take to your mentor:

- How do I . . . ?
- How did you . . . ?
- How do I raise issues to my boss?
- How do I navigate . . . ?
- What was your biggest challenge . . . ?
- What were you most proud of?

SO WHAT?

Coaches and mentors are two important relationships. What are the other collaborative relationships and people who can help you grow?

Tips for leveraging support of a professional coach like Mel (of the Digital Dozen). Coaches are often a valuable thinking partner to explore options and talk through tricky issues from an unbiased stance.

People find that coaching has many benefits including the following:

- Helping them articulate what's important
- Taking action in areas where they may not be moving as quickly
- Getting unstuck around difficult issues by getting clearer on the issues, breaking it down into chunks, taking action, or unearthing what's at the core
- Going deeper into problems

- Exploring available opportunities

- Sorting through the priorities

- Creating a plan that they can work with

Coaching may involve:

- Pausing to identify and analyze what's happening in complex situations.

- Acting as a shadow and observing you in a meeting, high stakes environment, and/or setting you seek feedback on. The coach can do some real-time coaching in the moment.

- Undertaking real-time work with you to polish and prepare for an upcoming presentation or conversation.

FIELD WORK—NOW WHAT?

Consider who you need to activate or add to your network in order to do your best work. Take a few minutes to focus on what you see as the role of each of these partners. What types of issues do you want to take to them? Complete the graphic shown a couple of pages back.

LIGHTBULB MOMENTS AND INNOVATION

"If you want something new, you have to stop doing something old."
—Peter F. Drucker

FOCUS QUESTION:

What does innovation look like in your work? What's going to help create new lightbulb moments?

WHAT?

The Oxford Dictionary defines innovation as "a new method, idea, product, etc." Innovation is also about responding to changes and doing things differently in the face of change and disruption. With this in mind, the landscape of coaching groups and teams around innovation is quite broad.

Innovation may refer to things that may not have been done before, or even created. What role does innovation play in your work?

Did You Know?

Here are a few ways to get new ideas percolating:

- Think about getting all your ideas out around a project by creating a mind map. Put it away and then look at it again later in the day, or the next day.
- Take a walk and see what new ideas bubble up.
- Connect with someone who works in a different part of your organization or works in a different industry. See what a conversation with them can invoke.

SO WHAT?

What's interesting about innovation for remote workers is the fact that many of the "lightbulb" moments people experience happen when we aren't necessarily thinking about things. Sometimes we need to step away, let our brain work on things, and then come back to them. This might involve a change of scenery or even a change of task.

What breaks do you want to give yourself? Are you replacing your commute time with more work, or with time to get away from your desk?

Where to Go?

In her book, *Design Works*, Heather Fraser[95] writes that the following skills are needed to build a mindset of innovation: empathy, openness, mindfulness, intrinsic motivation, embracing constraints, courage and vulnerability, positivity and optimism, and resilience.

Which ones are important for you to note?

FIELD WORK—NOW WHAT?

In what areas do you want to create new ideas?

_____

_____

_____

_____

What will help you innovate?

_____

_____

_____

_____

NOTES AND REFLECTIONS:

FLEXIBILITY

"A tree that is unbending is easily broken."
—Lao Tzu

FOCUS QUESTION:
Where do you need to be more flexible?

WHAT?

One of the most important skills for remote professionals today is flexibility. We have all needed to become more flexible, fluid, and agile.

Flexibility is a skillset that is hard to develop. Flexibility may be required when:

- You work across matrix teams who have competing priorities.
- You work with colleagues who are working in different time zones.
- Things are changing so quickly that you need to constantly be adjusting the way you do things.

Did You Know?

Flexibility and adaptability are key in today's teams. The business context continues to shift and change with the need to be agile and fluid. As team leaders, we can help our teams become more flexible and adaptable. Here are some actions we can undertake:

1. Model this in your own behavior in terms of how you approach changes.

2. Encourage contingency thinking—in many workplaces today, it is likely that things will not *work* as planned or will not *happen* as planned. Getting into the habit of thinking about "What else?" or "What other options are there?" is useful.

3. Encourage out-of-the-box thinking.

4. Get team members thinking about different perspectives and approaches.

5. Encourage both right- and left-brain thinking—both the creative and reactive way.[96]

SO WHAT?

It's easy to say we need to be more flexible, but what does that really mean?

Building more flexibility—knowing which work has the option for being flexible and when things realistically can get done.

Enrolling others with whom you partner, around a dialogue regarding flexibility and delivery dates—what is reasonable with both of your processes. This may lead to new timelines and options.

FIELD WORK—NOW WHAT?

Consider where you could benefit from being more flexible and adaptable.

_____

_____

_____

_____

What are the strategies you want to use?

_____

_____

_____

_____

RENEWAL/RELEASE VALVE/WELL-BEING

"We must always change, renew, rejuvenate ourselves; otherwise we harden."
—Johann Wolfgang von Goethe

FOCUS QUESTION:

What are you doing to renew? What release valves have you created?

WHAT?

From Microsoft's invoking a virtual-commute option for remote workers to acknowledgement six months into the pandemic that boundaries are a key issue, it's important to build wellness routines into your work.

The life of a remote worker can be very full, particularly for team members who work across distance and time and have a family. It's a 365-day, 24-7 world. Well-being and renewal are not always at the top of people's list. What are you doing to renew and be at your peak? What are you doing to blow off steam?

Did You Know?

Here are some strategies for creating more pause on an individual basis:

- Cultivate hobbies.
- Establish fixed start and end times.
- Switch off your screens.
- Dedicate a specific workspace for yourself.
- Put things away and power down at the end of the day.

SO WHAT?

Renewal—consider what's going to help you renew. How much is too much? No one else will tell you what you need to do and when you need to sign off. You can figure this out for yourself.

FAQ: Renewal—People talk about burnout. What does that mean?

A January 2021 *Harvard Business Review* article by Bobbi Thomason[97] noted that burnout was at an all-time high for work-from-home team members. They defined burnout as "chronic workplace stress that has not been successfully managed."

It's critical to address burnout before it happens. The cost of burnout from the pandemic has been huge. It was estimated that people were working 3 hours a week more in spring of 2020.[98] By 2021 this had risen further.

A 2021 Microsoft report, *The Next Disruption Is Hybrid Work—Are You Ready?*, noted:

> Workers in Canada are trending more toward burnout: in a typical workday, "47 percent of workers in Canada feel exhausted (versus the 39 percent global average) and 51 percent feel stressed (versus the 42 percent global average)."[99]

Queen and Harding's 2021 article, "Societal Pandemic Burnout: A COVID-19 Legacy," explores many ideas for combatting burnout.[100]

Today's text box invites you to consider some of the many strategies which can be employed to beat burnout. Another significant one is to build in what I term the "Power of the Pause."[101] Let's look at that now.

In today's digitally disrupted world, so many professionals are *on* all the time, with very few windows to **pause**, **reflect**, and **take action**.

As a virtual facilitator yourself, you too may have fallen into the trap of scheduling items right up to the last minute, or rushing from one call to another without even having had the chance to get up and stretch a little. If this is your reality, what about the experience of your clients?

How could you create more pause in your work? Here are a few ideas for creating more micro-pause:

- **Set a timer** and let people know that you will be moving through a series of reflective pauses. Check out this quarterly reflection session I led in early 2021, which shows I use it for extended periods. (See YouTube.com/watch?v=9f4ESiJN8ko)

- **Provide people with a chance to breakout** with others and talk through their insights and activities

- **Provide 2 minutes of silence** at the end of a call so that people can write things down or mind-map their ideas, and/or complete a One-Page Plan.

- **Provide a 10- to 15-minute window for people to get up stretch, and move around.** You might leave them with a question to reflect on during the process.

What action steps can you take around creating more pause points? It could even be as simple as exploring the chimes available on your phone to see what you could set the timer for.

FIELD WORK—NOW WHAT?

Consider what you are building in to create release valves for yourself.

_____

_____

_____

Relaxation Pursuits—what are the things that help you relax?

_____

_____

_____

What do you want to make sure you are building-in time for, with your work these days?

_____

_____

_____

What are the questions to be asking yourself?

_____

_____

_____

What are the things which can help you unwind?

_____

_____

_____

DAY 82

EXPERIMENTATION

"Don't be too timid and squeamish about your actions. All life is an experiment."
—Ralph Waldo Emerson

FOCUS QUESTION:

Where are you experimenting? Where does the experimental mindset serve you?

WHAT?

The experimental mindset is a core approach for many remote workers today. It is an entire approach to doing work. Embedded in the experimental mindset are:

- Trial and error

- Approaching things in different ways, sometimes radically different from each other—which may help to foster new ideas and approaches being discovered

- Creating a hypothesis—a guess to see what may happen

Experiments you may want to try:

- When is the best time of day to work?

- How much work can you get done in an hour?

- Noticing where your attention is? Where are you focusing? What is your attention span?

- Exploring what is the optimum length of a meeting?

- What type of reporting do you do best?

Did You Know?

An experimental mindset means that we are:

- Open to outcome

- Curious about what makes it happen

- Unattached to the end result

- In a learner's, or beginner's mindset—in other words, "I don't know everything; I am open to learning and seeing what happens"

- Focused on data; taking time to note what happens, the process we follow, and the outcome which is possible.

SO WHAT?

Experimentation is another mindset which can be very useful. Experimentation means that you are trying things out. Starting with an initial hypothesis, experimentation may mean that we are seeing how things work. It may involve doing things more quickly, trying things out, or even building a prototype, rather than doing things over a longer term in depth.

Ongoing learning is a critical mindset. It's likely that the context will continue to change, just as the remote world is changing rapidly every day.

More has been written on this topic from Carol Dweck and her growth mindset material.[102] Return back to Day 50 for more on the topic of Mindset.

EXPERIMENTATION AND "GOOD ENOUGH"

As a remote professional, you may find it challenging to be well rounded in everything. Experimentation can be helpful in creating greater ease for ourselves. It is not easy to be good at everything.

Knowing when things are "good enough" can save a lot of heartache. "Good enough" gets us out of the trap of things needing to be perfect. Having conversations with your colleagues around what *good enough* means is important, so you know when to move on.

While it can be useful to have tenacity and be persistent, there are some things you may want to outsource. This might include things like accounting, graphic design, administrative tasks. Just as we know in strengths, it's harder to develop skills in areas where we are not so proficient. What things do you want to let go of? Refer to the earlier focus on Delegation (Day 74).

FIELD WORK—NOW WHAT?

Consider what is important for you around the experimental mindset. Where could you benefit from more rapid iterations, learning, and some trial and error?

_____

_____

_____

_____

_____

_____

_____

_____

What does "good enough" mean for you?

_____

_____

_____

_____

_____

_____

_____

NOTES AND REFLECTIONS:

DAY 83

WHAT'S BEYOND THE SCREEN?

"Good leaders organize and align people around what the team needs to do. Great leaders motivate and inspire people with why they're doing it. That's purpose. And that's the key to achieving something truly transformational."
—Marillyn Hewson

FOCUS QUESTION:

What's happening in the world and context outside of your screen?

WHAT?

One of the challenges in today's remote and virtual workspace is that people see only a small window of our world. It is literally what we show them on our screen.

Did You Know?

As more people moved to the virtual conversation space, an increasing number of people focused on the 20-20-20 approach to rest in the virtual space.

This practice invites us to take a rest every 20 minutes by spending 20 seconds looking away from your screen to a distance 20 feet in the distance.

This practice is said to help with eye strain.

SO WHAT?

So, what's happening beyond the little 2 x 3 box on your screen?

This is a challenge given that *context* is so important for business today. Helping others understand our world occurs through the stories and information we share. It can also be influenced by what we choose to share.

Today's prompt gets you thinking about the question, "What do you want to share with others?"

Going beyond the screen could include:

- A different view behind you
- A snapshot of a project you are working on
- An illustration of the different people you liaise with
- A map of your key priorities for the next quarter
- Something related to your most important priority right now
- Sharing an inspirational message every day

If you are a remote team, it might be interesting to have everyone mix it up at your next team meeting. Ask people to dial in from somewhere different, or intentionally build in time to share a priority.

What do you want to share about your work right now with others?

This information was adapted from https://www.potentialsrealized.com/teams-365-blog/teams365-2093-effective-virtual-conversations-tip-112-beyond-the-screen.

In a team environment, sharing a little about our context can go a long way in building appreciation, empathy, and helping with prioritization.

What's important to note about your work?

FIELD WORK—NOW WHAT?

Consider the contextual issues beyond your screen that require attention. What's important to note?

_____

_____

_____

_____

_____

_____

DAY 84

WHAT DOESN'T GET SCHEDULED, DOESN'T GET DONE

"I recommend you take care of the minutes and
the hours will take care of themselves."
— Philip Dormer Stanhope, Earl of Chesterfield

FOCUS QUESTION:

What are you making time for in your schedule?
(What doesn't get scheduled, doesn't get done.)

WHAT?

What doesn't get scheduled, doesn't get done.

Michael Hyatt is said to have issued this phrase. In the remote space it is significant, given that its main intent is to keep things visible and top of mind. In the remote space it is likely that remote workers will find themselves with either too little to do or, sometimes, too much to do. What can get pushed off to the sides is the important work that people need to undertake.

Did You Know?

There are many different scheduling systems, including:

- The Franklin Covey methodology of considering what is urgent and what is important
- Covey's "Big Rocks"
- The ABC method of prioritizing

- The Eisenhower Method
- Michael Hyatt's Focus on the Big 3
- The *PlanDoTrack* Focus on the Top 5

SO WHAT?

What are some different ways for scheduling my calendar? I find that I'm working around the clock, but I'm not getting the important things done.

It can be very common to find that we are spending our time on the activities that really do not have the greatest impact. As I share in *Reconnecting Workspaces*, we can divide tasks down into several categories, including:

- *Quick wins*—projects that will give you traction and that, while they are important, may not always be the most impactful

- *Major projects*

- *Time fillers*—things like social media are time fillers which "seem" to have an impact, but may not be impactful

- *Must-dos*—Tasks that need to get done, often because they are important for others. Examples: taxes, reports, etc.

Where are you spending your time?

Are you blocking in time for the most important activities?

Action does not always equal progress.

Questions to consider:

- What core activities are critical to do?
- What kind of scheduling will benefit you daily? Weekly? Monthly?
- What is the benefit of putting pen to paper or fingers to keyboard?
- What will help you with visibility and focus?
- What really needs to get scheduled on a regular basis?
- What would your key stakeholders say needs to get scheduled in more?
- When have you scheduled in time for review?
- What chunks of work need to get scheduled because they keep getting focused on?

FIELD WORK—NOW WHAT?

Consider what tasks are most important for you to be scheduling in.

What isn't getting done consistently?

_____

_____

_____

_____

_____

_____

What is feeling like it needs more time?

_____

_____

_____

_____

_____

What parts of your schedule aren't working?

_____

_____

_____

_____

_____

_____

_____

_____

NOTES AND REFLECTIONS:

PARTNER	ROLE	ISSUES	OTHER

THIS WEEK'S FOUNDATION THEME WAS
EXPERIMENTATION

That's it for this week. What was it like? Describe it here in three words:

_____ . _____ . _____

Here are the areas we covered:

- Day 78—Leveraging Your Support Network
- Day 79—Lightbulb Moments and Innovation
- Day 80—Flexibility
- Day 81—Renewal/Release Valve/Well Being
- Day 82—Experimentation
- Day 83—What's Beyond the Screen
- Day 84—What Doesn't Get Scheduled, Doesn't Get Done

Wrap up theme:

_____

_____

_____

_____

_____

What are you looking forward to?

_____

_____

_____

_____

_____

_____

What questions do you have?

_____

_____

_____

_____

_____

_____

What To-Dos have surfaced? (List your top 3–5)

1.

2.

3.

4.

5.

Update your tracking sheet!

WEEK 13 · MOVING IT FORWARD/TRACK

> "Trust only movement. Life happens at the
> level of events, not of words. Trust movement."
> —Alfred Adler

Welcome to Week 13! This week is our last week of the quarter and this series. This week it is all about noticing what you have achieved, what you want to integrate, and how to move it forward.

You are encouraged to build in some time to take stock and review things this week.

There is also a *Bonus Day* geared to getting you to think about your learning throughout this process.

Here's our roadmap for the week:

- Day 85—Integration
- Day 86—Remote ≠ Disconnected: DNA of Remote
- Day 87—Track
- Day 88—Questions
- Day 89—Creativity
- Day 90—What's Next?
- Day 91—Bonus: Wrap It Up

WHAT ARE YOUR TOP 3 GOALS THIS WEEK?:

1. _____

2. _____

3. _____

By the end of the week I want to be sure that . . .

_____

This week's theme is on Tracking. Tracking is a key part of the learning process. It allows us to notice what has changed over time. This learning then helps to shape what ideas we want to integrate as we move ahead.

Metrics are an important part of the virtual work space. They help us note where things are at, at any given time. Data is power and can translate across time and space.

As we go to complete a process like this, it can also be useful to:

- Identify your major milestones along the way,
- Distill down your key learning, and
- Integrate it by putting it into practice.

What is important for you to note?

CONVERSATION WITH THE DIGITAL DOZEN

Everyone has a different process for learning and integration. In this conversation with the Digital Dozen, we check in on what's important for them. It includes:

> **Serge:** "As a serial entrepreneur, I've found it key to keep things moving by building in regular points to track and note my learning. It's also been important to harness what those key learnings are, so that I can continue to scale business and apply learning to new business ventures."

> **Mel:** "As a coach, I spend a lot of time supporting others through the reflective pause of a coaching conversation. Coaching is not just only about getting into action, it's about "doing the right things." In a super-charged world, a key process is to take time to pause and note what you have accomplished through what you are tracking around your milestones, in order to distill learning. Supporting people by creating ongoing checkpoints as they integrate their learning is a large part of my professional focus."

> **Sujit:** "As a project manager, I am always thinking about how teams can break their tasks down into smaller components. I am all about helping identify what are the tasks and activities which will help to shift into action."

> **Ned:** "As the newest member to remote work of the Digital Dozen, I have come to realize how important it is to focus on my tasks and activities."

D A Y   8 5
INTEGRATION

"Great works are performed not by strength, but by perseverance."
—Samuel Johnson

FOCUS QUESTION:
What do you want to integrate in order to move things forward?

WHAT?

Learning and insights are great, and they have to be put into practice. Part of moving things forward is taking time to integrate your learning, connect the dots, and put it into play.

PlanDoTrack's tagline is **Consistent Action + Daily Steps = Momentum**. In today's virtual and remote world, it is unlikely that we will get huge swaths of time to do things. With that in mind, what do integration and moving it forward look like or mean to you?

Questions to Help You Connect the Dots

- What patterns do you notice?
- What did you put into practice?
- What five themes stand out?
- How does it all connect together?
- What does moving things forward mean for you?
- Who can you activate to help you?

- What do you need to wrap up and complete?
- What do you need to focus on?
- What is going to keep you accountable?

SO WHAT?

Integration is a key part of the learning process. In the shift to a focus on 90-day windows of work, away from an annual cycle, we want to build in more time for integration points. It's grounded in the notion of integrative learning, which can be defined as follows:

> Integrative learning brings together prior knowledge and experience to support new knowledge and experiences. By doing this, learners draw on their skills and apply them to new experiences at a more complex level.[103]

This is important, as it allows us to get better and do things at a deeper level the next time round. You are encouraged to work through this at another layer, next quarter. Each time you pass through it, you will see new layers. Course Creator Marisa Murgatroyd likens it to moving up a spiral staircase. On each pass of the staircase, you see new details in the paintings on the wall.

Consider these questions to support your integration

What themes have emerged?

What do I notice about the connection?

Who else can support me with this learning, and action?

What can I do to put this into practice?

FIELD WORK—NOW WHAT?

Review your notes on what you said you would do.

What are the To-Dos you said you would do? Make a list. Schedule them in.

_____

_____

_____

_____

_____

_____

_____

_____

Who can help you with them?

_____

_____

_____

_____

_____

_____

_____

_____

Identify the roadblocks that might get in the way.

_____

_____

_____

_____

_____

_____

_____

_____

Identify the things that will help or enable you.

_____

_____

_____

_____

_____

_____

_____

_____

DAY 86

REMOTE ≠ DISCONNECTED: DNA OF REMOTE

"Remote work is the future of work."
—Alexis Ohanian

FOCUS QUESTION:
What's your core DNA? What is your presence?

WHAT?

Remote does not mean disconnected. In working as a remote worker, it is important to stay present in your conversations and focus.

In the book, *Presence*, Amy Cuddy defines *presence* as "the state of being attuned to and able to comfortably express our true thoughts, feelings, values and potential.[104]

Presence is how we show up. It is about being present.

Presence is about our focus and where we are placing our attention. Are you fully attuned to the people you are connected with, or are you focusing on something else?

Presence is also about the environment we create around us. Consider the calls you lead. What is the environment you want to create?

What do you want to imprint with others? What is infectious about your own team culture? What do you inspire others to do?

Our DNA is something that makes us unique. The DNA of a remote worker may include:

- Persistence
- Yearning for something different
- Yearning for connection
- Groundedness
- Yearning for flexibility
- Lone wolf syndrome—part of a pack but also able to go out on their own. Confidence in their own abilities. Deep trust with self. Knowing of their boundaries, which may have been weathered over time and shaped by feedback, journeys, and bruises.

What journeys have shaped you?

What are you calling others forward to do?

Did You Know?

As you think about your characteristics and what makes you unique, consider:

- Your strengths
- Your values
- What skills (technical, interpersonal, other) you bring
- Your philosophies

What makes you unique?

SO WHAT?

It's important to think about our presence in remote and hybrid work, given that things get magnified in the remote space. It's about thinking through how we show up and the environment we want to create.

Our DNA is unique to ourselves, and it helps to shape who we are. Understanding who we are is valuable with the many skills we've explored.

Another layer of our DNA is sharing our stories.

Taking time to share our stories has one of the most significant influences. Our stories demonstrate our *Why*—the thing that drives us forward. Our stories also are a unique tapestry of who we are. Our DNA, our journey, our aspirations and hopes, our learning and moments of defeat.

Our stories help to translate/transmit who we are, and what we take a stand for. Our stories will signal where we put our foot down. Where we say no.

Sharing our stories creates connection and creates a common ground.

Stories are part of a collective global process. What things do you want to communicate?

How can the team also share their stories? What might they do as a collective?

Creating a collaborative story—these are the things that make it work or not.

What does success mean for you?

FIELD WORK—NOW WHAT?

Consider how you are showing up in your conversations. Are you inviting or repelling people?

_____
_____
_____
_____

What is the environment you want to create with your calls? Consider everything from your background to the pacing.

_____
_____
_____
_____

What is the core of your DNA? Identify and note the characteristics which make you unique.

_____
_____
_____
_____

Review and note what you have learned about yourself during this 90-day journey:

What's been important for you?

_____

_____

_____

_____

_____

_____

What is at your CORE?

_____

_____

_____

_____

_____

_____

What elements make you unique?

_____

_____

_____

_____

_____

_____

NOTES AND REFLECTIONS:

D A Y 8 7

TRACK

"Tracking in the remote space is one of the most
important things we can do for high performance."
—Jennifer Britton

FOCUS QUESTION:
What does the data say?

WHAT?

One of the three tenets of *PlanDoTrack* is Track. As we move into the last few days of this series, what are you noticing about the activities and results you have achieved?

Note the trackers that you want to follow around your major milestones. They could be calls, sales, team huddles, etc.

Remember, there are several tracking tools available to you in the *PlanDoTrack* planner, including:

- **Monthly daily trackers**—with space to track more than 10 areas, consider some of the habits and consistent actions you want to get into this year, or the results you want to track. Complete these daily or at the end of a week.

- **Quarterly trackers**—this 90-Day Guide is a great example of how you might revisit this each quarter over the course of a year (4 x).

- **Content trackers**—use these to note what context you have created or shared.

- **Annual trackers**—use these to summarize key data in one source so you can see it.

Trackers can be a great way to get habits ingrained. What habits do you notice in your work and routine?

Did You Know?

We can track a variety of items, including:

- **Personal items**—reading time, time spent with loved ones, journaling
- **Fitness goals**—time spent walking, at the gym, swimming, minutes active, heart rate, sleep achieved
- **Business goals**—calls made, revenue in, program design time, product design time
- **Special projects**—components of the project, which might include elements of design or implementation

SO WHAT?

As you consider your annual or quarterly goals, what major milestones have you accomplished? Milestones are things we can measure or use as markers of our achievement.

If you have been working on creating a new course, milestones might be drafting and producing a certain number of modules.

Or maybe you have been working to increase sales and enrollment into a program you offer. In this example, your milestones might include a certain number of registrations *or* a number of marketing messages.

FIELD WORK—NOW WHAT?

Look at your top 3 goals this year, or quarter, and identify and write out what the milestones are.

_____

_____

_____

_____

_____

_____

_____

_____

Get granular with what milestone success will look like.

_____

_____

_____

_____

_____

_____

_____

_____

_____

_____

_____

_____

Mark the items and the milestone checklist in your calendar.

NOTES AND REFLECTIONS:

DAY 88
QUESTIONS

"The art and science of asking questions is the source of all knowledge."
—Thomas Berger

FOCUS QUESTION:

What questions are going to create new insights, action, relationships, and results for you?

WHAT?

> "Questions form the backbone to any great conversation."
> —Jennifer Britton, *From One to Many: Best Practices for Team and Group Coaching*

Questions are used for a variety of purposes in coaching. The most powerful are often *What? Why?* and *How?*

"What" questions are usually the most powerful. They are the questions that open up the space for insights and exploration. "Why" questions may cause people to justify their behavior or position. "How" questions put people into process.

As we go to wrap up the *Guide*, what questions can continue the conversations moving forward for you?

Questions to Ask Regularly

- What's possible?
- What else?
- What's another way of looking at things?
- What's going to create impact?
- What's going to create connection?
- What's important about that?
- What isn't being focused on?
- What's your priority?

SO WHAT?

Here are **17 "How-to" questions** you might be asking yourself:

- How to delegate in the remote space?
- How to provide feedback in the remote space?
- How to manage up in the remote space?
- How to prioritize in the remote space?
- How to support your team members moving through change in the remote space?
- How to coach in the remote space?
- How to problem solve?
- How to design a meeting that has impact?
- How to lead a conference call?
- How to design a memorable virtual presentation?
- How to get things done?
- How to figure out how much time a task is going to take?
- How to build trust and connection with your group
- How to build connection in the virtual space?
- How to stay at peak with your work?
- How to focus as a remote worker?
- How to ensure that the work you are doing is the best work?

And **3 What questions** to explore:

- What to simplify as a remote worker?
- What to prioritize?
- What can it look like?

FIELD WORK—NOW WHAT?

As you continue with your journey, what else is important to note?

_____

_____

_____

_____

_____

_____

Take a few minutes to flip through any notes you have taken during the 90-day process. What's important to note? What elements can you connect together?

_____

_____

_____

_____

_____

_____

_____

_____

_____

_____

DAY 89

CREATIVITY

"Creativity is just connecting things. When you ask creative people how they did something, they feel a little guilty because they didn't really do it, they just saw something. It seemed obvious to them after a while. That's because they were able to connect experiences they've had and synthesize new things. "
—Steve Jobs

FOCUS QUESTION:
What does creativity look like for you?

WHAT?

Creativity is an important part of remote work. Creativity can involve creating new products or thinking about new ways to do things.

Finding creativity when there's nothing left in the tap. What are the go-to items you can create and focus on as you go forward?

Why is creativity important in the virtual, remote, and hybrid space?

Reconnecting Tip—Creativity

"Connection fosters creativity." Think about all these ways that connection "sparks" you. They might include:

- Hearing about an idea from a colleague

- Attending a virtual event from another industry
- Participating in group coaching with others, and getting inspired from what they share
- Participating in a virtual co-working session

SO WHAT?

What can you do to integrate more creativity into your work? Michael Gelb indicates that these seven elements are critical in fostering creativity in his work *How to Think Like DaVinci*. These include:

- **Curiosity (Curiosità)**—an insatiably curious approach to life and an unrelenting quest for continuous learning.
- **Independent thinking (Dimostrazione)**—learning happens through experience, trial, and error, and learning from that.
- **Sensory (Sensazione)**—the continual refinement of the senses, especially sight, as the means to enliven experience.
- **Uncertainty (Sfumato)**—defined as "going up in smoke", it includes the encouragement to embrace uncertainty along with paradox and ambiguity.
- **Balancing Creativity and Logic or Art and Science (Arte/Scienza)**—using science and art, logic and imagination. "Whole-brain" thinking.
- **Body and Mind (Corporalita)**—cultivating elements such as ambidexterity and fitness.
- **Connections (Connessione)**— "a recognition of and appreciation for the interconnectedness of all things and phenomena. Systems thinking."[105]

When do you get activated? Consider these lightbulb moments for remote workers:

- When you realize that you really love your work
- When you realize that you will never commute again!
- When you realize that the people you have met are just as real as those you work with shoulder to shoulder

FIELD WORK—NOW WHAT?

What are the elements of creativity?

_____

_____

_____

_____

What do you need to have in order to be creative?

_____

_____

_____

_____

What can you do to weave together the different DaVincian elements of creativity?

_____

_____

_____

_____

NOTES AND REFLECTIONS:

DAY 90
WHAT'S NEXT?

"Doing the best at this moment puts you in the best place for the next moment."
—Oprah Winfrey

FOCUS QUESTION:
What's next for you?

WHAT?

Congratulations!

We are at the end of this 90-day process. If you are new to role, you are likely feeling well established, and you have passed your probation stage. If you are a seasoned remote or hybrid worker, you have likely wrapped up some key projects during this 90-day cycle and are ready to get going on another sprint. What's next for you?

Regardless of your role, my guess is that you are a lot more confident now around different skills, *and* a lot clearer on what you know.

In Review

- Week 1—Trust
- Week 2—Connection
- Week 3—Clarity
- Week 4—Learning by Doing
- Week 5—Resilience and Change

- Week 6—Loneliness

- Week 7—Leadership and Planning

- Week 8—Focusing and Getting Things Done

- Week 9—Additional Conversations to Have

- Week 10—Technology

- Week 11—Tricky Issues

- Week 12—Experimentation

- Week 13—Moving It Forward/Track

SO WHAT?

Here are some of the things you likely have accomplished:

- You know where to go around specific issues

- You have a much better sense of who the different players are

- You can tell what motivates you and what detracts from motivation

- You have mastered the Need to Know, Nice to Know, and Where to Go

- You have a mentor in place

- You know your peers—their preferences, their strengths

Take stock of your skills and see where you are on each of the ratings. Note that some of these may have gone down in terms of the number. This is not a bad thing. It simply signals that more things need to be done.

What is going to be your focus for the next 270 days of the year? What's going to help you do your best work?

Over the last 90 days, we've explored this very long list of topics, from things that will help you get results to how to build relationships; from things that will focus on work to helping you thrive personally.

Note your key ideas from each of the weeks of this guide:

WEEK 1		**WEEK 8**	
WEEK 2		**WEEK 9**	
WEEK 3		**WEEK 10**	
WEEK 4		**WEEK 11**	
WEEK 5		**WEEK 12**	
WEEK 6		**WEEK 13**	
WEEK 7			

Over the next phase, you may want to revisit these and think about what the next layer of learning is around these topics.

As you go to wrap up this process consider:

What is going to help you do your best work going forward?

_____

_____

_____

Who are you going to be accountable to?

_____

_____

_____

What capacity have you developed? What needs attention?

_____

_____

_____

What's going to take your learning deeper?

_____

_____

_____

What do you see as the next phase?

_____

_____

_____

Who can you pass your skills onto?

_____

_____

_____

What are the things which are going to help you scale your skills and experience?

_____

_____

_____

What will help you to continue to do your best work?

_____

_____

_____

What feedback cycles do you want to build in?

_____

_____

_____

For further learning, check out:

- The *Remote Pathways* podcast—Would you like to share your experience? Drop me an email and let's see if we could feature you as part of the Voices from the Field
- *Reconnecting Workspaces*: *Pathways to Thrive in the Virtual, Remote and Hybrid World*, my 2021 book.
- MOOCs (massive open online courses) related to remote and hybrid work
- Internal training opportunities
- Formal learning opportunities
- Joining us at the Leadership Lab for ongoing conversations and focus

What do you as a remote and hybrid worker likely need to learn more about?

- After your 90 days is done, your learning doesn't end. In fact, it likely is just beginning. Major areas still need exploration which haven't been touched on here.
- Policies, procedures—do I need an HR list?
- Technical skills

This book is geared as an introduction or primer to what is important in the realm of work.

Each quarter you can start the process again. Each time you may want to focus on creating a list of 3–5 items you want to learn over that 3-month period—it might include conversations to have with your mentor, podcasts to subscribe to, and/or elements to focus on. What does your boss flag as learning for your team or your role?

What things are going to help you most in continuing to grow?

HOMECOMING

As you prepare to wrap up your 90-day journey, here are questions to consider in several core areas.

Learning, goals, and action:

- What have you learned?
- What have you accomplished during our time together in this 90-day cycle?
- What are you clear on now, that you did not know before?
- What are the top-five go-to resources you want to earmark?
- What key milestones are you aiming towards?
- What is your vision for your work—this year, in 3 years, in 5 years?

You as a remote worker:

- Note your personal brand. What three adjectives describe who you are? How you show up?

- What compliments have you received?

- What habits have you developed in your remote work? What other habits do you want to form?

- What strengths do you want to lean into?

- What don't you want to overmagnify?

Relationships:

- No person is an island. What key relationships are important to cultivate?

- What communities are you now a part of?

- Who do you want to take under your wing as a new remote worker? How has your network expanded?

Wellbeing:

- What are you going to do to renew?

- What release valves will you use when things get stressful?

Passing the learning on:

- What one piece of advice would you pass on to others?

- What else is important to note as a remote worker?

- A year from now, where do you want to be?

Skills:

- What skills still need focus on?

- Where are you most confident?

- What else do you want to provide your learning around?

- What other things might be important?

- What else is important to note?

FIELD WORK—NOW WHAT?

Be sure to answer the questions posed above. You may want to journal on them, or share with your coach, boss, mentor, or peer partner. Use these following questions to help with your synthesis of learning.

- What needs attention?_____
  _____
  _____
  _____

- Where are your strengths?_____
  _____
  _____
  _____

- Who can support you? What could support and ongoing learning look like?_____
  _____
  _____
  _____
  _____

- What else?_____
  _____
  _____
  _____

NOTES AND REFLECTIONS:

DAY 91 · BONUS · WRAP IT UP

"Creativity is the production of meaning by synthesis."
—Alex Faickney Osborn

FOCUS QUESTION:
What will pull all the pieces together for you?

WHAT?

As you likely have seen by now, things never really have a firm boundary in the remote and hybrid space. I'm back for a bonus day to help you synthesize your learning. There's no new content here, just questions to get you thinking about your work.

Across the last 90 days, we've covered a range of topics, from skills to beliefs, from practices to what's below the waterline. We've looked at such topics as key relationships to invest in and things like your vision, that you can return to time and time again.

As you go to wrap up, what did you notice about what's shifted for you?

What's next with your work?

What are the nuts and bolts you feel are now internalized and part of your habits?

What are the various perspectives you have come to take into consideration, as you make decisions and prioritize?

Who is there like a ring buoy to provide support and help you float along?

How are things connected, like gears on a wheel?

What have you noticed about the scaffolding of your learning? What's the base, and what new pieces have you built up?

Your learning and growth will not end at this stage. In fact, it's likely just begun. Returning to your internal workshop will allow you to pause, focus on, and tinker with your results.

What are the things you know you will want to earmark for revisiting?

Grab your calendar. When will you revisit your insights and actions?

Where have you moved to? What's in the rearview mirror?

It's All About the Conversation!

Let's keep the conversation going:

Continue the Conversation as part of the *Remote Pathways* podcast. You can find it on your favorite podcast player or at www.remotepathways.com/podcast.

Let's have some live conversation—join us at the Virtual and Remote Visionaries Hub on Facebook at www.facebook.com/groups/314116869730339/.

Check out the Community Calls I host. You'll find recordings posted at my YouTube channel: youtube.com/effectivegroupcoach.

Bring me or one of the Reconnecting Workspaces Certified Professionals in as a speaker, coach, or workshop leader to work with you, your team, or your organization. Contact us at info@potentialsrealized.com.

SO WHAT?

What is now part of your everyday routine? What have you outgrown?

What still needs support or to be contained, just like a fence?

What will serve as a bridge to help you move from here to there?

What needs to be put away or prettied up?

What needs to be anchored down?

As you move forward, earmark times to reconnect with your learning and take a pause. Earmark times to renew and review.

Thanks for joining us for this adventure. Let's continue the conversation over at ReconnectingWorkspaces.com

FIELD WORK—NOW WHAT?

What are the core activities you want to dedicate time and attention to?

_____

_____

_____

_____

_____

What do you need to let go of?

_____

_____

_____

_____

What else is important to note?

_____

_____

_____

_____

What do you want to celebrate?

_____

_____

_____

_____

Who will you celebrate with?

_____

_____

_____

_____

What structures are going to remind you of this journey?

_____

_____

_____

_____

_____

_____

THIS WEEK'S FOUNDATION THEME WAS
MOVING IT FORWARD/TRACK

It's the end of another week. What was it like? Describe it here in three words:

_____ · _____ · _____

This week we explored the following topics:

- Day 85—Integration
- Day 86—Remote ≠ Disconnected: DNA of Remote
- Day 87—Track
- Day 88—Questions
- Day 89—Creativity
- Day 90—What's Next?
- Day 91—Bonus: Wrap It Up

Wrap-up theme for the week:

_____

_____

_____

_____

What are you looking forward to?

_____

_____

_____

_____

What questions do you have?

_____

_____

_____

_____

_____

_____

_____

_____

What To-Dos have surfaced? (List your top 3–5)

1.

2.

3.

4.

5.

Update your tracking sheet!

90 DAYS IN REVIEW

OVER THE 90 DAYS WE EXPLORED THESE AREAS:

WEEK 1	Getting started. What's the same and different. Vision. Office. Relationships. Team effectiveness.
WEEK 2	Goals. Core skills for success. Relationships—your boss. Relationships—your peers. Navigating VUCA. Strengths. Communication.
WEEK 3	Systems for working remote. Planning. Personal brand. Time management and staying at peak. Motivation. Prioritization. Teams in focus—types of teams.
WEEK 4	Styles. Metrics matter. Project management. Stakeholder, personal productivity, and boundaries. Focus and attention. Getting things done. Teams in focus—matrix.
WEEK 5	Values. Month-end check-in. Mentoring. Obstacles and Challenges. Troubleshooting and Decision making. Getting Unstuck Coaching. Team Identity and culture.
WEEK 6	Iceberg—beliefs. Boundaries. Getting organized. Change cycle and dip. Routines. Problem solving. Teams in focus—performance measures and roles.
WEEK 7	Habits. Perception reality. Messy middle—mid-point check in. Influence. Focus. Presentations 101. Teams in focus.
WEEK 8	Iceberg—assumptions/mindset. Ongoing learning. High-leverage activities. Meetings. Consistent action—get it done. Collaboration. Teams in focus—tools in the toolbox.
WEEK 9	Virtual conversation skills. Feedback. Difficult conversations. Troubleshooting and month two check-in. Pitfalls. Negotiation. Circadian Rhythm.
WEEK 10	Reliability. Alchemy. Visibility. Productive or busy. Conflict. To do/not to do. Chunk it down.
WEEK 11	Memorability. Micro-monitor, intercultural/global mindset. Delegation. Working across time zones. Simplify and keep it simple. Co-working.
WEEK 12	Leveraging support. Lightbulb moments and innovation. Flexibility. Renewal/release valve/well-being. Experimentation. What's beyond the screen. What doesn't get scheduled, doesn't get done.
WEEK 13	Integration. DNA of remote. Track. Questions. Creativity. What's next? Bonus--wrap it up.

Take some time to review your notes and what your next steps are. Enjoy the reflection!

END NOTES

1   Brie Weiler Reynolds, "159% Increase in Remote Work Since 2005: FlexJobs & Global Work-place Analytics Report," Flexjobs.com, https://www.flexjobs.com/blog/post/flexjobs-gwa-report-re-mote-growth/ (accessed June 30, 2021).

2   "Gartner HR Survey Reveals 88% of Organizations Have Encouraged or Required Employees to Work from Home Due to Coronavirus," Gartner.com, https://www.gartner.com/en/newsroom/press-releases/2020-03-19-gartner-hr-survey-reveals-88--of-organizations-have-e (accessed June 30, 2021).

3   Michael D. Watkins, *The First 90 Days: Proven Strategies for Getting Up to Speed Faster and Smarter*, Updated and Expanded Edition (New York, NY: Harvard Business Review Press, 2013), pp. 5–6.

4   Watkins, *The First 90 Days*, pp. 9–10.

5   Simon Sinek, *The Infinite Game, Portfolio: 2019, p. 106.*

6   Jennifer J. Britton, *Reconnecting Workspaces,* (Toronto, Canada: Potentials Realized Media, 2021), p 90.

7   Ibid, p.107.

8   Ibid, p. 107.

9   Ibid, p.108.

10   Jennifer J. Britton, *PlanDoTrack Workbook and Planner for Remote and Virtual Professionals,* (Toronto, Canada: Potentials Realized Media, 2021),. p. 8.

11   Michael Hyatt, "Put the Big Rocks in First," (February 14, 2011), https://michaelhyatt.com/put-the-big-rocks-in-first/ (accessed June 30, 2021).

12   Gloria Mark, Daniela Gudith, and Ulrich Klocke, *The Cost of Interrupted Work: More Speed and Stress*, https://www.ics.uci.edu/~gmark/chi08-mark.pdf (accessed June 30, 2021).

13   *The Year 2009* (The People History, n.d.), http://www.thepeoplehistory.com/2009.html (accessed February 23, 2020).

14   Christoforos Pappas. "Top 10 e-Learning Statistics for 2014 You Need to Know." *ELearning Industry*. January 25, 2015. Accessed March 25, 2017. https://elearningindustry.com/top-10-e-learning-statistics-for-2014-you-need-to-know.

15   Jennifer J. Britton, *Effective Virtual Conversations,* (Toronto, Canada: Potentials Realized Media, 2017).

16   "Is Your Organization Ready to Be Flexible?", *HRD,* 2015, Issue 4.3, p. 48.

17   Brie Weiler Reynolds, "The Environmental Impacts of Remote Work: Stats and Benefits" (Flexjobs.com, n.d.), https://www.flexjobs.com/blog/post/telecommuting-sustainability-how-telecommuting-is-a-green-job/ (accessed June 30, 2021).

18   https://www.cosocloud.com/press-releases/connectsolutions-survey-shows-working-remotely-benefits-employers-and-employees

19   https://www.wbur.org/hereandnow/2019/07/23/work-from-home-benefits

20   Bloom, Nicholas & Liang, James & Roberts, John & Ying, Zhichun. (2013). Does Working from Home Work? Evidence from a Chinese Experiment. The Quarterly Journal of Economics. 130. 10.1093/qje/qju032.

21   https://www.owllabs.com/blog/remote-work-statistics

22   https://www.cbc.ca/news/business/statistics-canada-commute-times-study-1.5038796

23   https://www.wbur.org/hereandnow/2019/07/23/work-from-home-benefits

24   https://remote.co/office-noise-remote-work/

25   https://wwf.panda.org/wwf_news/?364390/earth-overshoot-day-2020

26   Greg Kratz, "More Proof Remote Work Is Becoming the Norm" (Remote.co, May 8, 2019), https://remote.co/proof-remote-work-becoming-norm/ (accessed June 30, 2021).

27   Lin Grensing-Pophal, *Managing Off-site Staff for Small Business* (Vancouver, BC, Canada: Self-Counsel Press Ltd, 2012), p. 115.

28   Jennifer Britton, "Day 11 of 12 Days of Holidays—Creating Your Vision for the New Year" (Potentials Realized, December 22, 2016), https://groupcoaching.blogspot.com/2016/12/day-11-of-12-days-of-holidays-creating.html. (accessed June 30, 2021).

29   Simon Sinek, *The Infinite Game* (Portfolio, 2019), p. 34.

30   Sinek, *The Infinite Game*, p. 26.

31 Jennifer Britton and Michelle Mullins, "Top 10 Tools to Get Things Done in the Virtual, Remote & Hybrid World," *Remote Pathways* (Podcast Episode 32), https://www.remotepathways.com/podcast/ep32-top-10-tools-to-get-things-done-in-the-virtual-remote-hybrid-world (accessed June 30, 2021).

32 Amy C. Edmondson, "The Importance of Teaming," (Boston, MA: Harvard Business School, April 25, 2012), https://hbswk.hbs.edu/item/the-importance-of-teaming

33 *2016 Trends in Global Virtual Teams* (CultureWizard by RW3, LLC, n.d.), https://www.rw-3.com/virtual-teams-survey-0.

34 Amy C. Edmondson, "How to Lead Exceptional Teams: Four Pillars for Effective, Engaged Teams" (Benedictine University, January 30, 2017), https://cvdl.ben.edu/blog/4-pillars-effective-teams/ (accessed June 30, 2021).

35 Jennifer J. Britton, *PlanDoTrack Workbook and Planner for Virtual and Remote Professionals* (Toronto, Canada: Potentials Realized Media, 2019), p. 13.

36 Twist, *Remote Projects 101: The Remote Guide to Project Management* (North Pole, AK: Doist, Inc., n.d.), https://twist.com/remote-work-guides/remote-project-management (accessed June 30, 2021).

37 https://www.garyranker.com/global-mindset/global-mindset-leadership-what-it-really-means/

38 "Minimizing Email Overload for Remote Teams," *PoliteMail* (November 11, 2020), https://politemail.com/minimizing-email-overload-for-remote-teams/ (accessed April 18, 2021).

39 Sammi Caramela, "Working from Home Increases Productivity," *Business News Daily* (March 31, 2020), https://www.businessnewsdaily.com/15259-working-from-home-more-productive.html (accessed April 21, 2021).

40 "Surprising Working from Home Productivity Statistics (2021)" (Apollo Technical, June 2, 2021), https://www.apollotechnical.com/working-from-home-productivity-statistics/ (accessed June 30, 2021).

41 Tess Hanna, "Nintex Workplace 2021 Study Shows Remote Work Improves Productivity," *Solutions Review* (February 5, 2021), https://solutionsreview.com/business-process-management/nintex-workplace-2021-study-shows-remote-work-improves-productivity/ (accessed April 21, 2021).

42 Tony Crabbe, *Busy: How to Thrive in a World of Too Much* (London: Piatkus, 2014), p. 62.

43 Crabbe, *Busy*, p. 62.

44 Ibid, p. 71.

45 "Multitasking: Switching Costs." (Washington, DC: American Psychological Association, March 20, 2006), https://www.apa.org/research/action/multitask (accessed June 30, 2021).

46   David, "Signal v. Noise: Business" (blog), https://signalvnoise.com/posts/3768-clutter-is-tak-ing-a-toll-on-both-morale-and (accessed June 30, 2021).

47   "Multitasking: Switching Costs."

48   Sydni Craig-Hart, "Startling Statistics on How Multitasking is *Really* Hurting Your Business," *Smart Simple Marketing* (March 8, 2013), https://smartsimplemarketing.com/startling-statis-tics-on-the-negative-effects-of-multitasking/ (accessed April 21, 2021).

49   Joseph Grenny and David Maxfield, "A Study of 1,100 Employees Found That Remote Workers Feel Shunned and Left Out," *Harvard Business Review* (November 2017), https://hbr.org/2017/11/a-study-of-1100-employees-found-that-remote-workers-feel-shunned-and-left-out (accessed April 21, 2021).

50   Stephen Denning, *The Age of Agile: How Smart Companies Are Transforming the Way Work Gets Done* (New York, NY: AMACOM, 2018), p. 37.

51   Peter Economy, "This Is the Way You Need to Write Down Your Goals for Faster Success," *Inc.* (February 28, 2018), https://www.inc.com/peter-economy/this-is-way-you-need-to-write-down-your-goals-for-faster-success.html (accessed June 30, 2021).

52   *The Age of Agile—How Smart Companies are Transforming the Way Work Gets Done* (AMA-COM, 2018), pp. 34–36.

53   Jennifer Britton, "Remote Work Myth: Out of Sight Does Not Mean Out of Mind," *Teams365 Blog*, Episode 2081 (Toronto, Canada: PotentialsRealized.com, September 11, 2019), https://www.potentialsrealized.com/teams-365-blog/teams365-2081-remote-work-myth-out-of-sight-does-not-mean-out-of-mind (accessed June 30, 2021).

54   Scott Frothingham, "How Long Does It Take for a New Behavior to Become Automatic?," *Healthline* (October 24, 2019), https://www.healthline.com/health/how-long-does-it-take-to-form-a-habit (accessed April 21, 2021).

55   Jennifer Britton, "Working with Different Styles in a Team: Part 1," *Teams365 Blog*, Episode 1568 (Toronto, Canada: PotentialsRealized.com, April 17, 2018), https://www.potentialsrealized.com/teams-365-blog/teams365-1568-working-with-different-styles-in-a-team-part-1 (accessed June 30, 2021).

56   Brigid Schulte, *Overwhelmed: Work, Love and Play When No One Has the Time* (Harper Peren-nial, 2014), p.126.

57   Jennifer Britton, "Working with Different Styles in a Team: Questions to Consider," *Teams365 Blog*, Episode 1569 (Toronto, Canada: PotentialsRealized.com, April 18, 2018), https://www.potentialsrealized.com/teams-365-blog/teams365-1569-working-with-different-styles-in-a-team-questions-to-consider) (accessed June 30, 2021).

58   Lou Russell, *10 Steps to Successful Project Management* (Alexandria, VA: ASTD Press, 2007).

59 Sue McGreevey, "Eight Weeks to a Better Brain," *The Harvard Gazette* (January 21, 2011), https://news.harvard.edu/gazette/story/2011/01/eight-weeks-to-a-better-brain/ (accessed June 30, 2021).

60 Jennifer Britton, "Matrix Management: 4 Keys to Making It Work," *Teams365 Blog*, Episode 594 (Toronto, Canada, PotentialsRealized.com, August 17, 2015), https://www.potentialsrealized.com/teams-365-blog/teams365-594-matrix-management-4-keys-to-making-it-work (accessed June 30, 2021).

61 Daniel Goleman, *Focus: The Hidden Driver of Excellence*, (New York, NY: Harper, 2013), p. 16.

62 Elan Botelho and Kim R. Powell, *The CEO Next Door*, (Redfern, New South Wales, Australia: Currency, 2018), p. 87.

63 Ibid. p. 214.

64 Mike Oppland, "8 Ways to Create Flow According to Mihaly Csikszentmihalyi," PositivePsychology.com (February 15, 2021), https://positivepsychology.com/mihaly-csikszentmihalyi-father-of-flow/ (accessed June 30, 2021).

65 Goleman, *Focus*, p. 22.

66 Wikimedia Commons, https://commons.wikimedia.org/wiki/File:PSM_V54_D328_Optical_illusion_of_a_duck_or_a_rabbit_head.png (accessed June 30, 2021).

67 International Coaching Federation, *2020 ICF Global Coaching Study: Executive Summary*, https://coachingfederation.org/app/uploads/2020/09/FINAL_ICF_GCS2020_ExecutiveSummary.pdf (accessed June 30, 2021).

68 Sinek, *The Infinite Game*, p. 121.

69 Jennifer Britton, "The Dip in Mentoring (and Coaching, and Learning, and Change . . .," *Teams365 Blog*, Episode 756 (Toronto, Canada, PotentialsRealized.com, January 26, 2016), https://www.potentialsrealized.com/teams-365-blog/teams365-756-the-dip-in-mentoring-and-coaching-and-learning-and-change (accessed June 30, 2021).

70 Michael Watkins, *The First 90 Days* (Harvard Business Review Press, 2013).

71 James Clear, *Atomic Habits: An Easy & Proven Way to Build Good Habits & Break Bad Ones* (New York, NY: Avery, 2018), p. 143.

72 Robert Cialdini, *Influence: The Psychology of Persuasion,* Rev. Ed. (New York, NY: Harper Business, 2006)

73 Center for Creative Leadership, "The Importance of Empathy in the Workplace" (November 28, 2020), https://www.ccl.org/articles/leading-effectively-articles/empathy-in-the-workplace-a-tool-for-effective-leadership/ (accessed June 30, 2021).

74   Jennifer J. Britton, *Effective Virtual Conversations: Engaging Digital Dialogue for Better Learning, Relationships and Results* (Toronto, Canada: Potentials Realized Media, 2017), Chapter 7.

75   Jennifer Britton, "Empathy and Building Connection in Virtual Teams," *Teams 365 Blog, (March 13, 2018)* https://www.potentialsrealized.com/teams-365-blog/teams365-1533-empathy-and-building-connection-in-virtual-teams

76   Kendra Cherry, "How to Practice Empathy During the COVID-19 Pandemic," *VeryWell Mind* (March 30, 2020), https://www.verywellmind.com/how-to-practice-empathy-during-the-covid-19-pandemic-4800924 (accessed June 30, 2021).

77   Sridhar Ramaswamy, "How Micro-Moments Are Changing the Rules, *Think with Google* (April 2015), https://www.thinkwithgoogle.com/marketing-strategies/app-and-mobile/how-micromoments-are-changing-rules/ (accessed June 30, 2021).

78   Jennifer Britton, *Effective Virtual Conversations: Engaging Digital Dialogue for Better Learning, Relationships and Results* (Toronto, Canada: Potentials Realized Media, 2017), pp 104-105

79   Lauren O'Neil, "Rates of Burnout among Canadian Office Workers Higher than Global Average," *BlogTO*, (March2, 2021), https://www.blogto.com/city/2021/03/rates-burnout-among-canadian-office-workers-higher-global-average/ (accessed 6.23.21)

80   Jennifer Britton, "Solopreneur Myth: I Need to Do It All Alone," *Coaching Business Builder* blog (November 11, 2019), https://www.coachingbusinessbuilder.com/blog/solopreneur-myth-i-need-to-do-it-all-alone (accessed June 30, 2021).

81   Jennifer Britton, "Remote Team Toolbox: Helping Teams Connect, Get to Know Each Other and Focus," *Teams365 Blog*, Episode 2130 (Toronto, Canada: PotentialsRealized.com, October 30, 2019), https://www.potentialsrealized.com/teams-365-blog/teams365-2130-remote-team-toolbox-helping-teams-connect-get-to-know-each-other-and-focus (accessed June 30, 2021).

82   Heidi Grant, "The One-Minute Trick to Negotiating Like a Boss," *Harvard Business Review* (June 11, 2013), https://hbr.org/2013/06/the-1-minute-trick-to-negotiat (accessed April 21, 2021).

83   Daniel Pink, *When: The Scientific Secrets of Perfect Timing* (New York, NY: Riverhead Books, 2018), p. 26.

84   Keith Ferrazzi, "Getting Virtual Teams Right," *Harvard Business Review* (December 2014), https://hbr.org/2014/12/getting-virtual-teams-right (accessed April 21, 2021); originally published as https://www.keithferrazzi.com/blog/getting-virtual-teams-right (accessed April 21, 2021).

85   Jeanne Sahadi, "Dell *really* wants you to work from home … if you want," *CNN Money* blog (June 9, 2016), https://money.cnn.com/2016/06/09/pf/dell-work-from-home (accessed August 12, 2021).

86   Laura Hanrahan, "Downtown Toronto Office Vacancy Rate Will Surpass 12% in 2021," *Daily Hive* (February 23, 2021), https://dailyhive.com/toronto/toronto-office-vacancy-rate-2021 (accessed April 18, 2021).

87   Indeed Editorial Team, "Remote Work Can Bring Benefits, but Attitudes Are Divided," *Indeed* blog (November 14, 2018), https://www.indeed.com/lead/remote-work-survey (accessed August 10, 2021).

88   Ibid.

89   Jennifer Britton, "Navigating Conflict in Teams," *Teams365 Blog*, Episode 1196 (Toronto, Canada: PotentialsRealized.com, April 10, 2017), https://www.potentialsrealized.com/teams-365-blog/teams365-1196-navigating-conflict-in-teams (accessed June 30, 2021).

90   "Hermann Ebbinghaus," *Wikipedia*, https://en.wikipedia.org/wiki/Hermann_Ebbinghaus (accessed June 30, 2021).

91   W. Todd Maddox, "Training for Retention in Virtual Reality and Computer-Based Platforms" Training Industry (November 14, 2017), https://trainingindustry.com/articles/learning-technologies/training-for-retention-in-virtual-reality-and-computer-based-platforms/ (accessed June 30, 2021).

92   Geert Hofstede, "National Culture," *Hofstede Insights* (n.d.), https://hi.hofstede-insights.com/national-culture (accessed June 30, 2021).

93   Gus Lubin, "These 8 Scales Reveal Everything You Should Know about Different Cultures," *Business Insider* (January 20, 2015), http://www.businessinsider.com/the-culture-map-8-scales-for-work-2015-1 (accessed June 30, 2021).

94   Jennifer Britton, "Team Springboard: Virtual Co-Working Sessions," *Teams365 Blog*, Episode 1940 (Toronto, Canada: PotentialsRealized.com, April 23, 2019), https://www.potentialsrealized.com/teams-365-blog/teams365-1940-team-springboard-virtual-co-working-sessions (accessed June 30, 2021).

95   Heather M A Fraser, *Design Works: How to Tackle Your Toughest Innovation Challenges through Business Design* (Toronto: Rotman, 2012), p. 19

96   Jennifer Britton, "Teamwork Foundations: Flexibility and Adaptability," *Teams365 Blog*, Episode 910 (Toronto, Canada: PotentialsRealized.com, June 28, 2016), https://www.potentialsrealized.com/teams-365-blog/teams365-910-teamwork-foundations-flexibility-and-adaptability (accessed June 30, 2021).

97   Bobbi Thomason, "Help Your Team Beat WFH [Work from Home] Burnout," *Harvard Business Review* (January 26, 2021), https://hbr.org/2021/01/help-your-team-beat-wfh-burnout (accessed April 21, 2021).

98 Michelle F. Davis and Jeff Green, "Three Hours Longer, the Pandemic Workday Has Obliterated Work-Life Balance," *Bloomberg* (April 23, 2020), https://www.bloomberg.com/news/articles/2020-04-23/working-from-home-in-covid-era-means-three-more-hours-on-the-job (accessed April 21, 2021).

99 "The Next Great Disruption Is Hybrid Work: Are We Ready?" *Microsoft WorkLab* (2021), https://www.microsoft.com/en-us/worklab/work-trend-index/hybrid-work (accessed June 30, 2021).

100 Douglas Queen and Keith G. Harding, "Societal Pandemic Burnout: A COVID Legacy," *International Wound Journal* (August 2020), DOI: 10.1111/iwj.13441, https://www.researchgate.net/profile/Douglas-Queen/publication/342737980_Societal_pandemic_burnout_A_COVID_legacy/links/5fb50dc892851cf24cdc738d/Societal-pandemic-burnout-A-COVID-legacy.pdf (accessed June 30, 2021).

101 Jennifer Britton, "The Power of a Pause," *Effective Virtual Conversations* newsletter (October 2019).

102 Carol S. Dweck, *Mindset: The New Psychology of Success* (New York, NY: Random House, 2007).

103 "Integrative Learning" (Edith Cowan University, Australia, n.d.), https://intranet.ecu.edu.au/learning/curriculum-design/teaching-strategies/integrative-learning (accessed June 30, 2021)

104 Amy Cuddy, *Presence: Bringing Your Boldest Self to Your Biggest Challenges* (New York, NY: Little, Brown Spark, 2018), p. 24.

105 Michael J. Gelb, "Excerpt from *How to Think Like Leonardo da Vinci: Seven Steps to Genius Every Day,*" Penguin/Random House Canada, 1998), https://www.penguinrandomhouse.ca/books/58928/how-to-think-like-leonardo-da-vinci-by-michael-j-gelb/9780440508274/excerpt (accessed April 21, 2021).

CONNECT WITH US!

The Book: ReconnectingWorkspaces.com

Our Services: PotentialsRealized.com

For Coaches: GroupCoachingEssentials.ca

Planner and Productivity: PlanDoTrack.com

Remote Pathways Podcast: RemotePathways.com

@ReconnectingWorkspaces

@RemotePathways

Virtual and Remote Visionaries Hub, Effective Group Coaching

ClubHouse: @jennbritton

Email: info@potentialsrealized.com

Phone: (416) 996-TEAM (8326)

Set up a 15-minute conversation about your
coaching, consulting, or training needs at

calendly.com/jennbritton

ABOUT THE AUTHOR

A trusted ally to thousands of coaches, business owners, teams and organizations since 2004, Jennifer Britton has dedicated her professional work over the last three decades to enhancing conversations and supporting results for businesses, teams, and organizations in the virtual, remote, and hybrid space.

An expert in group and team coaching and a performance improvement specialist, Jennifer founded her company, Potentials Realized, in 2004. Since 2006, her Group Coaching Essentials program has supported thousands in scaling the coaching conversation beyond the one-on-one coaching modality.

A former leader in the international humanitarian sector, she spent most of the 1990s and early 2000s leading geographically dispersed teams across countries and regions of the world that took five days to traverse. These experiences shaped her passion and insights around what is possible in the remote, hybrid and virtual space.

Over the last few years, her *PlanDoTrack* and *Coaching Business Builder Workbook and Planner* have been used by hundreds. The work is also rolled out by PDT and CBB Facilitators.

Jennifer is also the creator of the 21 for 21 Virtual Co-working Sprints.

An award-winning program designer, Jennifer is dedicated to supporting groups, teams and organizations in the areas of leadership, teamwork, and performance. Since the late 1980s, she has supported professionals across a wide sector with a global client list that spans government, corporate and non-profit sectors, from financial services to education to healthcare.

Jennifer is a thought leader in the field of group and team coaching. Her first book, *Effective Group Coaching*, was the first book ever to be published on the topic of group coaching. It has been used as a text and/or recommended resource for many coach-training programs for the past decade. She is a well-known international speaker on topics related to coaching, leadership, teamwork, virtual conversations, and capacity building.

Credentialed by the International Coaching Federation, Britton was originally trained and certified by the Coaches Training Institute. She has also completed advanced coaching training in multiple areas including Organization and Relationship Systems Coaching, Conversational Intelligence, and Shadow Coaching. She is a Draw Your Future™ Certified Facilitator.

A Certified Performance Technologist (CPT) and Certified Human Resource Leader (CHRL), Jennifer also holds a Masters in Environmental Studies (York University) and a Bachelor of Science in Psychology (McGill).

A typical day in Jennifer's work takes her around the world, as she gets to connect with professionals and organizations with Zoom from before dawn to early in the afternoon. She physically divides her time between just north of Toronto, and beautiful Muskoka, where she enjoys time spent in nature with family.

www.ingramcontent.com/pod-product-compliance
Lightning Source LLC
Chambersburg PA
CBHW081758200326
41597CB00023B/4068